THE STRONG HORSE

Power, Politics, and the Clash of Arab Civilizations

Lee Smith

DOUBLEDAY

NEW YORK LONDON TORONTO

SYDNEY AUCKLAND

DD

DOUBLEDAY

DOUBLEDAY and the DD colophon are registered trademarks of
Random House, Inc.

LIBRARY OF CONGRESS CATALOGING-IN-PUBLICATION DATA
Smith, Lee, 1962–
The strong horse : power, politics and the clash of Arab
civilizations / Lee Smith.
—1st ed.
p. cm.
Includes bibliographical references and index.
1. Arab nationalism.   2. Civilization, Arab—20th century.
3. Civilization, Arab—21st century.   4. Nationalism—Arab
countries.   5. Group identity—Arab countries.
6. United States—Foreign relations—Arab countries.
7. Arab countries—Foreign relations—United States.
8. Lebanon—Politics and government—1975-
9. Lebanon—History—Civil War, 1975-1990.   10. Lebanon—
History—1990-   I. Title.
D63.6.S656 2009
956.05—dc22   2009012688

ISBN 978-0-385-51611-2

PRINTED IN THE UNITED STATES OF AMERICA

1 2 3 4 5 6 7 8 9 10

FIRST EDITION

*To my mother, my father, my brothers, Matthew and Kevin,
and my sister, Sasha*

*And to the other five from whom all good things came to me:
Manhattan, Brooklyn, the Bronx, Queens, and Staten Island*

When people see a strong horse and a weak horse, by nature, they will like the strong horse.

—OSAMA BIN LADEN

Contents

Acknowledgments

I would like to thank the various magazine and newspaper editors who over the last several years have helped make it possible for me to write about the Middle East. At *Slate*, Jacob Weisberg, June Thomas, and Meghan O'Rourke; William Kristol, Richard Starr, Jonathan Last, Michael Goldfarb, and Philip Terzian at the *Weekly Standard;* Thomas Goetz at *Wired;* Alex Star at the *Boston Globe* and then the *New York Times Magazine;* Kyle Crichton, Ethan Bronner, Amy Virshup, Laura Marmor, Mary Billard, Stuart Emmrich, and Maura Egan at the *New York Times;* Franklin Foer and Zvika Krieger at the *New Republic;* Michael Young at the *Daily Star;* Michael Karam, Faerlie Wilson, and Hanin Ghaddar at *NOW Lebanon;* Tariq Alhomayed at *Asharq al-Awsat;* Nathan Lump and Amy Farley at *Travel and Leisure;* Hugh Garvey at *Bon Appétit;* Eric Banks at *Bookforum;* Michael Tomasky at the *American Prospect;* Jim Nelson at *GQ;* Adam Shatz at the *Nation;* Sara Ivry at *Nextbook;* Jonathan Foreman at *Standpoint;* and Jose Guardia at PJM.

Among my friends and colleagues, I am deeply grateful to:

In New York, David Samuels and Virginia Heffernan; Casey Greenfield; Katherine Zoepf; Michael Caruso; Richard Chen; Tom Vanderbilt; Salle Colagi; Abdul Tabini; and Heather Caldwell.

In Washington, Harold Rhode; David and Meyrav Wurmser; my colleagues at the Hudson Institute, especially Ken Weinstein, Allan Tessler, Enders Wimbush, Nina Rosenwald, Grace Terzian, Rachel DeCarlo Currie, Katie Fisher, Phil Ross, Ioannis Saratsis, and Katherine Smyth; Nadia Schadlow; Samantha Ravich; Steven Peter Rosen; Sam Spector; Oubai Shabhandhar; Peter Theroux; David Schenker; Michael Doran; Rob Karem; Marsha Thaler-Smith; Carmen Lane; Eddie Becker and Joanie; Michael Veltri; Danny Kopp; Joseph Gebeilly; Hussein Abd al-Hussein; Amal Mudalalli; Firas Maksad; Hassan Mneimneh; Ammar Abdulhamid; Matthew Irwin; Noah Pollak; Joshua Pollack; Andrew Apostolou; and Zaynab al-Suwaij.

In Egypt, Raymond Stock; Hala Mustafa; Lobna al-Tabei; the faculty and staff at the AUC Arabic Language Institute; Awad and Marous; Josh Stacher; and Patrick Haenni.

In Lebanon, Mrs. Dina Fawaz, my mother away from home; Rita Aad; the faculty at Saint Joseph University, especially Rana Bakdache; the U.S. embassy and its exemplary staff during the Cedar Revolution, including Ambassador Jeffrey Feltman, Greg Marchese, Matt Pilcher, and Juliet Wurr; Andrew Tabler; Lin Nouehid; Norbert Schiller; Nick Blanford; the Quantum group, especially Eli Khoury, Elena Anouti, Lara Hajj, Makram Rabah, Jean-Pierre Katrib, Hussam Harb, Lina Mustafa, and Lina Silistily; Malek Mroue; Lokman Slim; Inga Schei; Hazem Saghieh; Nadim Koteich; Ahmad al-Husseini; Homer Lanier; Bill Harris; Michael Totten; Peter Speetjens; Jana al-Horr; Andrea Stanton; Charles Chuman; and Hassan Mohanna.

Elsewhere in the Arab states, Rana Sweiss; Ali abu Shakra; Malia Asfour; Jihad Fakhreddine; Sheikha Lubna al-Qasimi; Abdul Rahman al-Rashed; and Abd al-Rahman al-Alwani.

In Israel, Naomi Shultz; the Jerusalem Center for Public Affairs, especially Dan Diker and Dore Gold; Martin Kramer; Barry Rubin; Ami Isseroff; Richard Landes; David Hazony; Asgeir Ueland; Ezra Gabbay; Steven Alper; Maya Nathan; Avi Goldberger; and Stardust graduates.

Special thanks to my agent and great friend, Chris Calhoun, and all the Sterling Lord office; the staff at Doubleday/Knopf, especially the editor in chief, Bill Thomas, Stephanie Bowen, and, above all, my editor, Kris Puopolo, without whom this book could not have been written.

Tony Badran, Elie Fawaz, Jonathan Spyer, and Muhammad abd al-Raouf are great teachers all, and even better friends.

Greatest thanks go to Jim Surowiecki, a friend who sees the best in me and brought out the best in this book.

THE STRONG HORSE

The Clash of Arab Civilizations

I t was hard not to take 9/11 personally. I was raised in New York City, so when those planes flew into the World Trade Center, it felt like a direct attack on my family and friends and myself, on the neighborhoods where I'd gone to school, played, and worked, and on the Brooklyn block where I was living that beautiful summer day when the sky darkened with the ashes of other New Yorkers. It occurred to me more than once during the time I spent living and traveling in the Middle East after 9/11 that had I lived most of my life in some other American city or village, had New York not been my hometown, I might not have moved to the region some few months after to try to figure out what had happened. This book is an account of my time in the Middle East since then, and my understanding of it. My conclusion, without racing too far ahead, is that we all took 9/11 too personally.

The spectacular nature of the event was cause enough to see it as a declaration of war on America, so it is hardly surprising that Americans across the political spectrum came to think of it in the context of a "clash of civilizations." Even those on the left who disdained the phrase nonetheless employed a version of the conceit when explaining that the death and destruction were by-products of the legitimate grievances that Arabs had with the United States, which was finally just a way of delivering a verdict for the other side in the same civilizational war.

I see it a little differently. I believe that 9/11 was evidence of a clash all right, but the clash that led to 9/11 was less the conflict between the West and Islam than the conflict between the Arabs themselves. In that sense, strange as it sounds, the attacks on New York and Washington were not really about us.

To be sure, a significant part of the Middle East, including Osama bin Laden, is at war expressly with the United States. And there are genuine points of conflict between the lands of Islam and the West, including a religious rivalry that dates back to the appearance of the Quran and myriad regional confrontations to which the United States' strategic interests make us party. But these conflicts are just part of a system of wars that involves the entire Middle East. We are now incontrovertibly a part of these wars, but their causes and sources are to be found in the region itself, and not at the lower end of Manhattan, or even in the halls of the Pentagon. September 11 is the day we woke up to find ourselves in the middle of a clash of Arab civilizations, a war that used American cities as yet another venue for Arabs to fight each other.

If that assertion sounds implausible, it's because Americans are accustomed to thinking of themselves, in one way or another, as the source of the tumult in the Middle East. And that feeling was magnified after 9/11, when the continued eruptions of violence in the region made it hard for observers, from ordinary Americans to international affairs specialists, not to assume that the Bush administration was mostly, if not wholly, responsible for what was happening. But the problems of the region will not fade now that Barack Obama is in the White House, because they did not start when George W. Bush arrived there. Consider just a few of the clashes that preceded

Bush's tenure: the intrastate Arab crises like Saddam Hussein's 1990 invasion of Kuwait and Syria's occupation of Lebanon (1990-2005); the civil wars that wracked North Yemen (1962-1970) and Lebanon (1975-1990); wars between the state and non-state actors, like the Islamist insurgencies that ravaged Algeria (1991-2002), Egypt (1981-1997), and Syria (1979-1982), and the Palestine Liberation Organization's revolt against the Hashemite Kingdom of Jordan (1968-1971); the genocidal bouts of ethnic and sectarian cleansing, like Saddam's campaigns against the Kurds and Shia, Hafez al-Assad's mass slaughter of Sunnis in Hama in 1982, and the Sudanese government's campaigns against Christians and animists in the south (1981-2004) and now against non-Arab Muslims in Darfur. In all of these, the United States played, at most, a secondary role, and was often little more than a bystander.

Nor is this a new phenomenon. It's true, of course, that outside actors—including the United States and the Soviet Union and, before them, the European colonial powers—have helped shape the history of the Middle East. But ultimately their actions and policies have been less important than we imagine. If we think differently—if we think that we are to blame for what is wrong with the Middle East—it's because of two things: our own narcissism and the tendency of Arab nationalists to blame outside forces for the problems of their region. For decades now, the United States has been a convenient foil for those who believe that only the machinations of an evil outsider could keep the Arabs from becoming a formidable political, economic, and military bloc, just as we have become a convenient foil for Islamists seeking to explain why the Muslim world has fallen so far behind the West. But in both cases, focusing on the United States is a way of overlooking what's really happening. In this book, I shift that focus back to where it belongs: on the conflicts and divisions within the Middle East itself.

There are some, of course, who deny that these conflicts among Arabs and Muslims matter. For most of the past century, in fact, the mainstream American interpretation of the Middle East has seen it as a monolithic body, made up of people of similar backgrounds and similar opinions. (This misconception is frequently vented through the tidy journalistic cliché known as "the Arab street," which presumes that, say, a Lebanese Christian and an Iraqi Shia necessarily hold the same point of view as an Egyptian Sunni.) More important, this is how Arab nationalists also see the world. Arab nationalism is a political and cultural doctrine holding that the Arabs, by virtue of a shared language, constitute a separate and single people. It is a tribal pact raised to the supranational level: in projecting unity, it seeks to obscure local enmities and keep Arabs from making war against each other. Arab nationalists have hoped to coalesce the energies of disparate factions and concentrate their hostilities onto a common, distant enemy.

It is somewhat paradoxical that even while Arab nationalism, and then Islamism, has taken the United States to be its main foil for over half a century, all during that time the mainstream American interpretation of the Arabic-speaking Middle East has been Arab nationalist, from the American missionaries who first ventured into the Holy Land to the oil companies and the State Department, from the academy to editorial boardrooms and foreign bureaus. The United States has paid a steep price for misconstruing the region like this, but at one time our face-value acceptance of Arab nationalism had at least the advantage of being in line with American interests.

Arab nationalism is a Sunni Arab viewpoint. The doctrine's foundations are in a language considered holy by most Middle Easterners, and a history that holds the Prophet of Islam to be the greatest of all Arab heroes, and thus it is a sop to the status quo power of the Arabic-speaking Middle East that has ruled the region for more than a millennium, the Sunnis. Since the mid-1930s, the United States' most vital interest in the Middle East has been energy, and as the world's largest known reserves of oil are in Saudi Arabia, Washington has been guided by its need to accommodate a Sunni regime whose influence is proportionate to its wealth. America's Sunnicentrism has also been shaped by cultural and historical factors, but it is mostly the political and economic rationale that has given us our view of the region, a fact that allows us to derive a general principle: the Great Powers' view of the Middle East is shaped by their own interests.

Even before the discovery of oil, for instance, the British looked at the region much the same way as we have, as a Sunni fiefdom. With the British Empire comprising enormous numbers of Sunnis from Egypt and Palestine to Iraq and the Persian Gulf all the way to the crown's prize holding in India, London tinkered little after World War I with the skeletal remains of the Ottoman Empire's administrative structure. The Ottomans' Sunni Arab deputies were left in charge to protect and advance British interests, even in Iraq, where the Sunnis were, and are, clearly a minority. The French, however, saw the Middle East differently, partly because they were in competition with the British, and also because their Middle Eastern holdings included significant minority populations in conflict with the Sunnis, like the Maronites in Lebanon, the Alawis in Syria, and the Berbers in Algeria, communities that the French used to serve their own interests.

In the wake of 9/11, Washington found that the Middle East looked more like the way the French had conceived of it than how the British had ruled it. The U.S.-led invasion of Iraq changed the balance of power by pushing aside a Sunni strongman and empowering a national majority, the Shia, which, since they are also a regional minority, altered the nature of U.S. strategy. As descriptions of the Middle East go hand in hand with national interests, we need a way to understand the region in line with the reality now exposed, and this book proposes one. The Arabic-speaking Middle East is not a sea of some 300 million Arabs who all have common interests but a region with a 70 percent Sunni population and dozens of minorities. The size of the Sunni majority, and its concomitant power and prestige, have allowed it to rule by violence, repression, and coercion for close to fourteen hundred years. The Sunnis have been a bloc of force that has never known accommodation or compromise, but has rather compelled everyone else to submit to its worldview.

This does not mean that the Sunnis' reliance on violence to maintain their rule is the "root cause" of the problems in the Middle East. Rather, it is just the central motif in a pattern that existed before Islam and is imprinted on all of the region's social and political relations—whether the state is facing down insurgents, or nationalists are fighting Islamists, or one tribe is squared off against another, or two minorities are at war with each other. The order of the region is the natural order of things that the fourteenth-century Arab historian Ibn Khaldun describes in his masterpiece *Al-Muqaddima*: history is a matter of one tribe, nation, or civilization dominating the others by force until it, too, is overthrown by force. And it is this, what I call the strong horse principle—not Western imperialism, nor Zionism, nor Washington policy makers—that has determined the fundamental character of the Arabic-speaking Middle East, where bin Ladenism is not drawn from the extremist fringe but represents the political and social norm.

The war that Arabs are waging against the United States, some in deed as well as in word, is merely a massive projection of the same pattern of force, with a tribe bound as one to defend against and defeat the outsider. The Arabs hate us not because of what we do or who we are but because of what and who we are *not*: Arabs. But because of the size and heterogeneity of this putative Arab nation, that compact is not sustainable on so large a scale, civilization versus civilization. The wars waged between Arabs according to the strong horse principle make the Arabic-speaking peoples of the Middle East a much graver threat to themselves than they are to anyone else.

The *Strong Horse: Power, Politics, and the Clash of Arab Civilizations* is broken into three parts. The first part details the complex of issues—from tribalism to Arab nationalism, and from Islam to Islamism—spanning Arab history from before the advent of Islam through the nineteenth-century Muslim reform movement that have shaped the contemporary Middle East. And it is these issues taken as a whole that led to 9/11. The second part describes how the Bush White House responded to the attacks according to what it perceived to be the problems of the Middle East, and how the region in turn reacted to the Americans. At the core of the Bush administration's post-9/11 strategy was democratization, and thus the final third of the book looks at the challenge of making democracy work in a region that has little experience with it.

The first chapter deals with the tribal character of Arab societies, including jihad and its most famous contemporary practitioner, Osama bin Laden. The next two chapters take up Arab nationalism by sketching its history, introducing some of its most prominent ideologues, and describing the political, social, and cultural purposes to which it's been put. While those chapters deal explicitly with Arabism, this is a subject that runs throughout the book since I understand it to be the region's defining issue. In fact, I take Islam, at least in its initial thrust, to be little more than a variety—indeed the first manifestation—of Arab nationalism. Over time, as it extended throughout the Fertile Crescent, Persia, and North Africa, Islam clearly became something else and something more than just a pan-Arab ideology, but before anyone imagined the revelation embedded in the Arabic Quran could spread to faraway Spain or the Asian subcontinent, the "universality" of this religious and political doctrine applied to the various Arabian tribes to be unified under the rule of an Arabian leader, the Prophet of Islam. And for the conquered non-Arabs who converted to the new faith, as one scholar of the period explained, "membership of Islam was equated with possession of an Arab ethnic identity."[1] The early *umma*—or Muslim community—was an Arab super-tribe held together not by blood and kinship but by a religious idea that motivated and rationalized the Arab conquests by distinguishing between the tribe and all comers—Muslims versus infidels, *dar al-Islam* versus *dar al-harb,* or the abode of Islam versus that which is not under Islam, the abode of war.

Dar al-Islam's first modern encounter with *dar al-harb* was Napoleon's 1798 invasion of Egypt. The fourth and fifth chapters describe the intellectual and cultural ferment that came in the aftermath of this collision between the West and the Arab world, looking specifically at the rise of the Muslim reform movement. In the nineteenth and early twentieth centuries, Muslim intellectuals and activists took the West as their yardstick to measure how far the *umma* had fallen, and contended that the failure was due to the condition of Islam itself. They argued that the Islamic faith had been corrupted by centuries of fake customs and practices, leaving *dar al-Islam* so brittle that the infidels had overrun it effortlessly. The Salafist movement, as this reform current is called, is the precursor of what we know today as political Islam or, more frequently, Islamism.

It is a common misconception that Islamism is a deviant, radical ideology bearing little resemblance to the "real" or "traditional" Islam. I argue instead that Islamism represents the modern, progressive, and rationalist effort of Muslims to come to terms with the forces of modernity heralded by Napoleon's arrival. The terror and violence that mark what we've come to call Islamic radicalism are the products of the mixture of Salafism with traditional Arab politics, which has no mechanism for peaceful transitions of authority or power sharing, and therefore sees political conflict as a fight to the death between strong horses. Far from being deviant, the Islamists' reliance on violence is all too characteristic, not of Islam, but of the region. Consider the struggles we see played out today across the Middle East, with insurgents and oppositionists waging terror campaigns to win power, while the regimes use torture and collective punishment to defeat their domestic competition. Aside from the venue, September 11 was just the business of Arab politics as usual.

The second part begins by connecting the problem of Arab politics to the Bush administration's response to 9/11. When the Americans turned to the region and touched down in force, they found that the problem wasn't just bin Laden but bin Ladenism. The issue wasn't a shadowy network of rogue terrorists, or Arab regimes that jailed, tortured, and murdered their own people, but a political culture where insurgent terror and state repression were two sides of the same bloody coin. Indeed, as the Americans discovered, the most pressing strategic concern was less Al Qaeda than the collaboration between states and so-called stateless terrorist outfits. In particular, it became clear that the biggest threat to stability in the region was not bin Laden. It was instead a confederation led not by a Sunni Arab regime but by a Shia Persian power, Iran, alongside Syria, Hezbollah, Hamas, and various Iraqi groups. This confederation, which I call the resistance bloc, fought the United States and its allies on several fronts—Iraq, the Persian Gulf, the Palestinian territories and Israel, and Lebanon. At this point, the Middle East cold war, as it has come to be called, becomes a significant theme in the book, as Iran and the resistance bloc compete with the United States and its allies to impose regional order as the strong horse.

In the sixth and seventh chapters, I discuss the White House's program to change the nature of the Middle East, a program built around the top-down imposition of democracy or, more specifically, free elections. The Americans believed that giving Arabs a say in governing their own political, economic, and social lives was an antidote to bin Ladenism and the strong horse. What they discovered was that, as one Arab commentator noted, the problem with Arab democracy was not a lack of supply but a lack of demand. In failing to grasp that Arab political pathologies were organic—that is, the absence of democracy in the region is the result of Arab societies' conception of what politics requires—the White House's democracy promotion left the Americans pushing a set of ideas and values that most Arabs had no interest in. The trappings of democracy do not create democratic polities; free societies need to be built by men and women with a stake in their own futures. And so, in the eighth chapter, I look at the only indigenous cultural and intellectual idea in the Middle East that is capable of producing such people, namely, Arab liberalism. After 9/11, one major question in the Middle East was to what extent the American intervention in the region would empower the Arab liberals, or expose them to more danger.

In the final part of the book, I look more closely at the problem of democracy in the Middle East. My case study in the ninth chapter deals with Lebanon, the one Arab society where many of the ingredients for a democratic polity already existed. In 2005, Lebanon was the site of a remarkable, and in many ways unprecedented, upsurge of democratic sentiment, as Lebanese citizens of different faiths joined together in what became known as the March 14 movement. They mounted massive public demonstrations in favor of real democracy and brought about, for a time, what was labeled the Cedar Revolution. Yet even as it gave birth to this hopeful development, Lebanon was also home to one of the purest specimens of violence and strong horse tactics in the region, the Shia group Hezbollah, which was supported by Syria and Iran. The clash between the March 14 movement and the Hezbollah/Syria alliance offers an object lesson in the obstacles to making the Middle East democratic.

In chapter 10, I deal more directly with Syria, and show how successful it has been in its efforts to prove that democracy cannot work in Lebanon and that there is no serious alternative to strong horse politics. I argue that the only way to have stopped the Syrians from stamping out real democracy was for the United States to have played the role of strong horse itself. Once it refused to do so in Lebanon, the Cedar Revolution was doomed. Paradoxically, violence may be the only way to ensure that nonviolent politics can thrive in the region. Along those lines, I argue in the final chapter that Israel's two most recent wars—those with Hezbollah and Hamas—must be seen outside of the narrow focus of the Arab-Israeli arena and in the context of the power politics of the region. In effect, I suggest, Israel has been a proxy strong horse not just for the United States but also for Sunni Arab regimes like Egypt and Saudi Arabia.

The conclusion considers what may be in store for the Arabs and what is the way forward for the United States in the region. The Arabs are weak, and this frailty in turn reflects on their patron, the United States. Since the political nature of the region abhors a vacuum, I describe how Arab weakness may affect American regional interests, and how it has invited in other actors, like Iran, and may invite in more, like the Turks. If we lack resolve, others will force their own order on the region, an order in which American interests, and Arab ambitions, will matter little. One way or another, I argue, this is a future that should be avoided, for it would be disastrous, not for the United States so much as for the Arabs themselves.

This is a book about Arab politics, society, and culture, which is to say this is a book about some Arab ideas and the force they have on how people live from day to day in the region. I have tried to discuss those ideas as dispassionately as possible, although I recognize that the main thesis—that violence is central to the politics, society, and culture of the Arabic-speaking Middle East—is likely to cause unease. Nonetheless, the idea that people naturally prefer the strong horse to the weak one in this part of the world seems to me unassailable; it is impossible to understand the region without recognizing the significance of violence, coercion, and repression. That doesn't mean that I think the Arabs *only* understand force—a charge frequently leveled by many critics against, for instance, the Bush administration. It just means, I think, that force is at the core of the way most Arabs understand politics, and that therefore there is no way to understand how the Middle East works without understanding the concept of the strong horse. It is not a moral judgment but a description.

This is, to be sure, not a concept that comes naturally to Americans, because we are among the very few people in history who have been able to live our daily lives free, relatively speaking, from violence and the fear of violence. The various protections and liberties afforded us in our society have their roots in man's fear of violent death,[2] but we have come so far from that point that it is difficult for us to see that our form of political organization makes us not the norm but a privileged exception, the beneficiaries of a historical anomaly. We are so predisposed to ignore our freakish luck, as well as the blood spilled by our ancestors, that we imagine all men must have inherited essentially the same world that we have and are thus motivated by the same hopes and fears and ideas. In short, they are not.

Indirectly, then, this book is also about American ideas, or some American ideas, especially those about the best form of government and the possibility and desirability of bringing our political ideas and practices to societies and cultures that are vastly different from our own. It is also a book about my ideas and how they changed over time, what I had invested in certain ideas, and certain people, and why I was compelled to modify some and abandon others outright.

A few words about the style of this book are also in order. Like the Arabic-speaking Middle East, it is a heterogeneous affair, a book combining travelogue and policy, memoir and history, literature and revealed religion in an effort to give as full and dense a picture of a complex part of the world as possible in a tight space. I have limited the scope of this book by excluding the Maghreb (Mauritania, Morocco, Algeria, and Tunisia), as well as other African states (Libya, Sudan, and Somalia), to focus on the Mashreq, a region stretching from the eastern Mediterranean states—Egypt, Lebanon, Syria, Jordan, the Palestinian territories, and Israel—to the shores of the Persian Gulf. Several chapters are set in Egypt, the largest Arab state and the cultural and intellectual capital of the region where every major political and cultural trend of the last century has either its origins or its golden age, from Nasserism to the Islamist movement to Arab liberalism. Other chapters move on to the Arab Gulf states, and the Levant, especially Syria and Lebanon. This last I take to be the most beautiful country in the Arabic-speaking Middle East, as well as the most open and tolerant, most hopeful and tragic. Beirut, in contrast to Cairo (a Sunni-dominated society that offers mostly one perspective on the region), is a perfect crow's nest from which to watch the Middle East as the rest of the world comes into contact with it, a geographical, strategic, and historical vantage point. Almost every state in the region has a stake in Lebanon, from Shiite Iran to Sunni powers like Saudi Arabia, as do international actors like France and the United States, which for better or worse now represents the legacy of Western Christendom and its sustained interest in the Holy Land. Over the last millennium and a half, every imaginable crisis and conflict—sectarian, ideological, political, and civilizational—has had its day in Lebanon, most recently during the country's fifteen-year-long civil wars, which in summoning the region's historical furies also presaged everything we are now seeing in the Middle East.

I recognize that from an American perspective, the most prominent Arab state at present is still Iraq, and while this book discusses some of the ways in which the war and its aftermath reverberated throughout the Middle East, Iraq in this telling is something like the ghost of Hamlet's father. It is a significant presence that set certain events in motion, and motivates the behavior of significant players, but it is almost entirely offstage. So much of our attention and energy is consumed right now with Iraq that the sharp focus has dulled our ability to take in the Middle East as a whole; likewise, our knowledge of Iraq is incomplete without seeing it in the context of the rest of the region.

That other well-known center of conflict, Israel, I reach at the very end, for reasons that I hope will become increasingly clear. Unlike many in both the Middle East and the West, I give no credence to the idea that the Arab-Israeli crisis is the region's central issue. That a broad consensus of prominent policy makers, academics, analysts, and journalists so relentlessly advertise this conviction does not mean that they are correct, only that their obstinacy retards our understanding of the region, where the Arab-Israeli arena is merely one among many conflicts featuring the same problems that plague the entire Middle East. Regardless of what else one can say about America's post-9/11 policy, the one undeniable success of the Bush White House was to return the problems of the Middle East to the region itself, and it is there rather than in the southern end of Manhattan that the clash of Arab civilizations will be solved or managed or settled, in one way or another.

PART I

CHAPTER 1

The Strong Horse: Tribes

Osama bin Laden rightly observes that people naturally prefer the strong horse to the weak one, and Awad's was plainly stronger than mine. His horse was Assad, which means "lion," a purebred Arabian stallion of great beauty, conformation, and color—the boys at the farm said the old Arabs loved that shade of red. He'd studded several of the mares and once stripped a gold watch from a man's wrist with his teeth and swallowed it. He was flashy, a pop star among the barn's more honest horses like al-Ash'ar, "the Blonde," an endurance racer who took on the expensive mounts the Gulf oil sheikhs brought in for the daylong marathons around the Pyramids. Assad and Ash'ar, like all the horses in the barn with Arabian blood, had Arabic names, while the European horses carried foreign ones, usually American names, like Hogan, an eighteen-hand bully of a Belgian Warmblood named after the professional wrestler.

Another of the horses was a stout brown-flecked gelding we called Abloosa, which is how the boys said "Appaloosa" because there is no *p* in Arabic. They asked what it meant, and I said it was the horse of a great American nation. The boys didn't know there were tribes in America as there were in Egypt. The word *arab* comes from the verb for wandering, moving, or crossing space, and even farmers, the nomads' historical adversaries, are used to thinking that the Bedouin is the original man at the center of the world, in which there is nothing else like him.

Unlike the boys, Awad was raised in the city and only became a horseman during his tour of military duty some twenty years before. He was in his late thirties, of medium height, sensitive about his growing waistline, dark, handsome, and, like all men who spend the better part of their day on top of a horse, vain. In the winter months, he wore an olive green bomber jacket and with his black hair slicked back and big toothy smile affected the cool of an American movie star from the 1940s, while his thick black mustache made him look like a commander of a serious Arab military unit.

I knew no Arabic at the time, and Awad's Japanese was better than his English, which meant he knew ten Japanese words useful in equestrian matters rather than only five. And yet friendships don't really begin in talk, but rather with watching how someone else fills space and how the world repays that charisma. I imagine this is the main ingredient in women's intuition, and for men it is what makes us follow other men. And so I admired Awad even if all I knew about him was how he was with horses.

In time, of course, we talked. He had few opinions about the United States, and shrugged his shoulders when I asked if he knew where Green Bay, Wisconsin, was. Because that's a Green Bay Packers cap you're wearing, I told him. Eventually I gave him a Yankees cap to replace it, a curiosity he seemed to appreciate given New York's place in Arab history now. Obviously, Awad knew nothing about baseball, and neither did he care for any other sport, not even soccer, an Egyptian passion, or indeed any pursuit besides horsemanship. It was not just a sport, though it was the best of sports; it was a way of being in the world, learning how to master what parts of an environment you could control and how to use fear, real physical terror, as well as fear of contingency and chance, to your advantage, for the animal, as an ally or an agent of nature indifferent to man's success or failure, can sense both mastery and fear.

The horse I rode was Amina, a small gray mare with some Arabian blood, a type of mutt that the Egyptians call *baladi*, or "country," a word that refers to virtually anything, good or bad, that is authentically Egyptian. She was bred for the desert, her head alert in either direction and her nostrils flared, as though she had discerned the ghost scent of old enemies. She was carrying Assad's foal, which left her doubly handicapped that day, for while I weighed less than Awad, my teacher was by far the superior rider. The race started abruptly. We reached a flat stretch that seemed to go for a mile or so, Awad said, "*Yalla,* go," and all of a sudden I was watching Assad's haunches from more than two lengths behind. This continued for about a quarter of a mile, when Amina decided she would not let me make her lose. Awad looked over at us one more time before we ran past him and did not relinquish the lead.

Awad's cap had fallen off during the race, so after finishing, he turned back to retrieve it. I watched him dismount and bend down to scoop the blue hat out of the sand while he yanked on Assad's reins so tightly it struck me that we were in trouble if the animal bolted, and it made me tired to think of immensity like the desert's. An Arabian who only knows the desert is unlikely to willingly leave its owner's side for long, but these animals, tended by any number of farmhands, had their fealty fraternized out of them, and in any case loyalty didn't seem to be one of the manifest qualities God had bestowed on the haughty stallion. If he left, he'd run into other horses eventually, maybe a pack of flea-bitten mares rented out by tourists from one of the *baladi* stables by the Pyramids, or his pride would just keep driving him farther away and into the desert.

The farther you get from the Pyramids, the cleaner the desert becomes, void of the refuse from generations of tourists, travelers, and conquerors, the uncurated museum of the dunes, where the trash from Napoleon's troops mixes with candy wrappers scattered by a Russian tour group the day before. Awad threw a spent match in the sand, lit his cigarette with another, and then leaned over the two animals to light one for me. We walked through the *gebel,* or "mountains," as he called the high dunes of the desert, smoking in silence.

From this vantage point, I could see the road to the farm in the far distance, lined with tall date palms casting their shade across the narrow dirt road, surely one of the most beautiful places on earth, even if the corpses of oxen, horses, and donkeys filled the canal by the roadside. At some recent point in their five- or six-millennia-long history, the inhabitants of the Nile River valley learned to become ashamed of discarding their dead animal labor in the water supply, but instead of relinquishing the habit, they found it easier, or perhaps just less abject, to discourage tourists from photographing these liquid graveyards. The canal ended about a mile before a military base, which was also forbidden to photograph, forbidden by law, because an army that fights wars against its own people must keep many secrets. Awad and I kept the horses at a walking pace until we came upon a sun temple; it was from some period, I don't know which, in pharaonic history, unattended like most of the antiquity scattered throughout Egypt, and in ruins.

In English poetry, there is a genre of contemplating ruins that starts right around the beginning of the colonial era, when Europeans first became fascinated by all things Oriental, with Percy Bysshe Shelley's "Ozymandias" (1818). The narrator meets a "traveller from an antique land" who tells of a large monument in the desert "half sunk," bearing the inscription "Look on my works, ye mighty, and despair." The poem is set in Egypt, the colossal statue is of Ramses II, and the irony is that to *look on* this shattered monument is not to fear its *visage of cold command,* but rather to *despair* that all earthly ambition must meet the same desolate end.

Shelley's poem, like most of the subsequent efforts it inspired, is a comment on power, the vanity of men, and the passing of civilizations. But in Arabic poetry this stopping at the ruins, or *wuquf al-atlal*, begins more than a millennium before, in the pre-Islamic era, or the *jahiliya*, the age of pagan ignorance, and Imru al-Qays is credited as the poet who first employed the conceit. Qays, according to the Prophet of Islam, was the greatest of the Arabs' poets—and their leader into the hellfire.

The poet was a pagan and a prodigal, part Hamlet and part Prince Hal, a king's son who, as Qays's famous *mu'allaqa*, or "suspended ode," makes clear, spent much of his time chasing women. One of the poem's most colorful scenes, once described as "the most indecent verses ever spoken by any Arab poet,"[1] takes place when Qays is making love to another man's woman while she is tending to her infant child. In the same poem, he has slaughtered his camel for a group of young maidens, and while preparing the feast, the girls play catch with the animal's innards, *as white as Damascene silk*. The rare beauty of this strange and gruesome episode derives from the fact that Qays proposed such a thing was beautiful and made it so.

Qays's stopping by the ruins is not a moral dirge about the capricious nature of temporal power, and there is no irony here, but only flesh and love, tenderness and longing. He comes upon a deserted camp, the tents are packed away, the tribesmen are gone and with them his beloved, the fires are extinguished, and only their ashes remain. Qays is thinking not of death and the passage of time but of life and passion, and so his poem begins with an ending, *al-atlal*, "the ruins."

Qifaa nabki min dhikra habibin wa manzili . . .

These are among the most famous verses in all of Arabic poetry. "Stop, and let us weep for the memory of a lover and a dwelling." The imperative is in the dual case as he is addressing two figures, attendants who eventually come to rebuke him for his self-pity and remind him of his many other conquests. His interlocutors go unnamed in the poem, though one gloss, my favorite, suggests the two are his sword and his mount, apt companions for the poet known as the Wandering King.[2]

Qays's father disapproved so keenly of his son's pursuits—women, wine, and song—that he is supposed to have tried once to have him killed. Perhaps to plague him further, on his deathbed Qays's father charged the poet with avenging his death. The old man had been assassinated, and as he lay dying, he sent a messenger to inform the poet that he had chosen him rather than his brothers to perform the vendetta. Qays did not relish the burden of his father's blood, but meant to honor it nonetheless. "Wine today," he supposedly said, giving rise to one of the most famous aphorisms in Arabic literature, "tomorrow business." His revels lasted a week, after which he swore off all pleasures and vowed not to rest until he took his revenge.

"That's Khaled bin Laden's house," Awad said. He brought Assad to a halt and pointed to a large ranch at the bottom of the dunes where a strip of green divided the desert from Cairo in the distance. Awad saw my expression change and explained that Khaled was not like his famous brother. "He's a good man and an excellent horseman. He raises Arabians."

There is a story about Arabians relating how once after a long journey the Prophet of Islam turned his horses out to drink, but before they reached the water, he called for them to come back to him, and only five mares returned. The old Arabs preferred mares to stallions on account of their steady demeanor and quiet calm when preparing to ambush an enemy, so these five became Muhammad's chosen, *al-khamsa,* "the five," believed to be the bases of the five major strains of the Arabian horse. This foundation story tying the origins of the modern breed to the Prophet of Islam is of extremely dubious authenticity, but its popularity says something about the significance of lineage, affiliation, and legacy to the Arabs.

The strength of any society depends on its group cohesion, or what the fourteenth-century North African–born historian Ibn Khaldun described in his masterwork, *Al-Muqaddima*, as *assabiya*. Once *assabiya* starts to fade, the regnant civilization becomes easy pickings for a younger one still adhering to its martial ethos. As a result, history for Ibn Khaldun is an unbroken cycle of strong horses, not one Ozymandias but columns of them, one after another rising in the desert to replace his predecessor and rule until he, too, is put down by a more vital force.

This is the ethos driving jihad, but shorn of the jihad's triumphalist, religious rhetoric. Ibn Khaldun was a good Muslim and no doubt believed that armies of the *umma* were able to push far into Byzantium, Persia, North Africa, southern Europe, and India because, as Muhammad said, Muslims were the best of nations, enjoining good and forbidding evil. But in Ibn Khaldun's work, God is beside the point; he is not the agent of history but a narrative detail, the protagonist of one story that manages to motivate groups of men to kill and die.

The sacred book of the Arabs is the Quran, a difficult text written in an Arabic rarely spoken by most Arabs, except for the men of religion. Even for them, understanding and explicating some parts of the book require them to rely on certain passages from pre-Islamic poetry. This poetry was part of the pagan tradition that Islam was meant to replace, but without it Islam is incomprehensible, both as a text and as a cultural phenomenon. The message, as its audience is reminded several times, is an Arabic Quran, and it was revealed to an Arabian prophet. The same is true for Al Qaeda, as it cannot rightly be understood without accounting for its Arab roots, a tradition steeped in heroes, horses, and poetry that existed long before Islam.

That doesn't mean that bin Laden or any of his colleagues really intend to drag the *umma* or anyone else back to the seventh century. Al Qaeda is a military and political initiative to Islamize modernity, a concept espoused by almost every Islamist thinker of the last hundred years. And this project is in keeping with the initial thrust of the Quran, which was to transform the Arabs, to Islamize them. Islamization, though, did not mean de-Arabization.

Islam ameliorated some tribal practices, like the burial of infant girls, a custom that Muhammad outlawed; and it codified other Arab customs, like the raid, or *ghazu*, a word bin Laden and his peers regularly use to describe their operations. The *ghazu* was conducted against other raiding tribes, but more profitably against sedentary populations. While the Bedouin traded in livestock that wandered with them—camels, sheep, goats—farmers and merchants engaged in agriculture and industry, and a tribesman's interaction with these outsiders was not always regulated by tribal custom. More often than not, they were considered fair game.

In Ibn Khaldun's scheme, the Bedouin and the sedentary represent the two major groupings of civilization. The sedentary have their roots in the nomadic tribe, and the Bedouin's victories will invariably lead them toward a sedentary condition. Indeed, the raiders' military and political success is indicated by the extent to which the tribe is afforded luxury in its style of life, its manners, dress, entertainment, food, and drink, and yet these are also signs of its coming demise, for the more the tribe becomes accustomed to the good life, the farther it strays from the warrior ethos that initially motivated it. For a while anyway, the sedentary are capable of defending themselves, and later they hire others to do so, but they are merely postponing their inevitable end, for it is not only the actual fighting skill of the group that makes it strong but also the values that are derived from its young men, who will band together to protect the tribe. Once they lose their group feeling, their *assabiya*, the group is lost, and so one civilization or dynasty or nation falls when another rises to take its place and destroy it. What's radical about Ibn Khaldun's thesis is that he is not merely describing how one group expands at the expense of others, imposing its will with catastrophic consequences for the rest, but also suggesting that for history to have meaning, one tribe, one nation, must be stronger than the others. For if all groups are equal, then everyone is weak. The Islamist project can be understood in these terms: the Islamists want to restore the *umma* to its rightful place in world affairs, to be the strongest tribe. In their attempt to do so, they have reached farther back into the past than the great cultural, political, and military achievements of classical Islamic civilization and even before the revelation of the Quran. Jihad taps Islam at its source, its pre-Islamic roots, in the values of the raider, the *ghazi,* the Arabs.

Hence, it might be helpful to understand the Prophet of Islam as a type of pagan warrior-hero. We are accustomed to thinking of Muhammad as a holy man, and he is, but this hardly does justice to his career. He not only ruled a nation, the Islamic *umma;* he was also a wily commander, like Odysseus, who outwitted his often numerically superior opponents time and again. So, while his biography is usually seen in light of the tradition of the monotheistic prophets, he is also part of the literary tradition that includes epic heroes like Achilles, Beowulf, Cúchulainn, and Thor. As Muhammad turned the pagans of Mecca and then Medina into monotheists and created a nation, maybe it's most apt to think of him as a cross between Moses and Aeneas, pious Aeneas, who created Rome out of the remnants of what had been the people of Troy.

Of course, I do not mean that Muhammad is a fictional character. That his life serves as a model down to the present day is a consequence of his actual existence, a heroic legacy that partakes of the nearly universal tradition of the warrior-hero, the great father of all those who follow and look back to him constantly for reference and inspiration and the renovation of the nation's founding values. The contemporary West has no comparable figure—lawmaker, ruler, and warrior—at its origins. But Muhammad is not only the founder of Islam; he is also the culmination of the pagan Arabian tradition. The virtues of the tribal leader, his strength, wisdom, and cunning, are what gives him the power to enjoin good and forbid evil, to protect his own, to reward his allies, and to punish his enemies; this is why others are naturally attracted to him, and this is what makes him the strong horse.

In the case of Muhammad, he is further increased by his religious significance, his prophecy and direct relationship with the eternal creator of all things. Islam universalizes his role as tribal leader so that Muhammad transcends a narrowly Arabian context. The same is so for the pagan values of the Arabian Peninsula before Islam, the *jahiliya,* for the revelation binds those values and sacralizes them, giving them, too, a universal expression, one that transcends time and is coterminous with the God of all things. It turns Arab tribal values into eternal ones. For instance, there is the tribe, and there are all those outside of the tribe; after the revelation of the Quran and the founding of the *umma,* there is *dar al-Islam* and *dar al-harb.* There are no values more important to the tribesman than his ability and willingness to make war to protect his people and advance their interests. Jihad may be understood as holy war, but it is perhaps more accurate to say that it is the *ghazu* enjoined by an everlasting and all-encompassing God.

E very time we passed the house afterward, Awad pointed it out and smiled. I nodded back blankly. *Bin Laden.* Of course Awad wasn't with bin Laden any more than he said bin Laden's brother was, but so what? Those lines were easy to draw: *We are not with Osama. Osama is crazy. Osama is not a real Muslim—and besides, Osama didn't do it.* These were lines drawn in a desert.

It was the same when Awad brought Egyptian equestrian magazines to the barn and showed me photographs of Osama's sibling leading around one of his prize horses before an appreciative Arab audience. These small, fine-boned, neurotic animals weren't really bred to be ridden, but to be led around like large poodles and judged for their gait and conformation, their tail, their head. This is not what the tall, beautiful, and eloquent Osama meant by people naturally preferring the strong horse to the weak one, for strength is not simply in beauty or blood or the accumulation of easy applause. Strength, whether it issues from the body, intellect, or will, is the raw material that wedded to character becomes power imposing itself on the world. What more is there to say about one horse beating another in the desert when no one is watching? The stronger wins, and the other knows it has lost.

CHAPTER 2

"An Arab Regardless of His Own Wishes": The Idols of Arab Nationalism

Tribalism—the sense that society is, at heart, defined by the clash between groups (whether they be families or ethnicities or sects)—is a powerful force in Arab culture. At the same time, over the past century much of Arab politics has been defined by the quest to overcome tribalism, or, to be more accurate, by the quest to turn the myriad "tribes" that make up the Middle East into one super-tribe: the Arab nation. The origins of Arab nationalism date back to the second decade of the twentieth century. Until World War I, few Arabic-speaking Middle Easterners thought of themselves as Arabs, or subscribed to the logic of a political doctrine claiming that the Arabs constituted a separate nation just because they spoke the same language, or dialects of it. But as the Ottoman Empire began to totter during World War I, that started to change. Intellectuals and members of the bourgeoisie in search of a new political identity saw the Arabic language as a thread that connected hundreds of millions of Middle Easterners to each other and that could serve as the foundation for a pan-Arab project.

In the early days of the Arab nationalist movement, much of the impetus for it came from the Middle East's minority (non–Sunni Muslim) communities. For members of these minority groups, the notion of an Arabic identity was an appealing alternative to the oppression they felt under Islamic law and the rule of the Ottoman Empire. Islamic law, after all, relegated non-Muslims to the status of protected subject (*dhimmi*), making them effectively second-class citizens. This rule dated back to the seventh century, under Omar ibn al-Khattab, the second caliph after Muhammad, when the armies of the *umma* raced out of the Arabian Peninsula and swept through the region to create what we now know as the Arab Middle East. By the time Omar was finished, his conquests—or "openings" (*futuhat*), as the *umma* called those military victories that brought new lands and peoples into Islam—included all of Arabia, Egypt, North Africa, Syria, Mesopotamia, and a part of Persia. It was one of the most spectacular campaigns in military history, from the Persian Gulf to the westernmost reaches of the Mediterranean Sea, a martial progress that, like all imperial projects, left a river of blood in its wake and ruins where cultures once stood.

We are used to thinking that the imperial adventures of the West are largely responsible for shaping the contemporary Middle East. But the slogans that fueled France's and Great Britain's imperial classes in their march through the Middle East—"the white man's burden," "*mission civilisatrice*," and, more recently, "democratization"—were not more missionary than Islam, for the *umma* was an imperial power of the first order. To begin to understand the nature of the conflicts raging throughout the Arabic-speaking Middle East, we must go back to more than a millennium before Napoleon's 1798 invasion of Egypt, to the period when the Middle East was invaded by the Arabs.

After Omar's generals had laid siege to Jerusalem for a year, he entered the city in A.D. 637, a key date in Middle Eastern history, and not just because it consolidated the Muslim claim to a city already sacred to the Jews and the Christians. Muslim historians would come

to call the various laws and regulations by which non-Muslim subjects were allowed to conduct their affairs the Pact of Omar, a
reminder that it was under Omar, al-Farouq, he who distinguishes
truth from falsehood, that the Muslims came to rule so many non-
Muslims. Thereafter, the weight of the *dhimmis'* burden would
depend on the disposition of the particular caliph at the time, and
the local authorities, but their legal status was never equal to that of
Muslim subjects. Nor, logically, could it be.

Islam is not merely a personal religion but also the basis of a
political community. If non-Muslims were entitled to the same
rights as the faithful, then belief in God's final and perfect message
as revealed in the Quran through his prophet Muhammad would be
irrelevant, and the basis of the community would cease to exist.
Hence, full legal status is reserved for believers. Middle Eastern
minorities seized on Arab nationalism more than a millennium later
as an opportunity effectively to renegotiate the Pact of Omar and get
a better deal from the Sunnis. That was the promise of Arab nationalism, even as the reality was something else.

I had been in Cairo for about a week when I was invited to my
first dinner party with Egyptian aristocrats. Most of them
were baby boomers who were members of the Cairo elite, but the
older among them really were remnants of the days of royalty, and
their formative catastrophe was not the 1967 Israeli defeat, or even
Great Britain's long occupation of Egypt (1882–1954), but the 1952
Free Officers' coup, which had brought Gamal Abdel Nasser to
power. Nasser's ascendancy and the establishment of a quasi-
socialist Arab republic had cost them land, money, and prestige. If it
is customary to believe that Arab resentment is engendered by Western provocation, this was a class of Arabs whose humiliation consisted in having had to look on as an Arab demagogue sacrificed
their country—the Egypt they helped build and modernize, bilk

and misgovern—to the inchoate will of the resentful, illiterate masses.

At least that's how they saw it, the aristocrats. They served hors d'oeuvres on china bearing the once-royal colors of green and white, and spoke French, English, and Arabic fluently and all in the same sentence. As a belly dancer made her way around the large, bright apartment, the hostess and the rest of the women clapped along and pretended not to notice their husbands' eyes following her around the room. A recently remixed techno version of a famous Umm Kulthum song prompted some of the guests to debate the merits of tinkering with perfection. "You don't change the classics," one man explained. "You don't change Umm Kulthum." A younger man standing behind him shook his head for my benefit. "This is normal in Egypt," he confided to me. "People don't want anything to change, and nothing is better than the past."

The hostess walked me around to meet her guests—doctors, lawyers, designers, government officials, journalists, and, at the end of a long line of introductions, Omar Sharif. I looked up to see the gap between his two front teeth as he smiled warmly and shook my hand. I stood there speechless. "Why have you come to Egypt?" he asked. Because of you, I was tempted to reply, until he said it for me. "It's your Orientalist fantasy that's brought you here, isn't it?" He grabbed my jacket sleeve. "Tell me if I'm wrong," said Sharif, walking us over to the bar. "I'm not wrong very often, and I like to know when I am. But you are an Orientalist, no?" He threaded the word "Orientalist" with so much wit that I couldn't tell if he was poking more fun at me or at the catchphrase itself.

I said I was hoping to become one. "You are studying real Arabic?" he asked. Modern Standard Arabic, or *fusha*, is virtually the same as classical Arabic, with a vocabulary expanded in the nineteenth and twentieth centuries to account for scientific and political ideas imported from the West. The syntax is denser and the grammar stricter than the colloquial dialects of Arabic that are spoken in everyday exchanges throughout the region, and the pronunciation, since it is the language of the Quran, is more careful, and hence it is *fusha*—clear, fluent, and eloquent, like Omar Sharif. "It is a very difficult language," he said. "And I am sure all the Arabs here tonight have forgotten it."

Several of his friends had joined us by then, and Sharif tested his thesis, leading a small tutorial in conjugating Arabic verb forms. They sounded like half-drunken imams, rolling out sonorous verb endings until they finally broke down in laughter.

The odd thing was that the whole evening was a kind of Orientalist fantasy. In fact, sometimes it seemed as if no one cherished Arab culture and even its clichés more than the Arabs themselves. And it would have been hard for the evening to be more picturesque. Umm Kulthum was blasting on the stereo, and a belly dancer was coursing past us every few minutes just to bat her thick eyelashes at him, *Omar Sharif.* For a generation of Westerners, Sharif represented the ideal Arab. And the same was true for Arabs themselves, for whom the name Omar alone (Sharif was born Michel Shalhoub) recalled some of the giants of Arab history—Omar ibn al-Khattab, of course, but also Omar ibn Abi Rabi'ah (d. 712), a Meccan poet who is said to have watched female pilgrims unveil at the holy shrine as he stood astonished by the beauty of their bare faces. The poet was similarly enamored of his own appearance, and this uncomplicated narcissism makes him appear, in his work, to be a sort of Meccan movie star *avant la lettre*. Omar was one of the early masters of the *ghazal,* or love poem, a genre he stamped with a vanity so gallant that he permitted his conquests to sing his praises. In one poem, he offers his version of a conversation between three sisters as they watch him ride in from out of the blue:

> *While they were speaking of me, they saw me.*
> *I was galloping straight at them, proudly,*
> *When the eldest asked, do we know that man?*

The middle one said, "Oh yes—it's Omar!"
And the youngest, who'd fallen hard for me, said:
"Know him? Can you hide the moon?"

Sharif, it was clear, was also familiar with having people fall hard for him. He was the center of this large gathering of friends and their families, indisputably the star, but playfully ironic about his magnitude. His easy demeanor suggested he might have really believed the only difference between his successes and failures and those of his friends is that his were just more public. Sharif had used this vulnerability and intimacy to great effect throughout his career, especially in his first Hollywood film, *Lawrence of Arabia*, in which his character alternately shelters the weak and victimizes them.

The first time most Americans ever saw him on-screen was when the black-robed Bedouin noble Sherif Ali rides in from the distance (oddly evocative of Omar ibn Abi Rabi'ah's entrance) to shoot a rival tribesman for drinking from his water supply. It is a cruel introduction, but without his character *Lawrence of Arabia* would not be a classic. The movie turns on the gravity of his conscience, his ability to think, doubt, learn, and thus change. Lawrence is the hero of the story, and all the other characters are merely symbols of human qualities, like greed, brutality, and naïveté, or of national stereotypes (the American huckster, the French cynic, the generous and proud Arab, and so on). Sherif Ali is the only real human being in a picture over three hours long. It is he who questions Lawrence's decision to go to Aqaba and then rescue a man lost in the desert, and it is through his eyes that we appreciate the Englishman's courage. He is appalled by Lawrence's command to cut down a column of haggard Ottoman troops to take his personal revenge against the Turks, for although Sherif Ali killed a man at his drinking well, thirst for water is one thing, and thirst for blood is something else. And it is through his character that the screen version of Colonel T. E. Lawrence's colorful and often inaccurate retelling of the Arab revolt subtly makes an important point about Arab history. Once the Arabs have reached Damascus, and their representative council succumbs to chaos, Lawrence storms from the hall to take his leave of his former colleagues. His friend, however, is going nowhere. "I shall stay here," says Sherif Ali, "and learn politics." It's true that the Western powers, excluding America, carved up the former Ottoman Empire to satisfy their own interests, but it was the Arabs themselves who determined the political culture of the modern Middle East.

That notion—that the history of modern Arab politics is primarily the story of the actions of Arabs themselves—wouldn't, at first glance, seem all that controversial. Yet it is, thanks in no small part to the work of a man who was once an elementary-school classmate of Omar Sharif's: Edward Said. If Sharif represented, for Westerners, the ideal Arab man, Said, in a far more substantive fashion, came to be seen as the ideal Arab intellectual, the man Westerners looked to to make sense of the region. Indeed, no writer has had a bigger impact on the way Westerners see the Middle East than Said did over the course of more than three decades of work. The paradox is that while Said's work was devoted, in principle, to the idea that for too long Arab culture and Arab life had been misunderstood and misrepresented in the West, his own work often ended up fostering new, if different, misrepresentations. Most important, Said's work, inadvertently or not, lent itself to a kind of monolithic definition of Arab culture, and a view of the region's politics that in the end saw Arabs as more acted upon than acting.

I visited Said one afternoon at his office at Columbia University a few months before 9/11. The first time I had met him was in the mid-1980s, when I was in graduate school at Cornell, where he had come to give a lecture. He was one of the major figures in American academia, a reputation he clinched more than a decade before as one of the early Anglophone advocates of French post-structuralism, until his 1978 masterwork, *Orientalism,* vaulted him out of the rarefied world of literary theory and made him a public intellectual and a media star. In the years that followed, the Palestinian-American's stature only grew. His real-world activism as a member of the Palestinian National Congress enhanced his academic credentials, and vice versa. And his transition from scholarship to media criticism was seamless, for the methods he had used to categorize the prejudices of nineteenth-century artists, writers, and scholars were just as easily used to document the sins of late-twentieth-century newspapers and television networks, particularly since, in Said's view, little had changed in the way Westerners thought about and described Arab culture. "Every European," he wrote, "in what he could say about the Orient was consequently a racist, an imperialist, and almost totally ethnocentric."[1]

Orientalism was not a book about the contemporary Middle East. Nor was its thesis just reflexive anticolonialism, that the Great Powers had ravaged other societies through military, political, and economic means. It focused on the way Western authors and scholars had written about the region in the nineteenth century. But Said's conclusion—that the work of these writers and scholars had served as a handmaiden of the Western imperial endeavor to subjugate the Middle East—resonated with modern Arab concerns. The book was very much of its time, keyed to the self-image of a confident post-Algeria, post-Vietnam intellectual left for whom the Palestinian cause, with the paramilitary élan of Yasser Arafat and the youthfully glamorous violence of his Soviet-backed cadre, represented the revolutionary work that remained to be done. The book's success in influencing Western opinion of the Middle East was also enhanced by the fact that it gave intellectuals center stage. Even though Said was in effect charging writers, journalists, and scholars with conspiring to oppress Third World peoples, by arguing that they had played a key role in shaping history, he was also, paradoxically, flattering intellectuals.

Said offered me a seat. His office library held a huge collection of literature, philosophy, and history in many languages, including the more than thirty that *Orientalism* had been translated into. He sat across from me, squeezing his large athletic frame awkwardly into a chair to make himself less physically striking, more intellectual. We talked about what he was working on, his book on late style, or how some artists and writers achieve a certain refinement and power right before their deaths, which was certainly on his mind as he was fighting the cancer that eventually killed him in 2003. I gave him a recording of Palestinian folk songs I'd found in my Brooklyn neighborhood, and then, remembering halfway through the visit that he had written in his memoir of how he disliked Oriental music, I apologized for bringing him a less than welcome gift. I told him it was meant to thank him for introducing me to the Middle East and giving me access to a new world, a body of literature I knew nothing of previously, thousands of years of history, dozens of different cultures and languages. After all, the crucial and enduring insight at the heart of Said's work was that the people of the Middle East deserved to have their lives described as they were, and not as Westerners imagined (or hoped, or feared) them to be. He was touched, flattered, and a little embarrassed. It was the last time I saw him.

After 9/11, the ground literally shifted under his feet, the grounds of a city where he'd become famous for a thesis no longer supported by reality. Contrary to Said's argument, the West's fear of Islamic terror was not merely a projection of Orientalist stereotypes. In the introduction to *Covering Islam*, he had ridiculed "speculations about the latest conspiracy to blow up buildings, sabotage commercial airliners," based as they were on "highly exaggerated stereotypes," but he never emended his own caricatures of U.S. Middle East policy and the American media, a repertory rehearsed over a quarter of a century that, as the Arab response to 9/11 showed, was drawn from the lingua franca of Middle Eastern propaganda. Arab journalists and officials complained that Israeli prime minister Ariel Sharon had manipulated U.S. public opinion by likening suicide operations in New York and Washington to terror in Jerusalem and Tel Aviv. But it was Said and other Arab commentators who'd made the linkage between Israel and 9/11 by arguing that the attacks came as a result of legitimate Arab grievances over U.S. support for the Jewish state.

Said was the transitional figure between the academy and the world of mainstream Arab politics. And thus it was no accident that American academics came to sound like Arab nationalist and Islamist ideologues claiming that the 9/11 attacks were justified due to America's bad policies in the Middle East. As *Orientalism* had become the touchstone of Middle East studies, the academy could not help but see Washington as the dark angel of history. If you were not working to expose the racist lies fabricated for the purpose of destroying Third World peoples, then, willingly or not, you were collaborating with the state. It was this essentialism that allowed Said, the man who had accused scores of intellectuals of holding essentialist views of the Arabs and Islam, to write as though real-world events, like 9/11, never happened. If ideas or policies are not shaped in response to changing realities or interests but determined by immutable qualities, like anti-Muslim and anti-Arab racism, then information is irrelevant and debates are a waste of time, for the central issue is always the same—whatever is wrong with the Middle East is the fault of the West.

By attacking other writers with different points of view—his enmity toward the Middle East scholar Bernard Lewis was famous—Said helped set the terms by which Western intellectuals and reporters could write about the Arabs and Islam. Since in Said's view there was no such thing as disinterested intellectual work—all textual strategies served power—what mattered was taking the right side. If you were in the academic industry, jobs, publishing contracts, committee appointments, and such depended on it, and if you were outside of Said's direct sphere of influence, you were tarred as a racist, or for Arabic-speaking Middle Easterners like Fouad Ajami and Kanan

Makiya there were equally ugly formulations, like "native infor-mant," that is to say, traitor. Ajami is "a disgrace," Said wrote. "Not just because of his viciousness and hatred of his own people, but because what he says is so trivial and so ignorant."[2]

Said's litmus test for intellectual good faith was the Palestinian cause. Ajami and Makiya had at one time been safely within the fold, but then became preoccupied with their own concerns, which had nothing to do with Palestine and Israel or even the West. Ajami, a Lebanese Shia, became concerned with the outrages of Sunni supremacism, while the Iraqi Makiya dedicated himself to fighting Saddam Hussein, but from Said's point of view all they'd done by exposing rifts in the Arab consensus was to confirm for Americans the bad things that they had wanted to believe about Arabs, and Said's strategy was to credit Western intellectuals with all the sins they wanted attributed to themselves. His condemnations of the American media for its one-dimensional coverage of the Middle East were famous. "Very little of the detail," he had written, "the human density, the passion of Arab-Moslem life has entered the awareness of even those people whose profession it is to report the Arab world." But his accounts of the region were equally empty of human density and passion; the conflicting opinions of Middle Easterners, for instance, like the quarrels Ajami and Makiya had with Arabism, Said wrote off as apostasy.

Of course, intolerance of dissenting Arab opinion wasn't the only characteristic Said's work shared with Arab nationalism. Like many of the doctrine's major ideologues, he saw the Arab world as defined, largely, by the West and in its opposition to it.

Given *Orientalism*'s canonical status as one of the central works on the modern Middle East, it bears repeating that the book isn't about the Middle East. Rather, it is a polemical piece of cultural crit-icism about Western portrayals of it over the course of a brief period in Middle Eastern history. This wasn't a coincidence: the reason Said wrote about Western views of the Middle East, rather than about the region itself, was because, as he wrote, "I have no interest in, much less capacity for, showing what the true Orient and Islam really are."[3]

The notion that it is impossible to describe things as they "really are" was a postmodernist escape hatch that appealed to the book's more sophisticated readers, but was lost on much of a literate American audience that just wanted some sort of introduction to a complex part of the world. But consider how strange that line is: the person who, perhaps more than anyone else, has shaped the contemporary Western understanding of Arabism and Islam was uninterested in showing what the Arab world was really like. This had two consequences. First, in holding Western colonialism responsible for the conditions of the region, Said let Americans off the hook insofar as they didn't have to understand the politics, culture, and societies of the region itself. Second, it sent the message that Arabs were less responsible for what happened in the region than the West was. In effect, in Said's work the most relevant fact of modern Middle Eastern history is Western interference. He glided over the diversity, conflicts, and tensions among Arabs themselves, and painted a picture of an Arab community unified by Western oppression, a worldview derived from Arab nationalism.

There is a great deal of confusion about the nature of Arab nationalism, most of it arising from the idea that it is a secular doctrine. This misunderstanding results from the mirror imaging of Western scholars, the misplaced hopes of European and American officials, and the misleading descriptions of Arab nationalist ideologues who recognized that the Westerners feared Islam as a political force. Arab nationalism is secular in the sense that it does not derive its political legitimacy from divine revelation, but it is an absolutism nonetheless, enshrining the idea of the eternal and the unchanging not in an omnipotent creator but in the nation. This is profoundly different from Western secularism, which makes room for different, even opposing worldviews and lays no claims to absolute truth.

One of the major theorists of Arab nationalism was Sati' al-Husri (1879–1968), who played a leading role in Syrian and then Iraqi politics and education. Influenced by the Young Turks and their brand of Turkish nationalism, Husri also drew on the example of nineteenth-century German intellectuals and political activists and argued that the nation is a primordial force that impresses itself upon the masses whether they will it or not, and whether or not the state comes into being. The nation is different from the state, so even if the people do not create the legal and political foundations of an actual state, the nation exists nonetheless, a spirit with a destiny independent of the people's will. The task, then, of the Arab nation's political and intellectual leaders is to help the masses recognize and fulfill Arabism's destiny. As Husri explained, "Under no circumstances, should we say: 'As long as [someone] does not wish to be an Arab, and as long as he is disdainful of his Arabness, then he is not an Arab.' He is an Arab regardless of his own wishes."[4]

Husri, a Sunni, included minorities in his scheme, but there was never any real effort to detach Arabism from Islam, which would have been doomed from the outset in any event. "To define the Arab nation in terms of its history," as the Iraqi-born historian Elie Kedourie wrote, is "to come upon the fact that Islam originated among the Arabs, was revealed in Arabic to an Arab prophet."[5] The language of the Arabs, the defining feature that ostensibly made them one nation, is a shared tongue considered sacred by most Middle Easterners because it is the language of the Holy Quran. And hence Arab nationalism, as Kedourie writes, "affirms a fundamental unbreakable link between Islam and Arabism."

If the minorities had hoped that Arab nationalism would emancipate them, or at least deflect attention from their status, they were not nearly so naive as to expose themselves to the inevitable repercussions of challenging Sunni prestige and actively agitating against

Islam. Instead, they sought to court favor with the Sunnis, the sect that constitutes roughly 70 percent of the Arabic-speaking world and has ruled it for most of the last fourteen hundred years. In effect, the minorities were little more than smaller tribes aligning themselves with the Sunni strong horse, and so their goal was not to ditch Islam but to elide all other sectarian and ethnic identities by raising everyone to the level of Sunni Arabs. In keeping with the status-anxiety-ridden logic of the convert, many of the minorities became more Sunni than the Sunnis themselves. Michel Aflaq, a Syrian-born Greek Orthodox Christian, commended all the Arabs to "attach themselves to Islam and to the most precious element of their Arabness, the Prophet Muhammad."[6] A half century later, Said sounded the same note before an American audience in reaffirming the bargain minorities had made with the Sunni majority: "Islam is something all Arabs share in and is an integral part of our identity."[7] This overcompensation is perhaps yet another reason so many have been misled into believing that Arab nationalism is a secular philosophy—if non-Muslims express their devotion to Islam, then Arab nationalism can't really have anything to do with religious faith.

The Sunnis themselves were slow to embrace Arab nationalism. They owed their primary allegiance to the larger Islamic *umma* and the Ottoman caliphate, not to a linguistically separate sub-nation. And inasmuch as they also identified with their sect, there was no reason to give up their place and privilege on behalf of an *umma* that made no distinction between them and nonbelievers, Christians, Jews, and, worst of all, the heretical Shia. But with the dissolution of the empire, many former Ottoman officers and administrators, like Lawrence's comrades-in-arms, saw their main chance at hand.

The Sunnis refashioned themselves as Arab nationalists and in doing so strengthened their claims to govern not just their villages, cities, and districts of origin but also the entirety of the Arabic-speaking provinces—for after all, they were Arab, brother to those they meant to put under their dominion. Later they came to protest against the borders randomly imposed by the European powers, but those borders had given them sovereignty over lands they had no right to rule, except that the subject populations also spoke dialects of the same language. The Arabs complained of the new map of the Middle East and the powers that enforced it, not because they believed that the Sunnis should not govern Shia and Kurds in Iraq, or that the Saud clan of the Nejd had no claim to the Hejaz, but because it limited the scope of their infinite ambitions, and so they fought each other for larger shares, in Iraq, the Arabian Peninsula, Syria, Transjordan, and Palestine. Arab nationalism in their view was yet another heroic chapter, albeit unfinished, in the Sunni Arab triumphalist version of Middle Eastern history.

The mass graves throughout the region stretching from the Gulf to the Mediterranean testify to the willingness of Arab nationalist leaders to enforce Arabism. Arab intellectuals praised and exculpated the rulers by forging a narrative of the region that ignored more than a millennium of Middle Eastern history. Arab nationalism suppressed confessional, ethnic, racial, and tribal differences and brought forth a mythical Middle East where Jews and Christians were always treated as brothers, where there are no Kurds or Shia, Druze or Alawis, but only Arabs. It did away with the distinct legacies and contributions of those various communities while, as one scholar put it, "conveniently passing over the less than seemly episodes—the self-inflicted wounds; the civil wars, massacres, and human atrocities; the ethnic, linguistic, and religious cleavages and dislocations."[8] The purpose of Arab nationalist historiography was to coerce a single homogeneous identity from many competing, often antagonistic strands. The genre afforded its authors two types of apologetics: either accounts enumerating the legendary exploits of the heroes who fought for the greatness of the Arab nation; or epic narratives of betrayal and foreign subterfuge that had separated the Arabs from their destiny, like Said's *Orientalism*.

It is an index of Arab nationalism's hold over the American imagination, thanks in no small part to Said, that after 9/11 even those who didn't claim that U.S. policies led to the attacks nonetheless took the Arab nationalist worldview for granted—9/11 was about Us versus Them. "Why do they hate us?" we asked. Is it because of what we do or who we are? But in believing that 300 million Arabs had really lined up as one against America, we had been taken in by a mirage.

CHAPTER 3

"No Voice Louder Than the Cry of Battle": Arab Nationalism and Anti-Americanism

In the second half of the twentieth century, with the five-hundred-year-old Ottoman Empire dissolved and its British and French successors on their way out of the region, the Arabic-speaking Middle East seemed to be rushing headlong toward modernity. Ostensibly secular governments checked the rise of the Islamic revivalism best represented by Egypt's Muslim Brotherhood, and in the considered opinion of many nationalism rather than religion was the wave of the Arab future. So, what happened, and why was that advance checked?

There are a number of explanations, some of them drawn from the ideological biases of the region itself—such as the notion that the conflict with Israel siphoned off energies that would otherwise be used to build Arab societies and/or that the legacy of European colonialism prevented the Middle East from progressing. Other explanations were torn from the pages of Western sociology and political science textbooks—one side argued that Arab state institutions were too weak, while another contended that the Arab state was too strong and gave no room to civil society. In fact, the issue was much more elemental. What looked like secularization was merely a veneer laid over a society that had been proudly Muslim for over a millennium. Moreover, the ostensible engine of Arab modernization—Arab nationalism—was little more than an elevated tribal covenant. Arab nationalism was how Arab regimes made the various clans, sects, and tribes collectively called the Arabs cohere, and no one could galvanize the masses like the Egyptian president Gamal Abdel Nasser.

Mustafa told me that he had been Nasser's director of censorship twice. A short, balding bachelor in his mid-sixties with a large mouth that filled easily with laughter, Mustafa hardly radiated the kind of awful power that position would seem to require. He lived a short walking distance from me in the center of the city, overlooking the two major squares in downtown Cairo, Midan al-Tahrir and Midan Talaat Harb, where the noise, he complained, had gotten worse over the years, the crowds larger, and the streets dirtier. He had lived there with his sister long enough to remember when it was one of Cairo's most fashionable neighborhoods, with broad boulevards, large public squares, and mansions and apartment buildings designed by European architects, and just down the block was Groppi, a Greek café that virtually became a cinematic cliché so many directors had staged film romances there, with lovers discreetly reaching for each other's hand across a cup of Turkish coffee and a mille-feuille. Since then, the sun and desert winds had browned the buildings the same dun hue as the Pyramids, Groppi had turned into a dusty relic, and Mustafa had become a critic.

He ran a foreign film club, wrote articles on Egyptian and European movies, and published a book on the stars of the golden age of Cairo cinema, from the 1930s through the early 1960s. I met him through Sayed Badreya, a Hollywood-based Egyptian-born actor and filmmaker whose Web site featured his work with James Cameron on *True Lies,* the Arnold Schwarzenegger vehicle about saving the world, and his marriage, from a terrorist group named Crimson Jihad. It seems Sayed was so proud of his American-immigrant success story that it didn't occur to him that having worked on a film Arabs loathe for its depiction of them as violent, and hapless, fanatics would hurt his reputation in Cairo, the Hollywood of the Arabs. And so when Sayed tried to raise money for *Saving Egyptian Film Classics,* a documentary warning that the film stock of many of the country's cinematic classics was deteriorating, Mustafa was one of the few who came to the filmmaker's aid. The rest of the Egyptian film community was not eager to support what sounded to them like a catalog of their incompetence, for to note even the tiniest blemish in Egyptian society is typically perceived as an all-out assault against Egypt, the Arabs, the *umma,* and Islam.

Mustafa led me into the kitchen and poured us tumblers full of whiskey, the alcohol of choice for Egyptian intellectuals of a certain age and income bracket—not the fashionable single malts, but scotch blends, Johnnie Walker, Dewar's, Seagram's, real liquor with Western labels, holdovers from a different time, when modern Egypt was trying to integrate Western habits and brands into its own tastes and traditions. Mustafa was concerned that I wasn't going to get a very accurate picture of contemporary Egypt by watching Egyptian movies from that bygone age.

"The period idealized in those films is long past. It was a different moment in Egyptian history, different ideas about Egypt and its place in the world. Sayed is trying to preserve them lest the manner and style of life become as incomprehensible to future generations as the hieroglyphs were before the Rosetta stone."

Those golden-age films serve as an essential reference for middle-class Egyptians, less for those like Mustafa old enough to recall a Cairo that they remember as cosmopolitan as Paris or London, than for the younger generation who otherwise have little evidence besides their parents' and grandparents' reveries to prove that once upon a time the aesthetic ideal in Cairo was women in stylish skirts, French manicures, and impossible hairdos, not the veil, a black robe, and black gloves. Of course that glittering city of the past, an urban dreamscape of nightclubs, black-tie galas, and swimming pool parties, was unavailable to all but the wealthiest Cairenes, and yet the films themselves are self-conscious enough to recognize the class and cultural divides as well as the growing conflict between traditional Egypt and encroaching modernity.

Ghazal al-banat (1949), or "The Flirtation of Girls," is the movie George Cukor or Preston Sturges might have made had he been born on the Nile. It opens with a musical number featuring several young women on horseback singing, led by the famous Egyptian singer Layla Mourad playing an easily distracted young woman whose wealthy father has hired an Arabic tutor to improve his French-speaking daughter's classical *fusha*. The tutor, played by Naguib al-Rihani, is an elderly bachelor at first astonished by the girl's impertinence and then overcome with love for her youth and carefree ways. In the climactic scene, he follows her around an entire night desperate for her to end his loneliness as she leads him through a grand tour of golden-age Cairo, including a brawl at a nightclub and a random encounter with one of the giants of Egyptian cinema, the actor and director Youssef Wahby, playing himself.

It is well into the evening when the tutor and the girl stumble upon Wahby's home as he is putting the finishing touches on his newest screenplay while in another part of the mansion Egypt's greatest modern composer, Muhammad Abdel Wahab, also playing himself, just happens to be working on a melancholic love song for the movie. The director, the tutor, and the girl look on as Abdel Wahab rehearses his orchestra, during which the song seems to remind the tutor that the nature of desire is such that he will never win the girl. Leaving the director's home, the tutor and the girl hitch a ride with a dashing young airplane pilot whom she has fallen for, and he for her. The camera pans to the sad, silent, and suddenly very wise eyes of the tutor. It was the actor's last film; Rihani was dying while it was being shot, and *Ghazal al-banat* was shown after his death at the age of sixty, a real-life sad ending that only deepens the movie's rendering of love, loneliness, and longing.

At the time, the film must have seemed to be about the ongoing transformation of Egyptian society, mixing up as it did an aging teacher of Arabic, a flirtatious modern girl, and an airplane pilot in a madcap tumble from the country's past into its uncertain future. But in retrospect it seems to mark the end of an era. Three years after its release, a military regime came to power that would look to the West primarily for weapons, not culture, and the national temperament was less disposed toward the adventure of the new and fell into a self-crippling paranoia. For instance, Layla Mourad, born Jewish and later converted to Islam, was accused of collaborating with Israel, and while the charges were eventually dropped, the point was made. No one was above suspicion, and "traitor," "imperialist," and "Zionist agent" were the watchwords of the Arab nationalist consensus, as "infidel," "crusader," and "Zionist agent" would fulfill the same function for the Islamist movement decades later.

A friend claimed the apartment he rented used to be Mourad's, a luxury penthouse with panoramic views of Cairo all the way to the Citadel of Saladin and the Muhammad Ali Mosque. Downstairs was a brothel where the women shuffled in and out of the lobby in black robes and veils to deflect suspicion. Whores in burqas was certainly not the future that mid-century Egyptian cinema imagined. And yet there is no mystery as to what happened to that Egypt, or why a nation seemingly on the verge of modernity turned the clock backward on itself. Egypt has been a Muslim country for thirteen hundred years, and the half century or so nostalgically regarded as Egyptian modernity is most accurately regarded as a historical anomaly—albeit one that Egyptian cinema managed to capture in all its wit and glamour.

"Those films are not like American movies," Mustafa said. "It's small. But it's ours. The language, the music, the manners—it touches every Egyptian's heart. You Americans make movies that everyone across the world loves." Everyone except for his former employer.

"When Nasser was mad at the U.S.," Mustafa explained, "he wanted us to let in fewer American movies." As censor, Mustafa was responsible for vetting both Egyptian-made material and cultural imports. "My greatest achievement," he explained, "was getting *Blow-Up* shown in Egypt."

Michelangelo Antonioni's 1966 masterpiece includes a notorious scene with a photographer and two models rolling around on the floor. The camera cuts away before the orgy begins in earnest, but it was hard to imagine how Mustafa had managed to screen it in a Muslim country.

"There was silence in the theater," he said, his small body shaking with the laughter of a silent-movie villain who has just tied a maiden to the railroad tracks. "It was very uncomfortable."

It wasn't the movie's explicit sexuality that got him fired. "I wrote an introduction that appeared on the screen before the movie," he said. "I explained that this film is a comment on our own contemporary events." The movie was shown in the immediate aftermath of the June 1967 Arab-Israeli war. "I said the film is about things that aren't what they seem to be." In the movie's final scene two mimes are pretending to play tennis, and as the photographer walks away, he hears a tennis ball batted back and forth. "The analogy was obvious," Mustafa said. "During the war, we kept hearing that Egypt was destroying the enemy. Nasser told us that we were winning."

Israel had effectively taken Egypt out of the war on its first day by crippling its air force, the signature of Arab military modernity. Yet for several days Voice of the Arabs, Nasser's official radio station, continued to broadcast that the Arab armies were in the process of driving the Zionist entity into the sea once and for all. Nasser was well served by Cairo's advanced media technology, for long before satellite broadcasting made Dubai and Qatar Arab-world media centers, radio was the mass medium of choice, and its two biggest stars were Umm Kulthum and the Egyptian president. "After the war," Mustafa said, "anyone who wanted to know the truth listened to the BBC."

Maybe some did, but facts didn't seem to matter much to the Egyptian or Arab masses who begged Nasser to rescind the resignation he offered after the war's failure. They insisted that he not abandon them to their fate. It would be interesting to know exactly what ominous future the thronging crowds feared without Nasser to guide them. He had already steered them toward apocalypse; how could it get worse?

Historians of the period, Western and Arab, typically describe the 1967 war as the nail in the coffin of Arab nationalism, a catastrophe of such historic proportions that it compelled Arab elites, opinion makers, and intellectuals to reorient their ideological bearings from secular Arab nationalism to Islamism. And yet while the proportions of the two basic ingredients, Arabism and Islam, may have changed some in the wake of the 1967 war, the essential ideological recipe stayed the same—resistance against the West. The Arab nationalism that the twentieth-century ideologues advocated was an ideology built on both political and cultural pillars, and while the 1967 defeat shook the first, it did not bring down the edifice.

In part, that's because the allure of Arab nationalism seems to make its adherents impervious to the facts. The implausibility of an actual political union between Arab states had been proven before the 1967 war when the United Arab Republic, which joined Nasser's Egypt and Baathist Syria, lasted just three years (1958–1961), and it would be demonstrated yet again after a U.S.-led coalition kept Saddam Hussein from annexing Kuwait in 1991. Nonetheless, today, long after June 1967, Arabism and the hope of Arab unity continue to be a resilient cultural force that Arab leaders use to manage their domestic affairs, legitimize their regional ambitions, and create consensus out of dissonance and catastrophe. In doing so, all of these leaders— from Saddam to bin Laden to Hezbollah's Hassan Nasrallah—have sought to emulate one man: Nasser. Mustafa's boss remains the Arab nationalist leader par excellence, upon whom all others model themselves.

Given Nasser's stature, it seems peculiar that the Egyptians had a very minor part in early efforts to promote Arab nationalism. Intellectual figures like Sati' al-Husri had hoped that Cairo would come to play the leading role that its size, history, and cultural influence all warranted, but through the opening years of the twentieth century, as the Ottoman Empire was on its last legs, the energies of Egyptian thinkers were consumed by other intellectual and cultural currents, like pan-Islamism and Arab liberalism. It wasn't until the Arabs' 1948 war with Israel that the Egyptians entered the Arab nationalist arena when the country's decrepit monarchy went to war against the nascent Jewish state as a way to assert its Arab bona fides alongside Syria, Lebanon, Iraq, and the Hashemite Kingdom of Transjordan.

The Egyptians were especially wary of the Hashemites and calculated that they could not risk letting King Abdullah walk away with too large a share of the spoils should his well-trained, British-led Arab Legion actually defeat the Jews. There were domestic issues as well, and Egypt's King Farouk needed to shore up his legitimacy against local rivals, especially the Muslim Brotherhood, which had agitated on behalf of the Palestinians as a pan-Islamist cause for two decades. In declaring war against the Zionists, Egypt was also battling its Arab rivals (and putative allies) in order to check their regional ambitions.[1]

Nasser, a veteran of the 1948 war, came to power on a wave of popular resentment against not only Israel and the established Arab order that had lost the war but also the Western powers that underwrote both. His radio station tarred Jordan and Saudi Arabia as American stooges, even though the Egyptian president cultivated warm relations with the CIA throughout the 1950s.[2] President Eisenhower wondered why the Arabs loathed America when, after forcing France and England to stand down during the 1956 Suez crisis, it had handed Nasser his one success in a career of adventurist disasters.[3] But the reason is simple: with the eventual departure of America's two Western rivals from the region, only the United States was left for Nasser to use as a fulcrum to enhance his prestige by leveraging popular opinion against his regional rivals Jordan and Saudi Arabia, the so-called conservative—that is, pro-American—regimes. And even in the 1950s, it was clear that one way to unite the Arab masses was to attack the West. One of the ways Arab nationalism became a powerful and popular ideology, in other words, was by becoming fused with another powerful current of feeling: anti-Americanism.

It may seem surprising that there was a deep wellspring of anti-Americanism in the region five decades ago, since it's sometimes been made to seem as if Arab anger at the United States started with the Bush administration. The truth, of course, is that Arabs' anger at America long predated the invasion of Iraq. This was obvious immediately after 9/11, for despite the general goodwill that the United States was supposed to have enjoyed in the region following the attacks, in reality the most vocal Arab spokesmen celebrated or justified 9/11, while others charged that Washington itself had engineered the attacks in order to hurt the image of the Arabs and destroy Islam. The U.S. ambassador to Egypt at the time, David Welch, wrote an editorial in one of the Egyptian papers politely asking the press to stop accusing the American government of slaughtering its own citizens, a request that didn't go over too well with the Egyptian media, outraged that this self-styled proconsul had the nerve to try to dictate terms to them, a free press.[4]

As for the ostensibly sympathetic Arab opinion makers, they disguised their anti-Americanism by claiming that they felt bad for America until Bush's post-9/11 wars made Arabs despise America, which, while self-serving, was not entirely false. Just about the only thing that could really make America hatred noticeably worse is if

Washington decided to confront the anti-American ideological and political agenda that leads to attacks on U.S. citizens, allies, and interests—which is exactly what the Bush administration did, through diplomatic, political, and military means. It was only natural that America's image started to trend even farther down in the Arab world once all the post-9/11 crocodile tears had dried: fighting back never earned anyone the love of those who wish them harm.

Nonetheless, an entire social science rose from the ashes of 9/11, a growth industry with public opinion polls and surveys, along with man-on-the-street interviews and consultations with Arab officials and intelligentsia, churning out data to explain why Arabs were angry with the United States—or, to be more precise, why Arabs hated U.S. policy since it was clear that they had a high regard for America itself and its people. Alas, it never dawned on those American researchers and journalists who reported back to the home front with their dire findings that separating a people from its leaders is one of political warfare's oldest stratagems: *We have no quarrel with your great nation, only your bad government and its vile policies, so stand aside and let us finish our work, after which there will be a time of great understanding and comity.*

Liberal democracies should be immune to this kind of propaganda, but it never occurred even to those the White House tasked with public diplomacy and "re-branding" America to explain to the Arabs, and some Americans, that the essential feature of our republic, what distinguishes our form of governance from theirs, is that we *choose* our policy makers. The Arab conceit that there is some wide gap between Americans and the leaders they elect became even more ludicrous after the American people showed exactly how far they were from the policies of the U.S. government by electing George W. Bush to a second term in 2004.

Still, it's not hard to see why tracking surges in anti-Americanism with hard numbers, even if they didn't mean anything, became attractive to those who wanted to illustrate that the best way to keep Arab youth from killing Americans was to change American policies in the Middle East. If it was only a matter of tweaking a few policies, then 9/11 could be written off as a misunderstanding of sorts, and there was no real conflict between Americans and Arabs. The problem, however, is that there is no real correlation between most U.S. policies and Arab anti-Americanism. Consider the two policies for which America is most famously hated throughout the region, and for which it was attacked by Nasser more than a half century ago—its support of Israel, and its backing of "corrupt" Arab regimes.

While it's true that Washington immediately recognized the Jewish state at its inception in May 1948, it was only after Israel's victory in the 1967 war that the two nations consolidated an alliance when Washington came to see Israel as a potent counterforce to Soviet influence in the Middle East. Until 1967 it was France that supplied Israel with most of its weaponry, including Mirage fighter jets, a detail that did not stop Nasser from broadcasting the lie that American pilots had flown missions against Arab targets in the 1967 war. The Egyptian president could count on the outraged Arab response because he as much as anyone had seen to it that the United States was despised by the Arab masses.

As for the second complaint, U.S. support of despotic Arab rulers, the premise is that Washington's backing is the only thing that allows these regimes to stay in power, a notion so prevalent that it became a cornerstone of Al Qaeda strategy. It's true of course that Egypt receives some two billion dollars in U.S. aid annually, but regime maintenance is a relatively inexpensive affair, where some of the most lavish expenditures are devoted to feathering the retirement nests of high-level military and security officers. And what it costs an Arab regime to defeat an Islamist insurgency—torture, murder, assassination, collective punishment—hardly requires the beneficence of the U.S. taxpayer. Two of the most repressive regimes in the region, Iran and Syria, terrorize their own populations quite competently without any American support at all, as did Saddam for the last two decades of his career. The "U.S. support for despots makes the Arabs angry" is a red herring: after 9/11, the Bush administration apologized for supporting Arab despots, and then it went out and deposed one, but all that happened was that Sunni Arabs across the region became outraged that the United States had taken down an Arab champion like Saddam.

Regardless of what the United States does, or how Washington changes its policies, whether it targets Arab despots or supports them, anti-Americanism is an Arab constant. It's so ubiquitous, in fact, that you can find it even at places like the American University in Cairo, one of the manifest strongholds of U.S. "soft" power in the Middle East.

Opened by American Episcopal missionaries in 1919, the AUC intended to provide the Egyptian ruling classes with the intellectual foundations of democratic governance. Today, the school is a regime citadel, the alma mater of Egypt's First Lady, Suzanne Mubarak, and her two sons, Alaa and Gamal, where the ruling classes pay close to ten times the average Egyptian's annual salary to get their children an American-style education and imprimatur. Nonetheless, one warm winter afternoon I saw dozens of students demonstrating in the courtyard, heavily muscled boys in brand-new black T-shirts bearing the legend, in English, "Jihad Is the Only Language They'll Understand." This was more than a year before the invasion of Iraq, and American military force was limited to Afghanistan, where the Taliban's Arab guests were plotting against U.S. citizens, interests, and allies, including Hosni Mubarak and his Egypt. How had the boys and girls destined to inherit the regime taken up the slogans of the regime's chief rivals? Because anti-Americanism is the region's lingua franca, and from Nasser to Nasrallah it has not changed in over fifty years.

The United States is hated not because of what it does, or because of what it is. The United States is hated for what it is *not*, not Arab and not Muslim. America plays the part of the utterly alien force that puts the Arabs at existential risk unless they cohere as one.

The United States is the most powerful embodiment of the non-Arab other, and as any tribe is galvanized by the present threat of its rivals, anti-Americanism is the easiest method available to consolidate the Arabs and create consensus. Fear of the outsider clarifies Arabism, and war against him unifies the whole—or, in Nasser's formulation, "No voice louder than the cry of battle."

Arab nationalism is how the state retraces the limits to individual expression already drawn by Arab societies, including parents, families, and friends. Mustafa was fired as censor and then hired a second time to regulate the morals of moviegoing Egyptians for the simple reason that it just wasn't that sensitive a job. It doesn't take much to quiet the masses where self-censorship is a habit of mind; to step out of the consensus is to weaken the one, and if the integrity of the whole, whether it is family, tribe, or nation, is compromised, then there is no protection against the outsider. Arab nationalism is an expression of these same ideas raised to the supranational level; it is not merely a political doctrine but also a tribal value, an Arab value. Anti-Americanism is not the effect of American policies, but is organic to the region. Arab rulers have certainly played a role in fostering it, but its existence does not depend on them.

This is not something that's generally accepted in American press and policy circles, where the governing assumption is that the regimes are single-handedly responsible for inciting their people against America. The general thesis goes something like this: to deflect attention away from their corruption and incompetence and lay the blame elsewhere, Arab rulers use mosques, media, and educational systems to brainwash an otherwise-moderate Arab citizenry that would naturally be predisposed to like the United States were it not for the incitement of their rulers. This narrative is so widely accepted that the Bush administration based its democratization strategy on it: if Washington could circumvent the regimes and speak directly with the Arabs themselves, then it could make plain that America was not their enemy. This was a delusion. Nasser and his Arab nationalist followers have connected with the Arab masses, while the United States has failed, because Arab nationalism is a variation on a theme with which they were already familiar and comfortable—resistance to the West, or opposition to another tribe.

Arab mosques, media, and educational systems reflect the societies of which they are a part, as do Arab rulers. Nasser didn't invent anti-Americanism; his success, like that of any regime chief, was the result of his understanding the habits and wants of his people, and knowing when to manipulate them—and when to repress them. Indeed, Arab rulers are not wholly untruthful when they warn Washington policy makers that they're the only thing standing between the United States and the unfettered passions of the masses.

Consider the case of the Egyptian pop idol Shaaban Abdel Rahim. His premiere hit, "I Hate Israel," catapulted the overweight, pockmarked former shirt ironer to a fame and fortune surprising only in that no one had ever thought of such an obviously profitable tune before. In addition to hating Israel, Shaaban sang that he loved Amr Moussa, Egypt's then foreign minister, which caused Hosni Mubarak enough concern to push his putative rival over to a new post as secretary-general of the Arab League. This was a telltale sign not only of that organization's relative insignificance but also of the amount of respect the regime had for Shaaban's ability to move the masses. And so when he recorded his next song, a number that was sure to rival the success of "I Hate Israel," it was blocked from the airwaves lest millions of Egyptian youths humming a catchy pop tune about Sheikh Osama less than half a year after 9/11 send the wrong PR message to the Americans. The top political (and musical) echelons denied there ever was such an anthem to bin Laden, even if all of Cairo was already singing the chorus.

"**B**in—bin—bin—bin Laden!" sang the waiters at Pub 28, a small Cairo bar and restaurant. It was the early spring of 2002, and Pub 28, seemingly modeled after an alpine ski chalet, was always packed with expatriates and wealthy Egyptians with second,

European or American, passports. It was a melting pot of a different order of anti-Americanism, the anger and resentment of deracinated elites: Americans too young, confused, or rich to love or respect their own country; and wealthy Arabs, trust-fundamentalists, whose foreign education caused them embarrassment about the civic and moral deficiencies of their native land, a shame they turned into hatred of the world's center of cultural, economic, and political gravity, America.

When my tablemate started singing along to the bin Laden song, I chucked him in the shoulder. Jason looked at me as if he'd just come out of a trance. He was a twenty-four-year-old from Memphis with thick glasses and Elvis sideburns who'd worked for one of the wire services before coming to Cairo. We met at the AUC and roomed together for a while before he got into an altercation with a neighbor and broadly hinted he worked for the CIA, a vocation all Egyptians assume of all Americans in Egypt anyway. The neighbor called his bluff by claiming he flew Mubarak's private jet, which he did.

Jason inherited his gambling skills from his father, and weekend nights we pooled a small sum of money that he doubled after several hours of careful betting in the casino at the Marriott in Zamalek. It was a palace built in 1868 as a guesthouse for the empress Eugénie when she came to open the Suez Canal, and it was turned into a hotel a dozen years later when European creditors came to collect Egyptian debt for the canal. The casino was in a large gilded hall with a guard checking passports to make sure no Egyptians got in, though much of the crowd consisted of Egyptians carrying second passports. The rest were all Saudis, who along with Americans are the Egyptians' other favorite scapegoats.

Shortly after 9/11, as the extent of Saudi involvement in the global jihad became clearer, world opinion came to hold petro-fueled Wahhabism responsible for everything wrong with the Muslim Middle East. But the Saudis weren't the problem; they were merely the wealthiest clan of a super-tribe that is bound together to take on the other, and for the most part fought among themselves. And so in the fleshpots of Egypt, Jason and I cursed the custodians of the two holy shrines of Mecca and Medina only if they took a card we needed.

The Saudis were always the high rollers at the card tables and invariably the worst players. They bet clumsily and cursed their bad luck, even as Jason reminded them that it wasn't their luck that was drawing a card on fifteen. As we counted our meager winnings in the early morning hours over a plate of pancakes at the hotel restaurant, Jason often spoke of starting a gaming tutorial for elite Gulf clients. They admired his skill, and we liked hanging around them. We talked college football with the younger ones in nylon jackets bearing the insignia of some Texas school where they'd studied petroleum engineering. And we joked with the most ostentatiously Bedouin among them, the older, coarser Saudis with cheap rubber sandals rather than English brogues and Italian loafers under their dish-dashas, happy and worldly with a tumbler full of whiskey, a Moroccan girl in each arm, and looking to split a pair of tens.

We saw them in the nightclub boats moored along the banks of the Nile as well, drinking in packs or alone late into the night as evening turned to morning and one twenty-piece orchestra changed places with another and then another, with so many string and wind players and percussionists moving in and out of these large, dark halls it seemed there must have been entire Egyptian villages whose industry was the manufacture of band members. Waiters shuffled back and forth, rushing heaping plates of vegetables, hummus, and other Oriental dishes to diners at 3:30 in the morning, overcharging for Egyptian beer and wine and foreign whiskey while an MC in a threadbare evening jacket cased the room, chatting up guests to check their sobriety and disposable income. He circled back around to the stage and serenaded those he thought most likely to tip the entertainers by calling out their nationalities, like Amr Moussa taking a head count at the Arab League—"Oh, Lebanon," he intoned soulfully, "Oh, Algeria," and so on, invariably reserving the biggest spenders for last, "Oh, Kingdom of Saudi Arabia."

At 5:00 a.m., millions of Egyptians throughout the city of a thousand minarets were preparing for dawn prayers, while in the night-clubs the Saudis were still fresh in their bright white dishdashas, swinging their prayer beads over their head scarves as they improvised a Bedouin sword dance onstage and threw Egyptian pound notes at some half-naked belly dancer's powdered face. The beautiful bills amassed in a small pile at her feet—red, blue, green, and gold money stamped with the images of pharaohs, kings, and khedives, a hundred U.S. dollars' worth or more, maybe twice what the young Egyptian stagehand who stooped to collect it for her would see in a month.

The Egyptians are right; the Saudis are hypocrites, the missionaries of an austere Islam, Wahhabism, who come to Cairo on holiday to drink and whore while their wives sleep off a big day of shopping. But Egyptian piety comes cheap; without money there are few temptations, and if they resented the Saudis for the blessing bestowed on them in the form of vast energy resources, the Egyptians did their best to empty their wealthy co-religionists' oil coffers, charging them sometimes even twice what the clueless Americans paid for hotels, taxis, food, drinks, and entertainments.

The Egyptians contemptuously called the Gulfies "Arabs," drawing a line between themselves as the inheritors of a great and classical civilization and a bunch of lizard-eating Bedouin. It was hard not to sympathize with the Saudis since anti-Saudi sentiment was virtually indistinguishable from anti-Americanism. The Egyptians hated the Saudis because they were rich and because they were not Egyptians, and they blamed them for their problems and resented them, the profligate and arrogant tribesmen whom God had blessed in order to curse the Egyptians mired in their poverty. For the Egyptians, it was a zero-sum calculation, like all Bedouin math: we are poor because the other tribe is rich and they have kept to themselves the key to all the treasure.

The Egyptians even blamed the Saudis for radical Islam. No one questions the fact that the kingdom handsomely funds jihad throughout the world, but what had the Egyptian authorities ever done to stem the flow of Saudi cash into Egyptian pockets and bank accounts? For years all of the Arab countries had depended on Gulf money from guest-worker receipts, tourism revenues, luxury real estate investment, and direct aid, which kept Arab economies afloat, regime wheels greased, and complaints about Wahhabi meddling to a minimum. And whenever a journalist in one of the Cairo papers did try to point out the dangers of Saudi influence, someone with instructions from above and an envelope full of cash put a red line through it. You could refer vaguely to the doings of "some Gulf states," but no direct criticism of the house of Saud was permitted. It was only after 9/11, when the Americans came around asking questions, that the Egyptians pointed at Riyadh.

Saudi money was an explanation tailor-made for the Americans, especially the materialists among the U.S. policy makers, analysts, and journalists whose default ideological setting is to discount ideology and attribute everything to economic causes. Accordingly, the Cairo version of radical Islam holds that Wahhabism would have died out long ago of its own accord on the Arabian Peninsula had it not been for the discovery of oil, which allowed the Saudis to export their creed. In this telling, radical Islam has no roots in the land of the Nile and only took hold there after Egyptian professionals, doctors, lawyers, and engineers who had come to work in the Gulf, had been brainwashed by the Wahhabis, and returned to Egypt as radical Islamists.

In reality, many of those Egyptian naïfs employed in the Gulf during the 1950s and 1960s were Muslim Brotherhood cadres whom Nasser had released from prison or exiled from Cairo. And so there was another, private story that Egyptians told about the rise of Islamism. In this version, the Saudis were just ignorant billionaires who didn't even know how to write their own names with the expensive gold pens that they carried for show in the pockets of their dishdashas. Cairo on the other hand was the intellectual and cultural capital of the Arab world—and indeed it was, the birthplace of Salafism and all its leading lights, like the nineteenth-century mufti of Egypt Muhammad 'Abduh; Hassan al-Banna, founder of the Muslim Brotherhood; and Sayyid Qutb, the preeminent modern theorist of jihad. All the Saudis had done was fund the Islamist movement. The Egyptians had given it life.

CHAPTER 4

The Muslim Reformation

Cairo, and not the Arabian desert, was ground zero of the Muslim reform movement. It had been one of the seats of Sunni authority since Saladin, and Napoleon's 1798 invasion touched off tremors resonating throughout the Muslim world. Political and religious leaders were forced to confront the fact that, in military terms at least, their world was no match for the foreigners. The nineteenth- and early-twentieth-century reform movement was Islam's effort to meet and match the newness of the world revealed by the Christian West. The reformers took Muhammad and the early *umma* as an example, not in order to turn back the clock, but rather to rid Islam of the impurities that had accumulated over the centuries and restore the faith to its rational essence as practiced by the Prophet of Islam, his companions (*al-sahaba*), and the first four caliphs (*al-rashidun*). They were collectively known as *al-salaf,* the righteous forebears, and from them the reformers took their name, the Salafis.

The Salafi laboratory was Cairo, a living museum of Islamic civilization whose architecture tells a story unfolding over a millennium. Ibn Tulun Mosque was completed in A.D. 879 and named after the

Abbasid commander whose Mesopotamian origins are commemorated in the mosque's most salient feature, its ziggurat-shaped minaret. Sultan Hassan Mosque, finished in A.D. 1363, is one of the masterpieces of Mamluk mosque building, including separate schools for each of the four major traditions of Sunni thought— Shafi, Maliki, Hanafi, and Hanbali. Al-Azhar, the mosque and university complex, was established in A.D. 975, when the city was under the Fatimids, a Shia dynasty that named the structure after the daughter of the Prophet of Islam, Sayeda Fatima al-Zahra, thus Al-Azhar. The Citadel of Saladin, high atop the Muqattam, was fortified by the Ayyubid ruler famous for defeating the Crusaders and, just as important, for wresting Cairo from the Shia and bringing Egypt back under Sunni control, where it has remained ever since.

Cairo is the flesh and blood of Islamic civilization, from the eternal structures of the pharaohs to the urban sprawl of Nasser City. The Salafis wanted to return Islam to its origins, but there is too much history in Cairo, too much unruly humanity, too much life in the streets, people, ideas, song, smell, music, Islam, sex, beef, lamb, sugarcane, mangoes, guavas, voices, dirt, sand, and animals—a pack of camels idling through traffic on the way to the camel market; the indefatigable, noble donkeys pulling the garbage and remainder carts; the weathered mares and geldings dragging the knife sharpeners' wagons; cats, Cairo's lithe and desperate one-eyed predators; and wild dogs.

Dogs had overrun the garden of a large deserted villa across the street from my apartment. A few months after 9/11, I had moved into an eight-story building a block from the Nile where, a neighbor told me, you used to be able to see as far as the Pyramids in Giza. But with the construction boom of the past few decades, now not even the river was visible, though we were easy pickings for the mosquitoes generated in its shoals a block away. The dogs were at the other end of Pail of Milk Street, a pack of semi-feral strays the same golden brown as the Pyramids and the decaying colonial-era villa they inhabited. They stretched out lazily on the roofs of parked cars under the hot midday sun, and after dark owned most of the small street from sidewalk to sidewalk. But even when the animals were most affable, they were a problem for observant Muslims.

"They are filthy animals," said Muhammad the doorman, or *bawwab*, of the building I lived in. "It's in their saliva."

The *bawwab* is one of the central figures in Cairo life. A good one can make your life comfortable and a bad one difficult, and Muhammad was both. Squat, powerful, and walleyed, he had been a tae kwon do champion in his enormous working-class neighborhood that journalists nicknamed the Islamic Republic of Imbaba, where many of the Islamist cadres were semi-reformed street toughs adept in Asian martial arts. Muhammad was in his late thirties and like much of the city's working class supported three generations: his parents, his wife, and three children. His education was minimal, though he could read and write Arabic and knew several other languages, like the Polish he had picked up working on an Eastern European construction crew in Libya. He'd risen to manager of an auto shop until a run-in with a superior cost him his job. Now he was reduced to this, he said, pointing to his light blue *galabeya*, a long cotton robe almost like a nightgown, the traditional garb of the fellah and the uniform of Cairo *bawwabs*. Most *bawwabs* don't give the robe a second thought, but Muhammad hated the garment. "I used to wear a shirt and pants to work."

He had slid back down the few rungs it is possible to climb in Egypt, and believed that learning English would help him back up. We sat in front of the building at night trading verbs, one English for one Arabic, sharing a piece of watermelon or a pastry from one of the neighborhood stores, while he kept his one good eye on the dogs across the street.

"They have dirty bacteria in their mouths," he explained. Of course, all the Cairo bestiary was steeped in the same dirt and refuse, and if it is not clear why God had gone to the trouble of creating an existence that by its very nature was unclean, Muhammad the door-man explained his hatred of them by citing Muhammad the Prophet of Islam. "It is a filthy animal," Muhammad the doorman said Muhammad the Prophet said. "It says so in the Quran." In reality, the bad reputation of the dog seems to come from a hadith of questionable transmission.[1]

The hadith, or the sayings or traditions of the Prophet, is one of the sources of the sunna—in Arabic the word means "the way" or "the path"—and the basis of what over the years has become Muslim orthodoxy, Sunni Islam. Each hadith consists of two parts, the text itself and the chain of transmission by which that text has come down from one source to another, or *isnad*—that is, A said B said C said D said X—which establishes the genealogy and probity of the hadith. The *isnad* is something like a game of telephone, and Muslim scholars know that many links in the chain of the approximately 600,000 hadith were less than credible. The two most reliable collections of hadith, both known as *al-sahih*, or "the genuine," were assembled by two ninth-century scholars, al-Bukhari and Muslim ibn al-Hajjaj, who whittled down the numbers to get the most authentic specimens. Bukhari ended up with more than seven thousand hadith, and Muslim some nine thousand. Their editing task was surely made yet more arduous by certain hadith like the one that has Muhammad saying: "You must compare the sayings attributed to me with the Koran; what agrees therewith is from me, whether I actually said it or no."[2] As this patently self-referential example suggests, hadith were frequently forged years after the death of Muhammad to advance different political and religious agendas.

The nineteenth-century French historian Ernest Renan claimed that unlike other religions, Islam "was born in the full light of history." Renan, one of Edward Said's favorite Orientalist targets, was famous for his biography of Jesus, the difficulties of which he must have had in mind when he wrote of Islam, "The life of its founder is as well known to us as those of the Reformers of the sixteenth century."[3] The analogy is imprecise, for while there certainly is a lot of material about the early days of Islam, much of it is of questionable veracity and unlikely to stand up to the rigors of Western scholarship.[4] And yet it is clear why Renan, critical of all revealed religion, would want to cite the Protestant Reformers.

Even in Renan's time, the notion that Islam was in want of a reformation was a commonplace. It is not quite accurate to liken the Salafis to the sixteenth-century Protestant movement that sought to loosen the Catholic Church's authority and the grip of its clerical establishment and return the gospel to the people for whom it was intended, but the Muslim reformers did chip away at the past, in order to throw into greater relief the Prophet of Islam and the Quran, God's last and perfect message to mankind.

Al-Quran means "the recitation." Muslims believe it is a holy text that descended to Muhammad from God by way of the angel Gabriel, not at once but bit by bit. According to Muslim tradition, it was only after Muhammad's death, during the reign of the caliph Uthman, that the text of the Quran was compiled and bound in a book, or *mushaf,* which is said to be the same edition we have today. The book opens with an invocation, or opening prayer, *al-fatiha,* and is thereafter laid out in no apparent order except that the longer chapters, or *surat* (sing., *sura*), are at the front of the book and the shorter ones at the back. There are 114 *surat,* some of them believed to have been composed when Muhammad was in Mecca, and others when he was leading the first Muslim state after he brought his followers to Medina. It was during this period of governance that the majority of verses, or *ayat,* dealing with legislative matters appear, including *al-baqara,* "The Cow," the second and longest *sura,* with many famously violent passages. The Quran is further divided into thirty parts, the last of which is where children usually begin their first attempts at memorizing the book since these *surat,* all Meccan, are shorter, as are the verses, many of them rhyming, like the chapter *al-rahman.* That was Muhammad the *bawwab*'s favorite.

If it is thought inappropriate to value some parts of the Quran more than others—it is a sacred text and not a songbook—the reality is that *al-rahman* is widely cherished as one of the most musical of all the chapters in a text famous for its ability to enchant listeners. Many Muslims know the book not as a written text but as a recited one, with many of the most famous reciters enjoying a status somewhere between religious figures and pop stars.[5] Sometimes Muhammad would break into impersonations. "This is how Tablawi sounds," he said, reciting a verse in the style of that Egyptian sheikh. Then, changing the pitch and rhythm, he rehearsed the same verses in a different manner. "And this is Abd el-Basset," he said, shutting his eyes and riffing on his hero like a Mississippi bluesman.

I listened to Abd el-Basset's version of *al-rahman* until I knew not only the *sura* by heart but also every modulation of the man's voice and where it most dangerously tempted song. For even the most poetical passages of this *sura*, or indeed of the entire Quran, are expressly neither music nor verse. Rather, they are written in a rhyming prose called *saja'*, and the edifice of Islam rests on this distinction between poetry and revelation.

Islamic tradition holds that Muhammad was illiterate, the point being that since he could not have written the Quran, nor could he have read from the Torah or the Bible to copy it, he was not the author of a text but the vehicle of a revelation. And yet in the Arabic tradition, poets also were inspired by external forces, like desert spirits, jinn. So, to prove that Muhammad was not merely a poet but a prophet—a man spoken to by God and not by a desert spirit—passages in the Quran challenge any man, or jinn, to compose a *sura* like those found in God's final and perfect message. If the style of the Quran can be copied, then Muhammad is at best a poet; and if Muhammad is not a prophet, then the Quran is not a revelation. The inimitability of the Quran is proof of Muhammad's prophetic vocation as well as Islam's central miracle. God is one, says the *shahadah*, the Muslim profession of faith, but his message and his prophet depend on each other, like the rest of the world, as in the *al-rahman sura,* where all is in manifest balance, pearls and coral, sun and moon, jinn and man.

Muhammad the *bawwab* had never seen a jinn, but he fought once with an afreet, a smaller and less menacing desert spirit, when he was in the Libyan Desert. "One night I was in my tent reading," he said, "and I felt this hand hit me in the back of the head." He reenacted the drama, throwing himself forward, reeling, and staggering a few steps on the sidewalk. "I turned around to see who did it," he said, his head pivoting and eyes widening. "And then I got slapped in the face!" His head jerked back, and he grabbed at the front of his own robes. "Then it shook me and I tried to push it away, and finally it let go and I ran out of the tent." I asked him if he saw it. He looked at me as if I were crazy—did I really not know that it is because the afreet is invisible that makes it an afreet? Hearing my account of Muhammad's encounter with the afreet, my Quran teacher rolled her eyes. "You've never seen an afreet?" Dalia asked, tilting her head and smiling. "Are you sure?"

Dalia was in her mid-twenties and strikingly beautiful. She had sharp Turkish, aristocratic features, was fair and slender, with pale olive skin, a strong, aquiline nose, long, elegant fingers, and a smoky, tremulous voice that held the attention of her male students as long as she liked. She was veiled and wore long, colorful embroidered robes that fell past her ankles, allowing a glimpse of the high heels she'd matched to her outfits, a seemingly different veil-and-robe combination for every class, a wardrobe that included every conceivable hue of green, the color of Islam. Her glamour reflected her confidence in her ability to put Islam's most modern face forward to Western students.

I tried to memorize as much of the Quran as I could muster, starting with the thirtieth and final part of the book, as a child would. Dalia brought me a recitation of the entire Quran recorded on a few dozen cassette tapes by a Saudi sheikh. "It is much more modern than the Egyptian reciters," she said.

Still, I much preferred the Egyptians, even as I understood why

Dalia liked the sharp and austere Saudi rendition. It was a version that was the product of a purified, intellectual, and urbanized Islam that was meant to replace what the Muslim reformers came to criticize as an emotional and superstitious faith that subscribed to folk beliefs, feared dogs, and believed in the reality of jinn and afreet—in other words, Muhammad the *bawwab*'s Islam. Dalia, on the other hand, was a Salafi.[6]

Two hundred and fifty years ago, the apostle of the Islamic reformation walked out of the Nejd, a province in what is today Saudi Arabia, no less passionate, bigoted, and God-delirious than Martin Luther. Muhammad Ibn Abd al-Wahhab (1703–1792) is the very sheikh critics of Islam, Muslim and non-Muslim alike, typically blame for everything that has gone wrong with the religion. Those who follow his instruction chafe at the term regularly used in the West to describe them, "Wahhabi," and opt for *muwahhidun*, or those who observe *tawhid*, the "unity of God."

Tawhid is Islam's chief theological principle. Since Islam's self-description holds that it is a correction of its two monotheistic precursors, *tawhid* challenges the bases of Jewish and Christian belief. Judaism contends that the covenant God made with his people only applied to the Jews, for better or worse. *Tawhid* undercuts the particularism of Judaism. It holds that the message of the one God cannot be limited to one tribe only, a chosen people, but is universal, applicable to all men at all times.

Christianity, which preaches that God sacrificed his only son to redeem the sins of all men for all time, is universalist like Islam. Both are also exclusivist—either you accept the gospel of Christ, or the message of Muhammad, or you are damned. The similarities between the two faiths end there. For Christians, Jesus was God's son and the Messiah. For Muslims, Muhammad was a prophet, albeit the final messenger. Islam teaches that Jesus was also a prophet, a Muslim prophet, an important figure in the long line beginning with Abraham and reaching its conclusion with Muhammad, but he was not the son of God. He was not resurrected, because he did not die on the cross, but is waiting to return on Judgment Day. And thus from an Islamic perspective, Christianity is nonsense flirting with heresy.

Tawhid holds that the one God is by definition indivisible and eternal, and therefore the Christian doctrine of the Trinity, consisting of the Father, Son, and Holy Ghost, is *shirk,* or associating other entities with the one true God. God is not triune but one, and he does not father children, never mind sons who die. In the words of another *sura, al-ikhlas,* Islam's most concise statement of *tawhid:* "God is one. God is everlasting. He did not give birth and He was not born. And there is nothing to be likened unto Him." To be sure, Islam emerges from the Abrahamic tradition, but it represents a sharp rebuke to its two predecessors, and its doctrinal differences with them were at the origins of the long-standing enmity between Islam and Judaism, and Islam and Christianity.

Muhammad Ibn Abd al-Wahhab, for his part, did hold that Christianity and Judaism were infidel creeds. But his baleful eye was focused mostly on other Muslims, and in particular on the two rival Muslim sects on the Arabian Peninsula, Shiism and Sufism. The former he faulted for various heretical beliefs, but most especially for its veneration of the Shia imams, starting with Ali and ending with the twelfth or occluded imam, whose return would, from the Shia perspective, redeem mankind and initiate an era of justice. In imparting a semidivine status to men, the Shia were held to be *mushrikeen,* "idolaters," or those who commit *shirk.* So were the Sufis, adherents of a syncretic Islam that borrowed from different intellectual and spiritual traditions, including Greek and Hindu philosophy, Neoplatonism, Christian theology, and folklore. For instance, the Sufis took from Christianity the notion that an intercessor, or *wali* (pl., *auliya*), with special spiritual access can help a person's prayers be heard by God, a talent that made the *wali* something like a Muslim saint.

Shrines throughout the Arabian Peninsula, including those of

the Prophet's companions, were pilgrimage sites for Muslim travelers, and anathema to the *muwahhidun,* who in the early nineteenth
century destroyed the shrines and waylaid travelers on the annual
hajj and the 'omra, a lesser pilgrimage that unlike the hajj can be
made at any time during the year. Religious pilgrimages were a major
source of income for the Ottomans (as they still are for the Saudis
today), and so the Ottomans sent Muhammad Ali Pasha, an officer
of Albanian origin who had become ruler of Egypt after Napoleon's
departure, to put down the Wahhabi insurrection. He and Ibn Abd
al-Wahhab are the two key precursors of the Muslim reform movement: the latter was the wellspring of religious renovation, while the
former blazed the way for cultural and political renewal.

In Egypt, Muhammad Ali witnessed firsthand the scientific and
military superiority of the West, and decided to learn as much as he
could about this awesome infidel power that had defeated the Muslims so handily. He dispatched military cadets to France and Italy to
study the latest in technological advances, while other delegations
returned to Cairo with stacks of books from Europe's leading figures
on literature, drama, philosophy, and political theory. Although
Muhammad Ali Pasha and his heirs rated these texts less highly than
technical and military manuals, they were also translated into Arabic, making Cairo the undisputed cultural center of the Muslim
world and attracting intellectuals, ideologues, and intriguers, like
Jamal al-Din al-Asadabadi (1838–1897), the controversial and charis-
matic founder of the Salafi movement.

It is one of the ironies of Middle Eastern intellectual history that
the architect of what would become a patently Sunni movement was
a Shiite who used an assumed name to conceal that fact: Asadabadi,
better known as Afghani, was not from Afghanistan but Persia. However, unlike Ibn Abd al-Wahhab, Afghani was little concerned with
sectarian differences. He believed that the real threat came from outside: the West, which he saw as a dangerous enemy that the Muslims
must learn from or lose to. He taught that rather than just blindly

imitating Europe, the *umma* could find salvation within Islam itself, if it would only abandon its stultifying tradition and draw directly on the example of early Muslim society, the time of the righteous forebears, the *salaf.*

There is some speculation that Afghani was an atheist who merely used Islam to market his reform ideas in an idiom familiar to his Muslim audience. For instance, in responding to Ernest Renan's contention that Islam and science were incompatible, Afghani seems to have conceded the point to his contemporary, only adding that the same is true of Christianity and all religions. "So long as humanity subsists," Afghani wrote, "the struggle will not cease between dogma and free enquiry, between religion and philosophy, a bitter struggle from which, I fear, free thought will not emerge victorious."[7]

Obviously, free thought did win out in the West, or else Afghani would not have been able to publish in French his riposte to Renan, which was not translated into any Oriental language. But by comparing Islam to Christianity, Afghani had harmonized his ideas with the prejudices of his European audience. His conflation of all religions as essentially dogmatic and intolerant was a message the Western secular elite was as predisposed to hear in the nineteenth century as it is today.

No Western intellectual thinks fascism and communism are the same, nor does anyone with a literary sensibility argue that a James Patterson thriller and a Don DeLillo novel are similar just because they are both prose fictions; yet this same intelligentsia is content to believe that all religions are fundamentally the same. To understand why the Muslim reform movement did not follow the same path as the Protestant Reformation, we must recognize the differences between faiths and take them seriously, or else fall prey to the moderate/fundamentalist fallacy. That is, if all religions are essentially the same, and the specific character and quality of religious ideas are irrelevant, then the only way to explain why some people under the influence of religion act one way while others act differently is to break down each religion into a moderate camp and a fundamental-ist camp—that is, there are fundamentalist Muslims just as there are fundamentalist Christians, Hindus, and Jews. However, it is only Western intellectuals who distinguish between moderates and fundamentalists; people of faith distinguish between believers and non-believers, and Muslims are no exception.

The nonbelievers, as Napoleon's conquest had shown, were more powerful than the faithful. How was that possible when the *umma*, according to the Prophet of Islam, was supposed to be the best of all nations? The point of reform was not to make Islam more "moderate," or more amenable to the West, but to revive the *umma*.

During his time in Cairo, Afghani won many disciples. The most important of them was Muhammad 'Abduh (1849–1905), a native Egyptian, a journalist, educator, and scholar. 'Abduh, who became the mufti of Egypt, was perhaps the greatest of all Egypt's Muslim reform intellectuals, and it was under his stewardship that Salafism reached its apogee. Openly acknowledging the backwardness of the lands of Islam and seeking to catch up to and surpass the West, 'Abduh established the central themes that would inspire generations of Muslim intellectuals and activists, including Al Qaeda.

'Abduh was raised in a traditional, rural community and came to believe that the practices and beliefs drawn from folklore, as well as Sufism, were part of what had retarded the *umma*. He promoted an activist Islam that engaged the world around it, including politics, and challenged the fatalism, superstition, and resignation that had corroded the *umma*, for he argued that without reform and renovation Muslim societies would never be able to meet the challenges of modernity that the West had made clear. In order to restore the *umma* to its rightful place in human affairs, Afghani and 'Abduh looked to the ideal model, the first Islamic *umma*, and surmised that the lands of Islam were struggling because Muslims were not practicing the real Islam as set down by the Prophet and his companions. In 'Abduh's view, the entire edifice of Islam, its religious endowments, mosques, universities, and scholarship, had long fallen into a state of decay.

There is no official "church" in Islam, but by the nineteenth century the accumulation of hundreds of years of doctrine and practice based on imitation (*taqlid*) had essentially become an institutional body. What 'Abduh sought was to shear away all of that accreted dogma and practice, and return the faith to its original essence. In his view, the true Islam was well suited for the modern age since it was infinitely more rational than Christianity. The gospels, after all, were full of fantastic tales of supernatural feats performed by the son of God, whereas Islam had only one obvious miracle, the Quran, an extraordinary event, yet one consistent with the tradition of the Hebrew prophets, all of whom delivered messages from the one true God. There was no reason for Muslims to abandon their faith to join the modern world as the Europeans had because Islam was essentially rational. 'Abduh admired the West for its material progress, but thought that success had brought with it a spiritual malaise that issued from the gap between science and Christianity. In Islam, he thought, this divide did not exist, since God's word and his creation, revelation and reason, could not be in contradiction.

'Abduh's move in asserting there was no conflict between reason and faith was provident. If it were otherwise, if reason stood on its own and acted independently, then it could accept no authority above itself, neither the sultan nor God. A regime of Arab reason, like the Enlightenment, would therefore have to be a political project that would reject Islam and overthrow the established order. By insisting that Islam and modernity were compatible, 'Abduh promised the best of both worlds: Muslims could remain true to their faith and enjoy the fruits of science and rationality.

It was a clever attempt at a solution. But 'Abduh's strategy for reform did not, in the end, revive the *umma* or liberate Muslims from their backward mental habits; rather, it has sentenced them to cultural and intellectual servitude. 'Abduh's error, common not only in

Muslim circles but in Western ones as well, even down to the present day, was in failing to see that it was the cultural values of the West—the very values he rejected—that had led to its success. What 'Abduh wanted to separate, science from the values of the culture that produced science, cannot be split; and what he sought to unify, revealed religion and empirical science, cannot logically cohere.

Dalia, the Quran teacher, was not convinced of this. She was embarrassed by the notion that some Muslims believed in afreet, but she also thought that the Quran contains nuclear physics, astronomy, and biology, including details of the origins of human life, from insemination through conception and childbirth. She had our class read *al-alaq*, the ninety-sixth *sura* in the Quran, though thought to be the first that came to the Prophet, where the angel Gabriel's first injunction to the terrified Muhammad is *iqra*, "recite," the root word for Quran, "the recitation": "Recite in the name of your Lord, who created—created man from a clot of blood."

"Blood clot" is the standard translation for *alaq*, but since the verb *alaqa* means "to hang," some modern writers allege that *alaq* refers to the human egg suspended from the ovary waiting to be fertilized by the sperm. I told Dalia that I didn't think any scientist would consider the highly figurative and rhyming language of *al-alaq* to be real science.

"There are a lot of people," she said, "who believe it's one of the miracles of the Quran." I asked if she thought so, too. "I think it's at least remarkable."

This was simply apologetics. The argument that there is science in the Quran is a long-standing literary genre representing one defensive posture toward the West that evolved out of 'Abduh's contention that revealed religion was compatible with science. Since God's word and his creation must complement each other, 'Abduh reasoned that there must be signs in the holy book (*aya* also means "sign") illuminating the natural order. And if the mysteries of God's creation are included in his revelation, then it was not much of a stretch for those after 'Abduh to claim that Islam had described scientific phenomena long before Western scientists presumed to illuminate the natural order. This claim allows Muslim apologetics to assert the superiority of Islam to Western modernity even where the West is most proud of its own achievements.

S till, Salafism is not antimodernist, nor is it even anti-Western, except in the sense that it is a typical manifestation of a society that tends to define itself against the other. Salafism, in fact, represents the progressive and rational current of Islam, one that sought to reconcile a society marked by fatalism and backwardness with the forces of modernity embodied by the West. Salafism is not deviant but the mainstream of contemporary Islamic thought—even if some of its adherents do not always put it into practice.

For instance, Muhammad the *bawwab*'s belief in supernatural creatures that pulled pranks on mankind was folkloric Sufi in origin, but the Salafi preachers from his neighborhood had filled him with loathing for the Sufis. "Sufism is not real Islam," he said. Ahmed, a neighbor, was careful never to raise the issue when the three of us were together, for he was a Sufi.

Ahmed was a student, tall and thin with nervous hands. Every time we walked on the street together, he took my hand in his, customary among middle-class Cairo men. His father was a law school professor from a well-educated family that lost land and money when an uncle crossed the Nasserists, so Ahmed avoided politics and kept to philosophy, Western and Islamic. At Cairo University he majored in philosophy and specialized in Sufism. "Sufis believe that you don't change anything," he said. "If there's a problem with someone else, leave it alone. The point in Sufism is to change yourself."

That peaceful self-improvement program is precisely what the Salafis read as quiescence and Oriental fatalism. Instead of the jihad of personal growth, the Salafis preached a jihad that recognized real enemies in the world, enemies who needed to be defeated for Islam to survive and the *umma* to flourish. An even greater foe than the West, many of the Salafis thought, were the Westernized collaborators who corrupted Muslim societies from within. Those Muslims who did not share Salafi beliefs were subject to *takfir* (the accusation of apostasy), and the militants, starting with the Muslim Brotherhood in 1928, resolved to wage real jihad against them, no matter how many innocents were caught in the cross fire. Paradoxically, the Salafi crusade against apostates sent some Egyptians looking for relief from such bloodshed in the name of Islam, and they found it ready-made in the Sufi orders, or *tariqat* (sing., *tariqa*), communities of faith built around a firm core of tolerance and a history of openness toward other traditions and cultures.

The Sufi-Salafi dialectic was the topic of Ahmed's graduate thesis. He had counted almost one hundred different Sufi brotherhoods flourishing now in Egypt as part of the renaissance of Egyptian Sufism. He was a member of a *tariqa* and invited me to join him for one of its meetings. "They will not divulge any secret knowledge to you as an outsider," he warned. As an outsider, I told him, I wouldn't be able to distinguish what was secret from what wasn't.

The mosque was on the second floor of a commercial building near Al-Azhar. Some of the men were already there, a few praying on cushioned mats in the middle of a room the size and pale hue of a middle-school cafeteria. Others were sitting in the back, chatting quietly and smoking. Ahmed introduced me to a friend of his, a classics professor from Cairo University who regarded the sheikh with great reverence. "He knows everything," the professor said. "He's a *wali*."

I asked him, if Sufi wisdom is an advanced form of Islamic knowledge, why aren't more Muslims interested in pursuing Sufism? "It is an advanced spiritual stage in Islam, and not too many people can do it," he said. "And thank God, because we don't want it as crowded in heaven as it is in Cairo," he said, laughing. That was just the sort of elitism that turned people off of the Sufis and won the Salafis large constituencies across the region.

Still, the Sufis were a kindly-looking bunch, from college students in baseball caps to workingmen in *galabeyas,* and a few braved business suits in the hundred-degree heat that seemed that much worse with the large crowd of maybe two hundred packed into the small room. The women were in an adjoining hall watching on a live video feed. When the sheikh entered the room, Ahmed and I scrambled to find seats on the floor up front.

Sheikh Mukhtar was a short, roundish man with a dark complexion and gray spiky hair. His bright blue suit, blue tie, and large silver wristwatch were evidence of his life outside the *tariqa* as a successful entrepreneur whose agricultural project had won him some favor from the government. The mukhabarat, or state security, regularly attended the meetings to make sure that despite his worldly ambitions he avoided sensitive political topics. Also, they were there to protect him, since there had apparently been an attempt on the sheikh's life a few years back. There were practical reasons for Sufi secrecy as well as spiritual ones.

The sheikh saw Ahmed speaking to me and asked who the visitor was. Ahmed explained I was an American, and the sheikh punned on my name—an Arabic construction meaning "I have"—and all the Sufis laughed. "Now you understand why we like this," Ahmed leaned over to whisper. "We have fun. Sufis are different from other Muslims."

"This isn't just for Muslims," Sheikh Mukhtar said, looking at me. "This is for people who are open to different ideas, Christians, Jews—even," and he paused for the punch line, "Marxists." He waited for the laughter to subside and then resumed. "We want peace with everyone. We don't want war, not with Jews, not with Israel, no matter what some people say. We want peace." It was a political opinion, but one in line with a regime that had a peace treaty with Israel, and the mukhabarat breathed easily.

The sheikh paced the small stage with a microphone, discussing spiritual salvation and telling an occasional joke. The *tariqa*'s elders sat behind him in large comfortable chairs nodding and smiling pleasantly. They stood and moved to the front to lead a group prayer resembling deep-breathing exercises when Sheikh Mukhtar paused for a drink of water. "Allah," the Sufis chanted, "Allah, Allaaaah, Allaaaah . . ."

At the end of the two-hour meeting, the sheikh retired from the stage, parting the crowd like a prophet, and Muslim men reached like Romans to touch his blue suit. Ahmed said that we had been granted an audience.

We waited at the end of a long line leading into a room in the back where Sheikh Mukhtar was seated in a large throne-like chair to receive visitors. "Don't be nervous," Ahmed told me nervously. He'd never met Mukhtar before. I offered to go first to give him some more time to prepare himself. "No!" he said. "You have to watch me and follow the protocol. Go up, take his hand, and bow, and when he gives you permission, then you can speak to him."

At last it was Ahmed's turn. He told the sheikh about his scholarly interest in as well as his spiritual devotion to Sufism. When he explained excitedly that his thesis was about the differences between Sufi *tariqat,* Mukhtar exploded with anger. "There are no differences among Sufis," he shouted. "We are all one!" Ahmed didn't even have time to apologize before the sheikh's men led him away. He was stunned, and his mouth hung wide open. The sheikh had yelled at him, and how would he live this down—the Sufi apprentice who had broken the composure of a *wali*?

I followed in line reluctantly. The sheikh looked down at me and asked if I was Muslim. "No," I said. "I'm in the Christian, Jewish, Marxist camp." He turned serious and told me there was little for me in Sufism if I wasn't already a Muslim. I didn't want to be a Sufi, I said. I just wanted to hear different ideas. I was quickly dismissed.

Ahmed and I went to a nearby coffee shop. He ordered *shisha* and then got a call on his cell phone from someone in the sheikh's inner circle. "Mukhtar's brother heads a different *tariqa*," said Ahmed after hanging up. "The two brothers have been arguing." He poked at the hot coal in his water pipe for a bit and then continued. "The sheikh was very sensitive when I asked about divisions in Sufism because the brothers started accusing each other of apostasy." The Sufis are doing *takfir*? I asked. Brother against brother? He nodded his head despondently.

One of the typical charges against Westerners, made by Arab thinkers from Afghani down to Edward Said, is that we think of Islam as a monolithic, static force that has not changed over its fourteen-hundred-year career and is incapable of changing now. But the truth is that it is Muslims themselves who are most likely to see Islam as static, or their own variety of Islam as the essential version and all others as deviations. Non-Muslims do not practice *takfir* and accuse Muslims of apostasy; Muslims do.

Because Islam is not merely a matter of personal faith but also the basis of a political order, these debates over what is the real or true Islam are of great consequence—not just to the individual believer but also to Muslim communities, which during the last century have torn each other to pieces in search of an answer.

CHAPTER 5

"The Regime Made Us Violent": The Islamists' War Against the Muslims

Raouf invited me to his house for lunch before our meeting with a terrorist lawyer. Raouf's sister was home, and since as a non–family member I wasn't allowed to see her uncovered (she took her veil off when she ate), his mother served us our meal in his room. Raouf's mother also wore a head scarf, one that swept her graying hair off her bare neck, a style different from the one that the young Islamist girls, like her daughter, had made fashionable with the veil covering everything but the face. Raouf was not an Islamist. He modeled his life not after the Prophet of Islam but after the German philosophers whose pictures he had taped to his wall. "My mother hates those pictures," he said. "They're too depressing for her. She would rather I put up photos of girls."

But Raouf's dream in life was to translate all of Kant into Arabic, an ambition that is not really as odd as it sounds. As the philosopher who tried to derive a morality separate from organized religion, Kant is an important figure for Arab liberals, especially young ones. Raouf was twenty-three when we first met in the spring of 2002, and just out of college, where he, like the Sufi Ahmed, had studied philosophy.

They'd never met before I introduced them, and when I did, they didn't like each other. Their chosen field was not one of the high-profile faculties at Cairo University, like medicine or pharmacology, and it offered no guarantee of a good job for the only son of a comfortable and educated middle-class family.

Raouf's sister was studying architecture at Cairo U. and made him drive her around the city to look at buildings. "She says she is going to take a sketch pad and go through all of Europe," he told me. "France, Germany, and England, too, and draw all the churches, and I told her it's going to take the rest of her life because there are thousands of churches in England alone."

I asked him how drawing churches fit with her fundamentalism.

"It doesn't," he said, laughing. "Muslims live contradictions that can't be reconciled."

Like how the same family managed to raise an Islamist daughter and a German Idealist?

Raouf credited his father, a successful businessman who'd inherited the family store when his father died, leaving three wives, dozens of children, and a family business, and had no choice but to abandon his law studies. When it came time for his son to go to school, he encouraged Raouf to study what he liked. Raouf's father spoiled him some, giving him an allowance until he found work, money Raouf stashed away all year for the Cairo International Book Fair, where he used his savings to purchase so many books that he had to buy lunch for the friends he brought along to carry his purchases. For his companions, the field trip was a chance to look at girls at the exhibition grounds, but Raouf cared for nothing except his books.

He was handsome and tall with thick shoulders, big Egyptian eyes, and a full mouth. The Egyptian girls giggled when he walked by, and the middle-aged British women on holiday said things about him out loud to each other that would've made him blush had he been paying attention to the attention paid him. Unlike American men with the same literary interests, he never assumed his interesting ideas were destined to win him the affection of interesting women, so he kept his thoughts to himself. His ideal job was to run a small book stand, like the one specializing in philosophy that we stopped by late one night in Azbakiyah Square, a large open-air mall. Business was slow. The bookseller, a man in his early sixties, had also studied philosophy at the university and told us that he had ambitions when he was younger, had convened discussion groups with some like-minded friends, but was satisfied to raise his family on a government salary and bide his time until he could retire and surround himself with books. He brought us tea, and we talked about Aristotle. Raouf thought the whole setup was perfect.

In the meantime, he was building his own formidable library. Along with his precious Germans, he had, among others, volumes of Gibbon's *Decline and Fall of the Roman Empire,* Stendhal's *The Red and the Black,* a collection of short stories by Edgar Allan Poe, a collection of Nasser's speeches, Foucault, Samuel Huntington, a history of the Baath Party in Syria, and *From Beirut to Jerusalem.* "I love this book too much," he said. "Thomas Friedman is great, but I don't agree with some of his neoliberal colleagues—that money and jobs will make everything okay across the world."

Raouf thought our faith in *Homo economicus* and materialism made us more dogmatic than the Arabs and led us to underestimate the power of ideas. If ideas mattered less to a man than having another ten dollars in his pocket at the end of the day, then why had all these Americans who believed man to be a rational economic actor pursued intellectual work as a career? Writers, journalists, professors, diplomats—they were all smart enough to become lawyers or businessmen and make millions. So why didn't they make a rational economic choice with their own lives? Because they are not slaves, ideas matter. Yet our political theory, he thought, was all typed on a cash register, especially when it came to the Arabs and Islam. We believe that poverty has so humiliated the Arabs that they have no choice but to suicide themselves and murder others—that is, the

Arabs lack money. Arabs kill Americans because they hate our free-doms—that is, the Arabs lack the opportunity to make money. Arabs are motivated by legitimate political grievances—that is, the way to stop the violence is to bribe them. But the Arabs, Raouf insisted, are not slaves, either. Ideas matter to them, too.

"The Americans worked with the mujahideen in Afghanistan because you thought it was pragmatic," said Raouf. "But it was ideo-logical because the Americans thought that Islam was not a big deal. You had no idea that Islam was a bigger threat than communism? Wow. The Soviets got people to fight for communism by threatening to shoot them in the back. But if I believe in God, a God that takes care of me in heaven and on earth, then it is very easy to get me to die for God."

Raouf didn't believe in God, at least not since his first year at col-lege. "I'd sit in classes and listen to my teacher's lectures about Aquinas and religious persecution, freedom of thought and Voltaire, and I realized they weren't just talking about the history of thought in Christendom; they were talking about the Muslim world now; they were talking about Egypt. You have to pay attention, because they can't be too obvious, but if you know what you're listening to, it's there."

Raouf specialized in texts of dissimulation, Muslim writers who used the language of Islam to criticize it. He handed me a book by a linguist who, as Raouf explained it, casually notes that there were many Persian words in the Quran. "And then, about a hundred pages later," Raouf said, "he mentions that Muhammad spent a lot of time with one of his companions, who happened to be Persian. The writer never says so explicitly, but his meaning is clear. If the Quran is an Arabic Quran, a message given in Arabic by God, then the Persian words in the text suggest that there was another influence on the Quran, not divine, but human."

He pulled another volume down from his shelves. "This is by an Iraqi Marxist who tried to separate Muhammad as a prophet of God from the political leader. So he writes that Muhammad's assassination of a Jewish leader was a wise political move, but the implication is that the assassination wasn't ethical. The writer gives himself away as a critic just by offering his own opinion, even if he praises the action. The fundamentalist scholars give no opinions; they just describe what happened. That's how you know when someone is not a fundamentalist—when they make a comment. And this is who the fundamentalists fear, scholars who know the history and the precedents as well as the fundamentalists themselves."

I told him he would make a good fundamentalist.

"I would be a great fundamentalist," he said. "I know all the texts; I know all the arguments against the texts. And I respect the fundamentalists. They know how to make arguments, and they understand the logic of the system they're working in."

"So what's kept you from becoming a fundamentalist?"

"Philosophy is my fundamentalism. Doubt, skepticism, and this isn't the subject of the fundamentalists."

"But since you know Kant, Descartes, Voltaire, you'd make an even better fundamentalist since you'd know those arguments and could put them down."

"Yes, but I believe those arguments. I can't refute them, which is why I'm not a fundamentalist. I am probably not really even a Muslim anymore. I tried to talk to my friends about things I'm interested in, about Islam, about our history, but I gave up. You can't talk about Islam or Islamic culture; all people want to know about is ritual, the right way to wash yourself before prayer, the correct way to pray or fast. I used to hate Islamic culture. I looked around and compared us to the West and saw we had no intellect and no material wealth. I was interested in Greek philosophy, Plato, Aristotle. But then I started reading more Islamic history, the early periods, and it was the first time I was proud. Muslims had wide experience of other cultures, including their own, and interest in them. I was so happy. I saw that in the past we had intellectuals, wealth, humor. Religion was just an aspect of life, not all of it. And now you have twenty-year-old women reading Ibn Taymiyya."

Ibn Taymiyya (1263–1328) was a Muslim jurist, and one of the intellectual forefathers of the Islamist movement, a predecessor of Ibn Abd al-Wahhab, the Salafis, and Sayyid Qutb. Ibn Taymiyya's current popularity in Egyptian intellectual life rests largely on a single fact: he gave a ruling seven hundred years ago that was used by Islamist militants to justify the assassination of the Egyptian president Anwar al-Sadat. "The Islamists said he collaborated with an enemy of Islam in signing the treaty with Israel," Raouf says.

Sadat was murdered on October 6, 1981, the eighth anniversary celebration of the war with Israel that Egypt counted as a victory. Sadat's assassin, a junior officer in the Egyptian military, Khaled al-Islambouli, approached the reviewing stand at Cairo Stadium and opened fire on the president, whose peace treaty with Israel and realignment from Moscow to Washington spelled the end of Nasserism. Sadat had restored Egyptian pride with the army's performance in the 1973 war and with his recovery of the Sinai in his peace deal with the Israelis, although that agreement also set him at odds with the rest of the region and his domestic rivals. Riddling Sadat's body with bullets, Islambouli, a member of Islamic Jihad, shouted, "Death to the pharaoh," a protest against the Egyptian leader's ostensibly non-Islamic values, and also, strangely, an echo of the Hebrew Bible, where there are no Muslims for the pharaoh to repress but only Jews.

I asked Raouf if his sister justified Sadat's assassination. "No, she's not interested in politics, just in how to be a good Muslim. She reads Ibn Taymiyya on personal conduct, like how to pray, how to wash before prayer. Islam is good for her. She does social work for the poor; I respect her. We just have different ideas."

When it was time to go, Raouf restacked his books on the shelves. "I don't like to leave these books out for my sister to find them," he said. "I don't want to hurt her feelings." We were going to meet one of the Islamists who had been rounded up in the aftermath of Sadat's murder. Raouf was more excited than I was to meet him, one of the public faces of the group whose war against Egypt shaped his childhood.

By the time we got to Montasser al-Zayyat's law office downtown, the reception room was already filled with clients, almost all of them women, whose husbands, brothers, sons, and fathers were being held as members of al-Gama'a al-Islamiyya, an Islamist group that throughout the 1970s, 1980s, and 1990s targeted politicians, policemen, intellectuals, foreign tourists, and the Coptic Christian minority. The Islamist war against the Egyptian state and Egyptian society left more than thirteen hundred dead in the 1990s alone. Many Gama'a members were still being detained illegally, even though the organization's bloody career had essentially ended in 1997 when it declared a unilateral truce with the government. Al-Gama'a al-Islamiyya's unofficial membership was at one point reckoned in the tens of thousands, drawing recruits mostly from prisons and universities, like Cairo University, where Zayyat was studying law when he became affiliated with them after a stint in the Muslim Brotherhood. Since it is against the law to belong to al-Gama'a al-Islamiyya, or any political group based on religion, Zayyat describes himself as a spokesman for the group.

"Our fight now is not to be excluded from society," Zayyat said, multitasking. He was fielding phone calls on his land and mobile lines, answering e-mails, and checking the Web site of a local soccer team. "Our aim is to get back to our original message of peace and preaching, and to reconcile with the Egyptian people."

A barrel-chested man in his late fifties with a fistful of beard modeled the way the Prophet of Islam supposedly wore it, Zayyat spent three terms in prison, one during which he befriended Ayman al-Zawahiri, long before the emir of Egyptian Islamic Jihad signed on with bin Laden. "We met in '81 and spent three years together," said Zayyat. Both of them had been rounded up with hundreds of other suspects in the aftermath of Sadat's assassination. Zayyat said he still considered Zawahiri a friend, even though he had publicized his disagreement with the Al Qaeda lieutenant in an e-mail exchange a year after 9/11 and then later written a book about his former prison-mate, *The Road to Al-Qaeda: The Story of Bin Laden's Right-Hand Man.* While Zawahiri and the former Gama'a head Omar Abdel Rahman, held in a U.S. federal penitentiary for his role in the 1993 World Trade Center bombing, continued to preach armed struggle, Zayyat was now against it. "I refuse violence," he told me. "I denounce it from conviction."

This was what jailed Gama'a leaders said, too. They insisted that religious study led them to reject their violent legacy, but there's little doubt that their self-reflection was at least partly prompted by the Egyptian government's own ruthlessness.

Hosni Mubarak famously warned that the U.S. invasion of Iraq would give birth to a hundred more bin Ladens, that a crusade against jihadis would just recruit more jihadis from all over the Muslim world. However, the fear of breeding Zawahiri clones never deterred the Egyptian president from conducting a brutal campaign against his own Islamist enemies. He operated under the conviction that overwhelming force stops those determined to do violence and gives everyone else good enough reason not to try it. And he was right. It is not violence against jihadis that recruits jihadis. (Had the United States not invaded Iraq, Abu Musab al-Zarqawi would not have been content to stay home in his native Jordan and watch TV.) It is jihad that recruits jihadis, bringing them into a perpetual war against the nonbelievers: it is a fourteen-hundred-year-old political institution that is like a bottomless cup filled to the brim with the martial energies of young men who, as all Arab rulers know, must be either used to advantage or killed, lest they turn on the ruler. If we want to know how Arab rulers deal with jihad, we should ignore

Mubarak's self-serving warning to the Bush administration and take note of his actions. Any Egyptians who might have been motivated by Mubarak's violence to take up arms against the regime soon discovered that the government's capacity for violence and cruelty was much more formidable than their own.

"There was no way to bring down the Egyptian government through armed struggle," Zayyat says. "We were losing this cycle of violence. It weakened us." With most of its leadership and military wing imprisoned, deceased, or exiled, Gama'a had no choice but to sue for peace. Its cease-fire, in effect a surrender, was in order by 1997.

At any rate, Zayyat insisted, it was the regime that made the Islamists violent in the first place. "Starting violence was the government's trap to make the people hate us," he explained. Raouf gave me a sidelong glance to remind me that I was listening to one side in what is effectively a family quarrel.

"The government pushed you into killing tourists, journalists, and Coptic Christians?" I asked.

"Starting violence was a trap," said Zayyat, looking back at his computer screen. "It stimulates anger and leads to counteraction against violence. The murders in prison, the detentions, made the groups want revenge."

Zayyat is a pretty affable fellow with a flair for self-promotion that's made him a darling of Cairo's foreign and Arab press corps—everyone's favorite Islamist, as one Egyptian reporter told me. He has given his version of Egypt's civil war to so many visiting journalists that he is perhaps the man most responsible for disseminating the myth that it was the cruelty of the Egyptian government that made the Islamists wage war. That version has been widely accepted not only by the press but also by foreign governments, including the Bush White House.

The idea goes something like this: the Arab ruling order is so corrupt and repressive that Arab citizens have no other outlet to express their political selves except through ideologies as bloody minded as the regimes themselves. Sayyid Qutb, Al Qaeda's intellectual godfather, was tortured in prison, which only made him angrier and more likely to preach armed revolt; and the same was true for Zawahiri, also allegedly tortured by the Egyptians. Like Qutb and Zawahiri, the 9/11 attackers were all in effect created by an Arab political establishment that refused to take responsibility for its own citizens and instead deflected anger at itself toward others, like the United States. As one American journalist neatly summed it up, 9/11 was born in the dungeons of Egypt.[1]

The assumption behind this theory, and all theories purporting to explain the root causes of Islamic terror—for example, that it is the product of dire economic conditions, or is an expression of legitimate political grievances against the West—is that political violence in the modern Middle East is a deviation from the norm that requires a theory to explain it. The reality is very different. In the Middle East, political violence is not an anomaly. It is the normal state of affairs.

Let us pick up the Salafi thread we left off last chapter with Muhammad 'Abduh. One of 'Abduh's chief disciples, also his biographer, was Rashid Rida, born in 1865 near Tripoli, the largest city in what is today northern Lebanon. In 1897, Rida came to study with 'Abduh in Cairo, where they started an influential magazine called *Al-Manar* (The Beacon) that Rida published until the end of his life in 1935. Rida's outlook was conventionally Salafi, holding, like Afghani and 'Abduh, that the lands of Islam were stagnant not because of the faith but because Muslims had "deviated from the principles of public law as they had been decreed at the time of the rightly guided caliphs,"[2] and that a reform effort embracing science and technology would bring the *umma* up to speed with the West.

For Rida, the origin of the *umma*'s problems went back to a specific historical moment in the seventh century, when Mu'awiya, the

Syrian governor who wrested the caliphate from Ali, handed the post to his own son. In the wake of that decision, the caliphate came to be decided by violence and bribes, sending Islam off of the true path.

With the dissolution of the Ottoman Empire in the aftermath of World War I, Rida saw that trying to save the Ottoman caliphate was a hopeless cause. If the caliphate were to continue in some form, Rida believed, it had to return to the Arabs, the lifeblood of Islam and whose language was the only tongue in which Islam could properly be studied and discussed.[3] Rida was not an Arab nationalist, though it is in his work that Salafism is first scored with a pronounced Arabist strain. But by casting a cold eye on the Ottomans, Rida began to consider the historical reality of the caliphate: there was the "ideal caliphate" of the *rashidun* that lasted about forty years, and the "actual caliphate" of more than thirteen hundred years in which tyranny was the norm.[4] Still, in spite of this dismal track record, Rida maintained that it was "the archetype of government." What it needed was a refitting for the modern age, which Rida provided by proposing that the caliphate be equipped with a prototype of representative government called *shura*.

In Rida's view, the problem with the historical caliphate wasn't just the corruption and fecklessness of sultans. It was also the *ulema*, or scholars, who had been merely subservient to power when it was their duty to ensure that the rulers were acting in accordance with Islamic principles and the best interests of the *umma*. In Rida's vision of the Islamic state, the *ulema* would elect the caliph, who would in turn regularly seek their counsel, or *shura*. The Quran and the sunna, depending on your perspective, either enjoin or just recommend that the ruler seek counsel, but, as Rida saw, in reality Muslim rulers have rarely sought anything but a rubber stamp from all but their closest advisers. And those courageous souls who were tempted to resist the unjust power of the sultan found themselves caught in a dilemma, calculating whether the advantages of rebellion outweighed the negatives. The annals of Muslim history show that in the face of a choice between tyranny and anarchy, most chose tyranny. For instance, Ibn Taymiyya, whose reputation Rida had helped revive, wrote that "sixty years of an unjust ruler is better than one night without a Sultan."[5] (It may seem odd that such a supporter of state power would be credited with providing the basis for Anwar Sadat's assassination, but in fact Ibn Taymiyya never argued that despotic rulers could be justly murdered. What he did say was that while it was not licit to kill a Muslim ruler, it was permissible to spill a ruler's blood if he was not really a Muslim. This was the claim the Islamists made about Sadat—who as "pharaoh," in his killer's formulation, represented non-Islamic values.)

Rida was a systematic thinker. His most famous disciple, Hassan al-Banna, who founded the Muslim Brotherhood in 1928, was not. Banna was more like a community organizer, a man intent on raising the self-esteem of a people that had lost its way, and later, as the ranks of the Brotherhood began to swell with the middle and the working classes, he became a political activist. Although Banna agreed with Rida that an Islamic state was the "archetype" of good government, he never theorized what such a polity might look like. He simply knew that a political order determined by the Quran, God's final and perfect message, would solve everything. Indeed, the Muslim Brotherhood's political program could be boiled down to its slogan "The Quran is our constitution." This was not just a statement of faith. It was also effectively a warning directed against those Egyptian intellectuals and officials promoting a system of government in which man, not God, would write laws.

Early on, the Brotherhood resolved to use violence to bring about this new order, embarking on a campaign of riots and assassinations, like the 1948 murder of the prime minister, an assassination that led to the apparently retaliatory killing of Banna himself a year later. So while Montasser al-Zayyat claimed that the government made the Islamists violent, the reality is that their murderous streak dates back to well before the Mubarak regime. In 1954, in fact, the

Brotherhood made an attempt on Nasser's life, after which the Egyptian president responded with a massive roundup and a period of severe repression that culminated in the 1966 hanging of the Brotherhood's chief theorist, Sayyid Qutb.

Since 9/11, Qutb has rightly been identified as a major ideologue, and perhaps the transformational figure, in the development of radical Islam. Western critics have likened the onetime poet and litterateur to European writers and intellectuals grappling with the existential issues of modernity.[6] For the existentialists, the question was how to find authenticity after God had turned his back on mankind; but for Qutb, it was the other way around—until man once again drank from the pure Islam of its prophet, he was doomed to live in a state of pre-Islamic ignorance, or *jahiliya*.

Most of the attention that has been paid to Qutb in the West has focused, understandably, on his profound hatred of modern Western culture. And yet while Salafism was indeed a response to the West, Qutb must be primarily understood in the context of Islamic modernism. Like his predecessors—Banna, Rida, 'Abduh, Afghani, and Ibn Abd al-Wahhab—Qutb looked back to the first Muslim community in order to restore the contemporary *umma* to its rightful place as the best of all nations. For the Salafis, what they were trying to achieve was not an imaginary utopia (like that of the communists) that could only be realized in the future, but a real Eden that had been lived in historical time and ruled by the messenger of God. To avail themselves of that model, the reformers had to rid Islam of the imperfections that had accumulated since its golden era, for the fault was not with the final and perfect message revealed by the creator of all things but with the Muslims who had abandoned or corrupted that message. The Salafis differed from each other in how much of the past they thought worth preserving—'Abduh's strictures, for instance, were less severe than Rida's in sweeping away large chunks of Islamic history and precedent. But their reference point and purpose were the same—they looked toward the past in order to save the present. What sets Qutb apart from his predecessors is his refusal to excuse his contemporaries for their culpability in Islam's fall from grace.

Qutb took Salafism, a Muslim current purging itself of Islamic history and sources, to its logical conclusion by rejecting not only the recent past but the present as well. If the problem with the lands of Islam is not Islam but the Muslims who have misunderstood and corrupted it, then the fault that must be eradicated is not exclusively in the past. The present is also blameworthy. For Qutb, that justified war not only against unjust rulers but also against the *jahiliya* societies that had produced them, for in the end Muslims themselves were in error. That is, the real problem with the Arabic-speaking Middle East, Qutb believed, was the Arab and Muslim societies that had lost their way. And that required an endless war against the *umma* to purge it of its non-Islamic impurities.

This willingness to use any means necessary to bring about the new order is the essence of Qutb's radicalism. But in the context of Middle Eastern history, what we have come to call radical Islam is actually not so very radical. Political violence and coercion, as Rida noted, had been the norm for over thirteen hundred years of Muslim history. They were also standard practice in modern Arab politics. From the 1960s through the time of his death, Yasser Arafat waged a campaign of terror targeting Europeans and Americans as well as Israelis and other Arabs, a campaign of terror that differed from bin Laden's only in its ideological packaging. The same was so for the Arab nationalist regimes of Syria and Iraq, which fought each other and other rivals with terror. Arab terror in the name of Islam is hardly different from Arab terror in the name of Arab nationalism. Radical Islam is only where the violence that is an inherent part of the Arab political order meets Salafism, Islam's reformist, progressive, and modern current that reaches its end point with Qutb's perpetual, purgative war against the *umma* itself.

Qutb's advocacy of takfirism—the war on apostasy—trickled

down into the Islamist mainstream, and became a catchphrase among younger militants who had begun to compete with the Muslim Brotherhood, which had become relatively moderate after Sadat came to power in 1970 and began releasing Islamist prisoners from jail, where they had been broken by torture and executions. The Brotherhood's members had also just grown older; the agents of almost all of the world's violence are young men, and jihad is no different. Newer organizations like al-Gama'a al-Islamiyya and Egyptian Islamic Jihad offered the young the chance to make headway outside the rigid hierarchy of the Brotherhood, and to take up the weapons that their elders had laid down. Still, while the newer groups and the Brotherhood differed in tactics, it is inaccurate to think of them as two separate currents when they are both part of one intellectual trend, the Islamist movement, and heirs to a history of armed insurrection, one that culminated, in some sense, with Sadat's assassination—"the one operation that al-Gama'a al-Islamiyya and Jihad did together," said the rehabilitated Zayyat, with the shadow of a smile crossing his lips.

It is said that those who live by the sword must die by it as well, a tautology in a society where political power can only be won through violence. This "cycle of violence" in the Middle East is thousands of years old, the defining characteristic of a political order that Ibn Khaldun described almost eight hundred years ago. Once a ruling class reaches a certain stage of decadence, another group that still adheres to a strong warrior ethos will come along and defeat it in war. The ideology of the group is finally beside the point, just so long as it binds them to one another and preserves their *assabiya*.

It is a common misperception that Arab regimes and the Islamists are sworn ideological enemies, when it is much more accurate to think of them in biblical terms as two brothers wrestling for the same share of power. (It was no coincidence, for example, that the organizational structure and elitist ethos of the terrorist group Islamic Jihad were almost identical to those of the Free Officers, the

Arab nationalist military clique that had put Nasser into power.) Political repression is not the root cause of Islamist terror. Repressive violence and terror are two aspects of a political culture that has no mechanism for either sharing power or transmitting political authority from one governing body to another except through inheritance, coup, or conquest. The Islamists make war to win power; the regimes fight to maintain it. And so in the end, there are only two laws of Arab politics: the first is to seize power, after which political legitimacy is granted provided that the second law is observed—to maintain power.

Sadat, for instance, is even today criticized for violating the second law by freeing Muslim Brotherhood prisoners, a whirlwind he reaped as blowback—a charge also leveled against Washington for supporting the Afghan Arabs who would later become Al Qaeda. This theory of the vicious result of unintended consequences, blowback, proposes that the victim is a sorcerer's apprentice touching off a chain of events that would not have otherwise come to pass without his foolish meddling. But the blowback theory assumes a political realm where there is no will to power except that which the victim unwittingly conjured by his own actions. This is nonsense. Political ambition is in the nature of human existence; it is a given in any society. The purpose of political institutions is to manage that struggle. Liberal democracies do it with mechanisms like checks and balances, separation of powers, multiple parties, and free elections. Arab societies have other methods. The most common, as Rashid Rida remarked of Muslim history, is the use of violence to do away with rivals. But there are other techniques as well.

It is impossible to murder and jail every pretender to the throne, for they are legion. So another method used by Arab rulers is to set potential challengers at each other's throats, in the Arab-regime equivalent of a steel-cage match. That's why Arab states have so many different, and redundant, security services. While their purpose may seem largely domestic surveillance and repression, in fact they spend most of their time competing with each other for money, prestige, and power, leaving them too occupied with each other to take on the ruler himself.

Another useful strategy for keeping political rivals at an arm's distance is jihad. To spread Islam through conquest is the religious injunction that pushed the *umma* to expand throughout the former Byzantine and Persian empires, then to North Africa and India. But jihad has other benefits, namely, that as the borders of the empire are pushed outward, the warrior class moves farther from the capital. Through jihad, the ruler turns the energies of the military elite to his advantage and keeps potential competitors far from the palace. In Arab history, the most ambitious commanders were dispatched elsewhere to conquer other lands so they would not be tempted to try their luck at home. And elsewhere was often Egypt: Amr ibn al-As conquered Egypt in the service of the second caliph, Omar ibn al-Khattab; the Abbasid commander Ibn Tulun was sent from Samarra to Cairo, where he founded his own dynasty; as did the ambitious Albanian infantryman Muhammad Ali Pasha, who nominally governed Egypt for the sake of the Ottoman sultan but was in reality a regional power unto himself. The price for not keeping the warrior class far from the center of power is loss of power. That's what happened to the Egyptian monarchy: after the Free Officers felt that the monarchy had betrayed them in the 1948 war with Israel, Colonel Nasser and his companions returned from Palestine to send the king packing in a bloodless coup.

In addition to keeping rivals away from power by directing their attention elsewhere, jihad serves another strategic purpose, namely, to advance the interests of the palace abroad. Just as the early Islamic conquests brought glory to the caliph back home in Damascus or Baghdad, and as the eighteenth- and nineteenth-century rulers of the Barbary States had their privateers and cutouts ransom European and American vessels in exchange for tribute due the palace, so Islamist groups' activities abroad have served (and continue to serve) the interests of Arab regimes. This is sometimes hard for Americans to see, because so many of us find the notion of a state being solely dedicated to its self-interest vulgar and outmoded. But the reality is that it is just normal foreign policy for states to turn their internal problems against rivals and even allies for their own security and prosperity. And Arab regimes have become adept at doing just that.

Nasser, for instance, may have crushed the Muslim Brotherhood, but he also used the Islamists to his benefit. He was not opposed to the Muslim Brotherhood on principle, as, say, the defender of a secular Arab worldview that had no use for Islam and its prophet, but only because it challenged his rule. And yet the Islamists were plenty useful when they went into exile in Saudi Arabia, where Nasser hoped that they would destabilize a rival regime. Sadat, similarly, got rid of his Islamist elements by dispatching them to Afghanistan, where they assisted his new U.S. ally in countering Soviet influence. And when Mubarak moved into the presidential palace, he followed the example of his predecessors and sent some jihadis off to die in foreign lands, even as those who stayed to challenge him were beaten militarily, broken in prison, and later used for regime propaganda. Mubarak's repentant Gama'a prisoners came in handy when the Americans confronted Egypt after 9/11. When the Americans said that the Islamists attacked the United States because the regime was ruthless with them—that 9/11 was born in the dungeons of Egypt— Mubarak's response was, *No, we're on good terms with them, we have a truce with the Islamists, their problem is with you.* This formula deflected Washington's furies and gave the Mubarak government common ground with its Islamist rivals: *America is our enemy, too—look at what it does to the Palestinians.*

Arab regimes always triangulate and spread their bets across the board; this is the only way to maintain power in a political system where survival, political and existential, is the objective. Democracies must fight their enemies in order to preserve the state, but Arab regimes are caught in a perpetual pincer movement, squeezed by foreign enemies on one side and their much more dangerous and always present domestic challengers on the other. Since all of these enemies cannot be defeated militarily, the regimes sometimes fight and at other times use different methods, as we've seen, like manipulating the unlikeliest of bedfellows or sending potential rivals to fight in foreign lands. On September 11, the United States was one of those foreign lands, a dumping ground for jihadis.

What was extraordinary about the attacks on lower Manhattan and the Pentagon was not the carnage—certainly not compared with some of the most vicious intra-Arab campaigns over the last several decades—but that the Arabs had shifted the field of battle to the continental United States. Washington's response was to try to fix a political system that it thought was broken, when in fact it was functioning just as it always had, for hundreds, perhaps thousands of years.

PART II

CHAPTER 6

Bin Laden, the Father of Arab Democracy

Until 9/11 it had been easy for Americans to forget that the first duty of the leaders of a liberal democracy is to protect its citizenry. If elected officials cannot ensure the security of their constituents, they will lose their jobs to others who are willing and able to defend the men and women who vote for their leaders. National security is built into the mechanism of liberal democracy. This is not the case with Arab regimes.

Over the last half century, Arab leaders have imprisoned, tortured, and murdered thousands of their own citizens, and waged foolish wars costing the lives of millions for the sake of a vain fantasy that, from Nasser to Saddam, and Arafat to Nasrallah, was always a variation on the same theme—the new Saladin would restore the dignity of the Arabs and redeem their humiliation. When the Bush White House made Middle East democracy promotion a keystone of its U.S. national security strategy, its goal was to bind the Arab masses together with their leaders in a democratic contract. The hope was that with a voice in their own governance, the Arabs would be able to make their leaders accountable to them. (Actually, the hopes for accountability went beyond this: insofar as elected Arab officials would be responsible for the welfare and actions of their own citizens within their states' borders and outside them, governments would also be made accountable to the international community. Arab regimes could no longer exculpate themselves by claiming they had nothing to do with the manufacture of terrorism and no way to stop it.)

Representative government, then, was coming to the Arabs, and the first direct multicandidate presidential elections in Egypt's history were held almost four years to the day after the event that kickstarted the Bush administration's Arab democratization program, September 7, 2005.

"I wish we had elections every day," said Raouf.

At 4:30 in the afternoon Cairo is usually choked with rush-hour traffic, but we were cruising easily through the city. Raouf figured that the government offices all emptied early when employees were bused en masse to various polling places throughout the city. As a reward for presumably performing their duty—that is, voting for their employer, Hosni Mubarak, to keep his job—they all got to go home early, so while the streets weren't exactly empty, life in Cairo, a city of eighteen million that's short on all sorts of space—personal, social, economic, and political—seemed manageable.

Still, it was not an easy day. Raouf's wallet holding his voter ID card had been stolen a few weeks before, so we spent hours looking for where he was supposed to vote. At one polling place, one of the presidential candidates showed up to cast his ballot and couldn't find his name on the register, as did many other Egyptians who had not registered in time to vote.

Whether or not Egyptians should vote at all has been a question for locals and foreigners alike going back to the British occupation of Egypt. In 1922, as Egyptian officials were petitioning for further independence from the crown, one Egyptian minister went against his colleagues and explained that a parliament would put the country "into the hands of the dominant class who would manipulate elections and purchase votes—the whole system of administration by baksheesh would start afresh and the fellah would undoubtedly be oppressed."[1]

The argument against popular political participation hasn't changed much over the last century: the masses of Egyptians are so poorly educated—illiteracy is at least 40 percent—that they are easy marks for the ruling elite, whose corruption would further increase the gap between rich and poor.[2] But even without the popular vote, the ruling classes had managed to keep the poor and illiterate in their place.

Another argument against democracy was that the Egyptian masses would elect the Muslim Brotherhood. The unhappy retort is that the Islamists had already shaped the social and cultural agenda over the last two decades. While the state had beaten the Islamist movement militarily, the Mubarak government co-opted the language and symbolism of the Islamists to shore up its legitimacy. As a result, the public rhetoric of the regime differed little from that of its religious rivals, with the notable exception of the peace treaty with Israel, which the Islamists rejected out of hand.

Still, while these arguments didn't hold up, there is a fundamental problem with holding free elections in Egypt, namely, that it isn't clear that the masses care all that much about democracy. Indeed it isn't obvious that Egyptians, who live in a country where much of the land is still farmed with ox plows, want anything to change at all. Nasser himself had confronted this problem when he tried to inspire the revolutionary aspirations of the countrymen on whose behalf, at least ostensibly, he had overthrown a king. After the Free Officers' coup, Nasser was reportedly frustrated to find that the Egyptians "weren't really motivated in any direction."[3]

"I don't know what the Egyptian popular will is," said Raouf. "We should take a year to drive all around Egypt and find out what democracy means to Egyptians. Does it mean more food on their plate? Then they would like it. Does it mean that their daughters all have to go to college, because then maybe many of them would not like it. A lot of people say they want the Muslim Brotherhood, but if they come to power and won't let Egyptians listen to Umm Kulthum or let girls smoke *shisha*, I don't think Egyptians will accept it. And if it just means they get to vote, I am not sure many people care that much."

Raouf was happily surprised that so many of his friends did care, when he assumed most of them would stay home. All of them voted for the two runners-up, one of whom was the liberal candidate, Ayman Nour, jailed by the incumbent shortly after the elections. Despite irregularities at the polls—Raouf's friend who was working at one of the many polling places we visited told us that party operatives were openly campaigning for Mubarak at the ballot boxes—and reports that the government "manipulated electoral laws, subverted judicial processes, beat up demonstrators, and blocked voters from the polls," the vote was relatively fair, by Arab standards anyway.[4] With 88.6 percent of seven million votes, about 22 percent of the thirty-two million registered voters, Mubarak's victory was competitive compared with the nearly unanimous triumphs for the elected presidents of other Arab republics, like Syria and Saddam's Iraq, who typically received 99 percent of the vote (as had Mubarak in the days before free elections). Mubarak's 2005 success reflected, as Raouf had surmised, that the mass of ordinary Egyptians were perhaps not so interested in democracy—or that they fundamentally trusted Mubarak to keep Egypt safe and steering a more or less steady, albeit impoverished, ship of state.

Mubarak must have figured as much because the well-oiled media campaign he ran before the election wasn't aimed at securing Egyptian votes. The man wearing an easy smile and pancake makeup in the slickly produced video ads was not an authoritarian regime chief, but a democratic leader in an open-necked collar who joshed easily with the press; this Mubarak was not a president for life sur-

rounded by corruption, but a man at ease with the Egyptian peas-
antry in all their folkloric splendor; he was not an Arab strongman
whose decisions consisted of winks and nods, but a commander in
chief sitting behind a desk, signing his name to official papers. This
was an American-style media campaign for American consumption,
because Washington was watching closely. And it seemed to work.
The United States had pressed the Egyptian regime to open up the
elections, and afterward the State Department called it a "beginning . . . that will enrich the Egyptian political dialogue for years to
come."[5] Egypt was among the many Arab states where U.S. pressure
for democratic reform appeared to be gathering some momentum.

Typically, it is that group of hard-charging ideologues known
as the neoconservatives, policy makers who were concentrated in the Bush White House's National Security Council staff,
the Pentagon, and Vice President Cheney's office, who are credited as
the intellectual architects of Arab democracy. However, the administration's policy was anything but revolutionary: the quest for Arab
democracy is a habit of the American mind, dating back to the earli-
est American travelers to the region, the nineteenth-century Christian missionaries. Once the proselytizers found there was little room
in the Holy Land for the Protestant gospel, they started to preach
America's civic religion—universal equal rights, freedom, democracy.
Our missionary calling in the Middle East underpins a long tradition
of American policy making, from President Woodrow Wilson's Fourteen Points speech promoting self-determination for all peoples,
to President Eisenhower's decision to stand against Washington's
"imperialist" allies France and Great Britain at Suez in 1956 and
demand they withdraw from Egypt.

Eisenhower later called his intervention at Suez the worst mistake he ever made,[6] and with two notable exceptions (Beirut in 1982
and Kuwait in 1991) subsequent administrations tended to play a less

activist role in the region, entrusting U.S. interests to regional allies inclined to repress their own people, a tendency the Americans noted with displeasure but did not correct. September 11 returned the White House to the missionary roots of U.S. Middle East policy, but were it not for the confluence of other unforeseen events, and unsuspected allies, it is unlikely that Arab democracy would have become the cornerstone of U.S. national security strategy.

The kernels of regional transformation were strewn before the invasion of Iraq, and its unwitting Johnny Appleseed was a career military man from the "realist" school of U.S. foreign policy. Secretary of State Colin Powell was opposed to using American might for the sorts of ideological and idealistic ends associated with the neoconservatives, but when he warned President Bush of the consequences of military action in Iraq, he set the table for the new policy. "You are going to be the proud owner of 25 million people," Secretary Powell told the president. "You will own all their hopes, aspirations, and problems. You'll own it all." This principle is derived from American retailing; Thomas Friedman called it the "Pottery Barn rule": "You break it, you own it."[7] It is not an idea that is readily traceable to the realist school of American policy making, which cares little for the hopes, aspirations, and problems of foreign nationals.

The fact is that the divisions in the administration weren't as clear as Washington insiders have made them out to be. Realists like Powell weren't as realist as they and their cheerleaders in the press let on, and for the neoconservatives Arab democracy came a distant second to American interests. The mantra often associated with the neoconservatives was "regime change," which did not necessarily mean that representative government would replace bad actors like Saddam Hussein, but only that the leaders of regimes across the region were put on notice that their days might be numbered.

As the Bush White House sought to prevent further attacks on the United States, the invasion of Afghanistan was little more than a policing action to round up those responsible for the attacks—the

Arabs led by bin Laden, who had in effect rented space from the Taliban to use as a base of operations. But a national security strategy is not the same thing as a criminal prosecution. The goal cannot be simply to apprehend wrongdoers after the fact, but to protect Americans against external threats, which means taking the initiative and going to the heart of the problem. And in this case, that was not Al Qaeda, and not Islam (as the White House tried clumsily to explain so as not to alienate the world's 1.2 billion Muslims). The heart of the problem lay in the Arab world. Nineteen Arabs had struck the United States on behalf of Arab causes—Palestine, U.S. sanctions on Iraq, U.S. troops in Saudi Arabia, and so forth—supported by Arab rulers and the Arab masses alike, which is why on 9/11 Arabs across the region, from the Palestinian territories to the Persian Gulf, passed out baklava in celebration. The Iraq adventure was a punitive war against the Arabs, or more specifically against those who fund, arm, and embody the causes for which Arabs are willing to kill Americans: Arab regimes.

While much of the public debate in the United States was focused on the grievances that motivated networks of rogue operators to murder Americans, even before the invasion of Iraq the leaders of Arab states had reason to fear they would come in the crosshairs of an angry White House, since they knew better than anyone that stateless terrorism is a fiction designed to conceal their hands-on relationship to violence beyond their borders. Libya and Sudan were quick to let the White House know that they had nothing to do with 9/11 and were out of the terror industry. A diplomatic cable from the U.S. embassy in Libya dated a week and a half after 9/11 says that Khaddafi was "hysterical in his telephone call to [Jordan's] King Abdullah as if only his personal intervention would prevent U.S. action."[8] Even Cairo, which interceded on behalf of Khaddafi and Sudanese president Omar Bashir, was scared of reprisals. In the fall of 2002, a state-owned Egyptian newsweekly carried an interview with imprisoned Islamist militants from al-Gama'a al-Islamiyya,[9] who explained that since they had repented of their violence and were no longer terrorizing ordinary Egyptians or foreign tourists, or taking orders from Sheikh Omar Abdel Rahman, neither they nor Egypt should pay the price for 9/11.

There were many other likely targets that the administration might have chosen in order to deter another attack on the United States. Both Syria and the Palestinian Authority, formerly the Palestine Liberation Organization, had long, amply documented histories of sponsoring terror dating back to the 1970s; Saudi Arabia, home to fifteen of the 9/11 hijackers, had funded and armed Islamists across the region (as we well knew, since the Saudis had done so often with our approval, if not our active cooperation). All of these regimes might reasonably have expected American reprisal attacks, from which they all would have taken the obvious lesson: Arab rulers who provide funding and support for terrorism are responsible for the actions of their citizens, and hence if Arabs attack American citizens, interests, or allies, Arab states will suffer the consequences.

Saddam drew the short stick. His regime could be toppled, the Americans had throttled his army only a decade before, and he more than any other Arab ruler embodied anti-American causes. Washington's justification before the world for singling out an Arab country that would have to pay for 9/11 was that Saddam was in possession of weapons of mass destruction, a conviction shared by every intelligence agency in the world, while the United Nations passed numerous Security Council resolutions concerning Iraqi armaments. It was not until six months after the invasion of Iraq—after the Americans failed to find the WMD—that the freedom agenda took pride of place in the administration's thinking: Iraq would be a forward base for advancing Middle Eastern democracy.[10]

I have already noted the American habit of seeing the Arab-Israeli crisis as the Middle East's central issue, which, once solved, would magically settle all the region's other problems as well. The Bush White House was wise enough to dismiss this idea. But it nonetheless believed that there was a link tying the region together, meaning that change in one country could have profound effects throughout the region. In their thinking, the road to peace didn't run through Jerusalem; it went through Baghdad. Democratizing Iraq would touch off a domino effect throughout the Arab states, turning them, one after another, into nascent democracies.

As it happened, there was a chain reaction, but it wasn't exactly the one the Americans had imagined. The Bush White House had correctly identified the culpability of Arab regimes in cultivating terror and using it as a political tool, but the Americans' biggest mistake was in believing that the regimes were the only problem. Since these rulers afforded their subjects no other option than violence, Washington would change the game, offering the Arab masses freedom instead of tyranny. The United States would no longer entrust its interests, or security, to allies like Egypt and Saudi Arabia, whose friendship was rightly in doubt. Instead, America would speak directly to the Arab people, who deserved to govern themselves. The White House knew democracy would prove messy, for a while anyway, but it was convinced that the Arab people would be so busy using their newfound political, social, and economic liberties to have a say in their own self-rule that they would have no time, and no desire, to kill Americans. As 9/11 showed, Arab political culture had only produced despair and exported terror, and so, as President Bush explained in a series of speeches starting in the spring of 2003, the answer was to uproot it and bring democracy to the region. "In an age of global terror and weapons of mass destruction what happens in the Middle East greatly matters to America," Bush said in a commencement address at the University of South Carolina on May 9, 2003:

> The bitterness of that region can bring violence and suffering to our own cities. The advance of freedom and peace in the Middle East would drain this bitterness and increase our own security.

So today I want to discuss with you a great goal for this nation. We will use our influence and idealism to replace old hatreds with new hopes across the Middle East. A time of historic opportunity has arrived. A dictator in Iraq has been removed from power. The terrorists of that region are now seeing their fate, the short, unhappy life of the fugitive. Reformers in the Middle East are gaining influence, and the momentum of freedom is growing. We have reached a moment of tremendous promise, and the United States will seize this moment for the sake of peace.[11]

In his November 2003 speech at the National Endowment for Democracy, Bush elaborated on his vision of what a democratic Middle East would look like:

Successful societies limit the power of the state and the power of the military—so that governments respond to the will of the people, and not the will of an elite. Successful societies protect freedom with the consistent and impartial rule of law, instead of selecting applying—selectively applying the law to punish political opponents. Successful societies allow room for healthy civic institutions—for political parties and labor unions and independent newspapers and broadcast media. Successful societies guarantee religious liberty—the right to serve and honor God without fear of persecution. Successful societies privatize their economies, and secure the rights of property. They prohibit and punish official corruption, and invest in the health and education of their people. They recognize the rights of women. And instead of directing hatred and resentment against others, successful societies appeal to the hopes of their own people.

The president argued that the West had to take responsibility for its past actions in the region and do better:

Sixty years of Western nations excusing and accommodating the lack of freedom in the Middle East did nothing to make us safe—because in the long run, stability cannot be purchased at the expense of liberty. As long as the Middle East remains a place where freedom does not flourish, it will remain a place of stagnation, resentment, and violence ready for export. And with the spread of weapons that can bring catastrophic harm to our country and to our friends, it would be reckless to accept the status quo.

Therefore, the United States has adopted a new policy, a forward strategy of freedom in the Middle East. This strategy requires the same persistence and energy and idealism we have shown before. And it will yield the same results. As in Europe, as in Asia, as in every region of the world, the advance of freedom leads to peace.

The advance of freedom is the calling of our time; it is the calling of our country. From the Fourteen Points to the Four Freedoms, to the Speech at Westminster, America has put our power at the service of principle. We believe that liberty is the design of nature; we believe that liberty is the direction of history. We believe that human fulfillment and excellence come in the responsible exercise of liberty. And we believe that freedom—the freedom we prize—is not for us alone, it is the right and the capacity of all mankind.[12]

In short, a president usually characterized as a swaggering cowboy, a warmonger, was pushing a Middle East policy that could only be described as liberal, if not leftist. Not only should the Americans bring democracy to the Arabs, but, as if taking a page from Edward Said's *Orientalism,* Bush said that Washington was at fault for not having done so before and ignoring the democratic aspirations of Arabs for sixty years.

Not surprisingly, Arab liberals were energized by Bush's efforts. The night of the president's second inaugural speech I was in Syria, in a middle-class Sunni neighborhood in Homs, a midsize industrial city some two hours north of Damascus, visiting my friend Abdul Rahman, a huge man in his early fifties, well over three hundred pounds, whose emotions come easily. He was sobbing as the American president spoke. "God bless you, Bush," he said, blowing kisses at the screen. "God bless you, the only man who's doing something for the Arabs."

The genuine Arab liberals, as opposed to the regime mouthpieces left out on display for the foreign press and visiting dignitaries, did not draw fine lines between what they believed were American ideals and U.S. policies. When the White House took the side of Arab people against their rulers, that was enough evidence for Arab liberals that American values and policies were aligned just right. "I'm more neocon than the neocons," said Abdul Rahman. He told me he cried when John and Robert Kennedy were killed, but his American role model now was Paul Wolfowitz, the undersecretary of defense and Bush's point man for Arab democracy. A few days later, on January 30, 2005, when ten million Iraqis risked their lives to go to the polls, I was sitting in a Beirut restaurant with a Lebanese friend, the political analyst Elie Fawaz. "I cried watching the Iraqis vote," he said. We lit after-dinner cigars to celebrate in spite of the protestations of Miss Lebanon at a neighboring table. "The courage it took for Iraqis was amazing," Fawaz said. "This was a great day not just for the Iraqis but for all the Arabs. This is historical. This is going to change a lot of minds about what Arabs can and cannot do."

It was also a great time to be an American in the region. Some of our countrymen living or working in the Middle East at the time, either driven by their anger at Bush or sympathetic with ostensibly pan-Arab causes, let their emotions shape their analysis and their political inclinations as well, leaving them on the side of dictators, Islamist militants, and regime lackeys. But for others of us there, witnesses to the massive demonstrations in Lebanon, colleagues of Arab bloggers and journalists, or friends of the men and women hopeful that if the Americans were serious, then things might really change in the region, it was a privilege to be represented by a U.S. government that had taken the side of freedom. It was a time of high optimism, and democracy really did seem to be on the march; the Bush White House was rolling up victories with the elections in Egypt and Iraq, the public demonstrations in Beirut's Martyrs' Square, and despots on the defensive from Riyadh to Damascus.

Soon enough, though, it became clear that Arab liberals and their Western supporters had let their hopes get ahead of reality. The Middle East is a part of the world where it is licit and even encouraged to reason with one's nerves, and the intensity that this brings to Arab politics—an intensity that has no counterpart in our, happily, secure and essentially rational Western societies—is part of the appeal that Arab politics holds out for foreigners. And while this temperament is usually specific to the millenarian and maximalist policies of the parties of resistance and no compromise, it engulfed even the pro-democracy forces, Arabs and foreigners alike, during this period. Swept away by the prospect of real change, we ignored the implausibility of a sustainable democratic revolution in a region where authority is vested in the strong horse.

In retrospect, the January 2006 Palestinian Authority elections that brought Hamas to power were a defining moment. Secretary of State Condoleezza Rice explained that the Islamic Resistance Movement's victory at the polls came as a surprise to her office, a bizarre claim seeing as how the main reason the United States had previously refrained from strong-arming Arab regimes for reform was because over the last three decades Washington had repeatedly been told—by its own analysts, the Israelis, and of course the regimes themselves—that more freedom would empower Islamists.[13] The Bush team refused to acknowledge that an Islamist militia with a rejectionist Israel strategy and an obscurantist domestic agenda could really win the affections of an Arab polity. In this instance, the Western media and the Bush White House found themselves on the same side, explaining that the election results signaled not a vote *for* Hamas's eliminationist war against its Jewish neighbors but a vote *against* the corruption and incompetence of Fatah. But in time it became clear that the Palestinians knew exactly what they were voting for: armed resistance. How else to explain the fact that just two weeks before Israel's 2008 siege on Gaza, 250,000 Palestinians, or a little less than 25 percent of Gaza's total population of 1.4 million, took to the streets to celebrate Hamas's twenty-first anniversary?[14]

If the Bush administration refused to come to terms with what Hamas's victory actually meant, it wasn't just because it wanted to cover up for its mistakes. It was also because it couldn't really accept the obvious implication of the election's result, which was that spending U.S. lives, money, and prestige in pushing democracy on the Arab world might, at the moment, be a fool's errand. In theory, Arab democracy was the antidote to bin Ladenism and the strong horse principle, offering the Arab masses a share of their own government and obviating the political grievances that presumably gave rise to violence. In practice, the administration's post-9/11 national security strategy rewarded precisely those whose freedom to operate in any political environment should have been most severely curtailed—the Islamists, or anyone who sounded even faintly like Osama bin Laden.

The administration hoped that the democratic process would moderate the Islamists by forcing them to maneuver in the messy realm of give-and-take politics. Yet there is little evidence that radicals are made moderate by having to solicit votes and govern. History shows that the reverse is true—radicals radicalize politics. For instance, Hitler did not become more moderate when he took over the reins of a parliamentary government; he liquidated opponents and onetime allies, turned Germany into a totalitarian state, and set it on a course for war. And at least the government Hitler took over, the Weimar Republic, was a consensual political system to begin with, whereas the Arab states that the United States pressured into elections, with the exception of Lebanon, had never known anything but authoritarian rule. So, what was going to compel the Islamists to become moderate in a climate of extremism and eliminationism— that is, the normal weather of Arab politics? Where did the Americans get the idea that Islamists could be made democrats?

Many decades ago, Western officials, analysts, and researchers were convinced that the future of the Muslim Middle East would consist of various forms of "secular" nationalisms that would eventually adopt more or less Western political norms. They were caught off guard by Iran's 1979 Islamic revolution. The revolution was an epochal event, a real revolution that, like all revolutions, changed the world—but it had scarcely any effect on how most Western experts looked at the region.

Even after the 1979 takeover of the U.S. embassy in Tehran, many in the Carter administration believed that because there seemed to be competing centers of power in the Iranian leadership, and because liberal and leftist secularists were part of the revolution as well, Washington could do business with the Iranians. Later, the Iran-contra scandal was premised on the idea that the Reagan administration had identified Iranian moderates that it could deal with. The notion that Iran could be engaged, provided that sufficient diplomatic energies were applied and the United States was willing to proffer incentives and show contrition for past indignities, has survived four U.S. administrations, from Reagan to Bush II; it was the major plank of President Obama's foreign policy platform. Thus on both sides of the aisle, policy makers and analysts refused to recognize the nature of the regime, and believed that Islamism was just a passing social movement, that no one could be that serious about religion and govern a modern state at the same time, that the corruption and self-interest of these carpet weavers turned statesmen would eventually bring them to the bargaining table, as pragmatists. Over time, the thinking went, once the Americans got their hooks into them, the Islamists would have little choice but to become free-market liberals.

All this was gospel for the same reason that a former State Department policy maker named Francis Fukuyama looked at the fall of the Soviet Union and decided that history had come to an end and liberal democracy had conclusively triumphed. For good reasons and bad ones, the American policy elite cherishes stability above all other values, and so it is apt to see stability on the verge of breaking out even in the unlikeliest of places. Unfortunately, the rest of the world is not always cooperative, nor does it agree that democracy is the highest and final stage in political organization.

Many Islamists, like Ayatollah Khomeini himself and the Muslim Brotherhood, were plainly contemptuous of Western forms of government and all efforts to co-opt the Islamic movement. Indeed, the Brotherhood's motto "The Quran is our constitution" underscores the irreconcilable contradiction between democracy and Islamism.[15] Democracy holds that the people are the source of political sovereignty, whereas the Islamists believe that any governance that does not make God the source of political sovereignty is an abomination and a recipe for disaster.

To be sure, there are other Islamists, like Hassan al-Turabi, bin Laden's onetime host in Khartoum, who have been happy to indulge Western fantasies about democratic Islamism.[16] And this had led Western analysts to try to distinguish between Islamist extremists and Islamist moderates, with the latter usually defined as such based on their willingness to submit their program to a popular referendum, as Islamists did in Algeria with great success at the polls in 1992. When the Algerian government nullified this victory, it touched off a civil war that lasted throughout the 1990s, leaving more than 150,000 dead. During the war years, the Clinton State Department pushed the regime to reconcile with the Islamists, arguing that if the government couldn't find ready-made moderate Islamists to dialogue with, it needed to create them through the political process.[17]

Ideally, analysis shapes policy, and in the case of Algeria the carnage left in the war's bloody wake should have shown to U.S. policy makers that a party that goes to war to protest an election result is at the very least no more likely to rule democratically than the government that canceled the results. Indeed, the analysis was shaped by an American policy that counseled rapprochement between the regime and the Islamists. And since describing the Islamists as well-armed cadres willing to kill and die for God could not lead to a policy of reconciliation, policy makers had to come up with an explanation of how Islamists might in time become more moderate.

As a result, Washington was flush with advocates of Islamist pluralism who found evidence of nascent democracy scattered throughout the Islamic canon—though admittedly none of this consensual governance had ever been practiced in the actual course of Muslim politics over the last fourteen hundred years.[18] The case for Islamist democracy was hypothetical: Might the Islamists govern justly and prudently the Arab societies that they had previously made war against? Sure, the Islamists might well become democrats—and in any case, what do *we* have to lose if they don't?

Looking at Algeria, some of the sharper American policy makers understood that once Islamists came to power at the polls, they would not likely be willing to cede authority in a subsequent round of elections—or, as the former assistant secretary of state Edward Djerejian put it, Islamist democracy means "one vote, one man, one time." In other words, the strong horse takes power in any way possible and keeps it by all means available. The fundamental problem with Arab democracy isn't Islam or Islamism but the norms of Arab politics and governance, of which Islamist politics is merely an aspect. The problem is systemic, organic.

In effect, the Bush administration's top-down approach toward regional transformation conceived of Arab reform as a debugging program that would go through and clean all the problems out of a flawed but basically sound piece of equipment. The White House proceeded as though democracy were a kind of technology, like the Internet, cell phones, or satellite TV, opening up new vistas, possibilities, and arrangements unimaginable to the tradition-bound Arab elders, but which the rising generation, Arab youth, would find so appealing that it could not help but be seduced by the Western way of life, utterly transforming the region, whether anyone willed it so or not.

CHAPTER 7

The Schizophrenic Gulf

The Bush administration's faith that it could turn Iraq into a beacon of democracy seemed to assume that once it brought the trappings of modernity and liberalism to Baghdad, the substance of these things would soon follow. And the fact that we had put American lives at risk in order to topple a dictator and support a nascent democracy, meanwhile, would help defuse anti-American hostility and demonstrate our bona fides in the region. The reality of the situation turned out to be very different: Iraqis may have welcomed the toppling of Saddam, but they despised the United States for invading their country. They turned out in throngs to vote, and yet seemed to see democracy as primarily a matter of legitimizing the rule of one sect over another. They wanted the Americans to leave, but they also thought that if the Americans left, the country would descend into chaos. America's intervention, in other words, produced a kind of schizophrenia among Iraqis. This should not have been surprising. After all, schizophrenia is the default condition of most of the Middle East.

Consider that Saddam Hussein had once seemed poised to overrun Saudi Arabia and the rest of the Arab Gulf states after his 1990 invasion of Kuwait; but with the Islamic Republic of Iran recuperating from its decadelong war with Iraq and ascendant throughout the region, the Arab states once again turned to Saddam as a stalwart defender of Sunni power. The Sunnis' other way to deter Tehran was to back the same militant organization that threatened to topple Arab regimes, Al Qaeda. Once the Americans deposed Saddam and dealt a withering blow to Al Qaeda in Iraq, the Arabs had lost both their local security pillars, and the Saudis and the Egyptians found they had no choice but to leave their fate in the hands of Israel—the Zionist entity that they had warred against for sixty years—to protect them from Iran.

But nowhere does Arab schizophrenia manifest itself more clearly than in the Sunnis' alliance with the United States. The relationship penetrates every aspect of the Arabs' lives, especially in the Gulf states, where the United States has basing rights in all six Gulf Cooperation Council (GCC) countries—Saudi Arabia, United Arab Emirates, Qatar, Bahrain, Kuwait, and Oman—in order to protect the oil that ensures the stability of the global economy. The Arabs are incapable of defending for themselves the resource that has made them rich, a wealth that has given them access to all of the most glamorous products of a world that they played no part in creating. Their dependency on the West extends beyond the military and political spheres even into culture, a fact that becomes evident strolling through any mall in the Arab Gulf states, where teenage boys in bright white dishdashas, baseball caps, and Converse All Stars wait in line for first-run Hollywood action movies, while their teenage sisters in black burqas and designer sunglasses balance armfuls of shopping bags from American retail outlets while chatting on their iPhones.

It is hard not to be charmed by an ice-skating rink in a Qatari mall, or admire the daffy ambition in building the world's largest indoor ski slope in Dubai. However, the Gulf interpretation of American pop has a seamier side to it, like the hotel lounge tricked out to look just like a college-town sports bar, with beer and burgers and ESPN on four large-screen TVs at the bar, where I was watching two preppy-looking couples playing eight ball and sharing a pitcher of beer—until I saw in the bright yellow light hanging over the pool table that they weren't flirtatious undergrads but two Saudi teenagers and a pair of thirtysomething Russian call girls.

It is hardly surprising the Arabs are deeply confused about the United States and their own feelings toward a civilization that has the wherewithal to enjoin good and forbid evil, as the *umma* once did. Their obsession on the one hand with the ornamental baubles of the American lifestyle as emblems of the values and ideals they say they admire, and their loud hatred on the other hand of the policies that protect and advance the interests of the country that makes those products, are the schizophrenic symptoms of a society exposed and vulnerable to the modern world to which it has mainly contributed two things: the fossil fuel that lies below its land and, of late, jihad. It is the vast wealth of the Arabs of the Persian Gulf that makes them especially susceptible to this bifurcating disorder: with access to everything America makes, they are afforded the luxury of believing that it is possible to distinguish between a culture's products and its policies, its technological prowess and the secular worldview underpinning the scientific method. But these items cannot be separated out, for no matter how diffuse and various are the individuals and institutions that make up a culture, a society is a coherent, holistic organism that reflects its values, contradictions, and convictions from every prism.

Of course a large number of Westerners as well as Arabs see it differently. One of globalization's articles of faith is that technology and consumer goods will bridge the gaps between different societies, including the West and the Arabic-speaking Middle East—as if a shelfful of DVDs, sitting behind the wheel of an SUV, or facility with a BlackBerry were the entry fee to the modern world. But because so many take the shiny surface of our society as the thing in itself, because they see no necessary relationship between the technological dynamism and productivity of our society and the ideas and values underlying our American gloss, it is likewise impossible for them to register the density of Arab culture. To the apostles of globalization it is inconceivable that an Arab, perhaps educated in the West, speaking Western languages, and doing business with Westerners, would hesitate to swap the values that have distinguished his society for generations in exchange for a ticket in the globalization sweepstakes. This ethnocentric fallacy that everyone wants our way of life just because they desire our consumer goods has led to the untenable conclusion that goods like the Internet, cell phones, and satellite TV are capable of transforming fundamental values and ideas. And so for the technology-is-social-progress crowd, the mix-and-match fashion bricolage of the Gulf Arab mall rat is not the armor of uncertain identity but the style paradigm for the one-world-brotherhood-and-security-in-globalization generation. This is the brave new Arab world where Islam commingles easily with the West, and its red-hot center is Dubai, where, as Sheikh Mohammed bin Rashid al-Maktoum, the ruler of this small Gulf emirate, says, "If you dream it, you can build it."

But that optimism reigned before the financial crisis hit Dubai full force in the winter of 2009, requiring Abu Dhabi, the largest and richest of the seven city-states that make up the UAE, to bail out its more visionary sister emirate. Dubai's population had surged from 30,000 to 1.4 million since the 1971 founding of the UAE, but with foreign labor, from Baluchi construction workers to British lawyers, forced to leave in droves, it's unclear where the numbers will settle once the dust clears. The construction cranes that dot the skyline more than minarets or date palms are mostly idle, and the future of many of the emirate's more audacious projects—like the amusement park under construction called Dubailand that was to double the size of Dubai itself, and the man-made islands where luxury condominiums were bought in advance by European celebrities like the soccer star David Beckham—is unclear.

Still, it's unlikely that Dubai will be forced to return to its origins as a small port village that depended on the pearl trade and commerce with India and Iran. In 1966 the emirate known as the pearl of the Persian Gulf struck oil, but its ruler at the time, Sheikh Rashid, understood that his oil had a shelf date and it was best used to bankroll other projects, like shipping, tourism, and finance, varied sources of income that earned the emirate high ratings from the World Bank and International Monetary Fund for economic diversification. What Sheikh Rashid sowed, his third son, Sheikh Mohammed, reinvested in ports, hotels, and several large industrial-park-type free zones not subject to UAE laws or tariffs, like Internet City, Medical Village, and Media City, which attracted regional and international tenants. The emirate's Arab critics—many of whom actually work in Dubai—said it has no authentic culture or history, unlike Damascus, Cairo, Beirut, or Baghdad. But to Dubai's admirers, that was the key to its success—the absence of history. Distance from the rest of the region and its problems made the Emiratis more flexible and adaptable than the ideological Arabs of the Levant.

"Here your ideas can make things change," says Dr. Omar bin Suleiman, one of a small group of Emirati natives in their thirties to forties who make up Sheikh Mohammed's kitchen cabinet responsible for managing the daily operations of Dubai Inc. The U.S.-educated bin Suleiman was CEO of Internet City before he was moved over to iron out some of the regulatory problems at the International Financial Center. "One businessman told me he was considering doing business in Lebanon," says bin Suleiman. "But he saw all these posters with the pictures of all of Lebanon's different leaders, and wondered, 'Who do I go to if there's a problem?' In Dubai you know who you go to, and the government listens." In other words, Sheikh Mohammed is the government, a tribal chieftain working on a global stage.

It was Ramadan, and bin Suleiman invited me over to break the fast. He lived in a large villa in a neighborhood that looks like a suburb of Los Angeles, where he got his graduate degree before returning home to the Emirates. The juices and dates set out on tray tables were the only color in a sparsely decorated living room with only a long white couch with gilded edges and matching chairs. He removed his white head scarf and white skullcap and went to pray. When he returned, the meal began in earnest, several different rice dishes, some with lentils and others with meat, like *mansaf*, which was not served with the head of the lamb resting in the middle of the dish, as it usually is in traditional Bedouin fashion.

The Gulf Arabs do have a real culture, even if the citified Arabs of the Fertile Crescent disparage them as uncouth bumpkins with none of the refinement that the storied Arab metropolises have embodied for over a thousand years. The Bedouin have neither ancient mosques nor great museums for the curious tourist to wander through; their culture is transmitted through poetry, the spoken history of the tribesmen, their heroes and feats of arms passed down to generations in an oral tradition's vast library of virtues, like loyalty, physical courage, and generosity. And without those virtues and the culture of the tribesman, the Arabs, the Bedouin, who gave rise to Islam, there would be no minarets owning the horizon from the Persian Gulf to the Mediterranean.

"Dubai is different from Egypt and the rest of the Arab world," says bin Suleiman. "I was at the duty-free in the airport, and an Egyptian fellah was looking at computers and wanted to know the best one. I asked him, 'You don't know how to use computers, do you?' He said, 'It's not for me, but for my kid. Whoever has one will have the best job.' See," bin Suleiman concluded, "even the fellah got it."

Dubai calls those savants who will master the new technologies "knowledge workers." The emirate had hoped to boost its population to five million knowledge workers within the next decade and become a major international service and sales hub, serving the Middle East as well as Africa and the Asian subcontinent. The big regional and international firms, universities, hospitals, and media outfits—like Microsoft, Apple, Cornell University Medical Center,

Purdue University—that leased space in the free zones saw Dubai as a forward position in a market that until the fall of 2008 showed no signs of weakening anytime soon thanks to India's and China's growing need for fossil fuels. But with history as a guide, cracks were showing long before the crisis hit.

The Emiratis saw Dubai much the way the father of modern Egypt, Muhammad Ali Pasha, understood Egypt: the latter sent delegations to France and Italy to learn the latest in scientific and military advances, while the former lured the West to bring its twenty-first century to the Arabs, but both believed modernity could be had on the cheap. Egypt's failure to join the modern world over the last two centuries was proof enough that this was a delusion: without the values and worldview that underpin the manufacture of technology, the Arabs will not only come short of catching up to the West but also end up living a schizophrenic existence. The gap between the West and the Orient is not geographical; rather, it is a rift between two worldviews, where the first is an open and free society that cannot help but constantly reevaluate and investigate its own premises, leading it to prize the empiricism and quest for the new that propel technological innovation, while the second is a culture that draws red lines around authority—political, religious, cultural, and even familial—as a matter of habit.

To be sure, Dubai advertised itself as an open Arab society eager to join the world community, but just as the impact of the financial crisis was starting to be felt, the emirate kept an Israeli tennis player from competing in one of the international tournaments that were meant to raise the emirate's profile. At the same time, Abu Dhabi's much-publicized International Book Fair banned a novel portraying a fictional Gulf sheikh as a homosexual. The Gulf Arabs were not less ideological than their brothers in the Levant. They were just more adept at straddling two worlds than the rest of the Arabs were.

Media City was central in promoting Dubai-style openness. Home to several Arab and international press outfits, with its most famous tenant the twenty-four-hour news station Al Arabiya, the ostensibly liberal alternative to Al Jazeera, the region's most notorious satellite network, Media City projected an image of Dubai that represented less the reality of the emirate than its economic program and political strategy.

At one time Cairo was the capital of Arab media, a position that enhanced Egypt's regional prestige with the sort of "soft power" rivals could only envy. On the strength of Cairo's advanced recording and film industry, Egyptian became the best known of all Arabic dialects and the region's de facto lingua franca. Even today some of the most popular Lebanese divas record their songs in Egyptian in order to tap the region's largest music-buying market. Cairo's reputation as cultural power broker, trendsetter, and opinion maker endured even as Nasser began to nationalize the press and turn it into a regime bullhorn. Others followed the Egyptian leader's example until the Arabic-language media essentially consisted of closed local markets from Morocco to Iraq that faced little internal competition and gave the regimes almost absolute control over the flow of information leaving or entering their countries. That slowly began to change as Western networks penetrated the Arab market with the advent of satellite technology, and when the first Gulf War broke out in 1991, Arabs flipped to CNN International for coverage of a conflict that was taking place in their own backyards. The BBC tried to piggyback on CNN's success by setting up an Arabic-language satellite network, and when it failed, much of the staff signed on with a start-up operation that began broadcasting from Qatar in 1996 as Al Jazeera.

As globalization cheerleaders see technology as an engine of political reform, many herald the Qatari network as the dawn of a new day in the Middle East. Social progress, they suggest, will invariably follow technological innovation, just as the printing press transformed Europe and the Gutenberg Bible sparked the Reformation. On this view, Al Jazeera is a breakthrough not just for Arab media but for all Arab society, pushing open public space and redrawing red lines. With all the information that satellite TV makes available to Arab viewers, the regimes now no longer have the last word on what appears in Arab living rooms and coffeehouses. Al Jazeera has made dissent and debate the order of the day, and with the Arabs talking openly for the first time ever, there's no way to put the genie back in the bottle.[1] In other words, the revolution *is* being televised, because television is the revolution.

In reality, there is little in tone or content to distinguish Al Jazeera from the rest of the region's standard media fare, certainly not the anti-Semitic and anti-American exhortations of the network's hosts and guests, though it is true that seldom before have viewers had the opportunity to repeat those same clichés themselves during live on-air phone calls. The station's most popular show is *Sharia and Life,* preaching and advice from the Muslim Brotherhood sheikh Yusuf al-Qaradawi, praised by Western academics for his relatively moderate social message,[2] while ignoring his mainstream, hard-line political positions, like his anti-Shia invective. Even as Al Jazeera may have made the Nasserist model of state-owned media obsolete, it features a popular talk show hosted by a Nasserist retread, Muhammad Hassanein Heykal, who served as the Egyptian president's onetime confidant, speechwriter, and publicist, and whose message has changed little since the immediate aftermath of the 1967 war. There's only one thing new about Al Jazeera, aside from its first-rate production values: it showed Arab regimes that while they could no longer manage words and images to control information internally, neither could rival governments. Paradoxically, what the rise of the new media has really done is increase the ability of Arab regimes to project power across the region and interfere in the workings of other Arab states.

Qatar's ruler, Sheikh Hamad bin Khalifa Al-Thani, overthrew his father in a 1995 palace coup. His first order of business was to figure out how to put Qatar on a regional stage without the huge quantity of energy resources of neighboring Saudi Arabia, or even the port facilities of Dubai. The latter served as something of a cosmopolitan model for Qatar, which like Dubai has leased space to Western brand names, like the Louvre Museum and the BBC, which bases its East-West dialogue, *The Doha Debates,* in the emirate. More significantly, Qatar has allowed the U.S. military to set up shop there with CENTCOM, which oversees American military planning in the region. Nonetheless, the Qatari emir's strategy is focused on the Gulf's principal Sunni power, Saudi Arabia, and his satellite network plays a key role.

In the 1980s, as Arab intellectuals were escaping from high-conflict zones in Lebanon, Iraq, and the Palestinian territories, they found refuge in London, making it a pan-Arab media hub in exile, where newspapers and magazines grew up alongside the first Arab satellite network, the Saudi-owned Middle East Broadcasting Center (MBC). In the British capital, aspiring Arab media figures learned that one of the surest ways to finance a project was to use their editorial space to insult a wealthy individual in the hope that the victim would pay for silence or even buy the medium outright. Naturally, Saudi Arabia's several thousand wealthy and often debauched royals made good targets. On a bigger scale, this became Qatar's model for Al Jazeera: by incessantly attacking Riyadh, the emir raised his country's profile by taking on the biggest kid on the block.

In time, political strategy followed insults and threats, and the Qataris lined up alongside the Saudis' rivals in Iran and their allies in the resistance bloc, including Hezbollah. For instance, in the summer of 2008 Al Jazeera threw a welcome-home party on live TV for Samir Kuntar after the Lebanese national was released from an Israeli prison where he had served twenty-nine years for bashing in the head of a four-year-old girl. This episode and other like-minded broadcasts set off alarm bells throughout Riyadh. It's not, of course, that Saudi Arabia is kindly disposed toward the Jewish state. But what Riyadh fears more than Israel is the Iranian-led resistance bloc and anything that bolsters its image, like the celebration of Hezbollah heroes on Al Jazeera, for Iran and its allies threaten the Saudi order of the region. The Saudi position rests not on brute strength but rather on its wealth and its political and religious clout. That makes it, in some sense, a paper strong horse, one whose power is proportional to its ability to shape Arab opinion.

Of the 300 million Arabic speakers in the greater Middle East, roughly 3 percent constitute what is known as the pan-Arab media market—the 10 million Saudi consumers out of the country's total population of 27 million wealthy enough to purchase what advertisers are paid to sell. There are elites with plenty of disposable income scattered throughout the region, and several states with populations equal to or larger than Saudi Arabia's—like Egypt, Iraq, Morocco, and Algeria—but no place has the same concentrated wealth, making Saudi Arabia the largest advertising market in the entire Middle East. Controlling access to that market gives Riyadh all the leverage it needs in the making of Arab opinion, much of which, surprising as it may seem, is liberal.

Almost all of the liberal press outlets, or print and electronic media and networks that prominently feature liberals alongside Arab nationalists and Islamists, are funded by Saudi Arabia, even if severe press restrictions compel media moguls to base their holdings outside the kingdom, like in Dubai and the United Kingdom. Members of the royal family own the two most esteemed London-based pan-Arab newspapers, *Al-Hayat* and *Asharq al-Awsat.* The latter is now edited by the Saudi journalist Tariq Alhomayed, who was studying for his graduate degree in Washington, D.C., when he was called upon to replace another liberal Saudi journalist, Abdul Rahman al-Rashed, when he was named to take over Al Arabiya.

As Al Jazeera is part of Qatar's business plan, Al Arabiya is a loss leader for its parent company, MBC. Having moved from London to Dubai in 2002, MBC makes a profit on its entertainment channels, especially MBC-2, whose earnings are due to its large roster of premier American movies, a fact that suggests U.S. public diplomacy initiatives in the name of "soft power" are a waste of money—the Arabs already pay top dollar for the privilege of being saturated with our cultural messages, so there is little new we can tell them if they don't already get it. In a manner of speaking, Al Arabiya is a function of Riyadh's public diplomacy that was meant to address Americans' ideas about the Saudis: in the wake of 9/11, and Al Jazeera's soaring popularity, Al Arabiya started broadcasting in 2003 to deliver what its investors hoped was a more moderate message.

"It seems ironic that the Saudis are behind all the liberal trends," Rashed told me in his office, a large glass box of a room looking directly onto the bright studio set. The slender, silver-haired journalist is one of the deans of Arab media, his visage familiar to the readers of the regular column he continues to write for *Asharq al-Awsat* even after coming over to Al Arabiya. "If you look at these media, Al Arabiya, *Asharq al-Awsat,* these are the biggest media names in the region, and they're owned by Saudi companies. These are definitely not fundamentalists. The liberal orientation reflects the private sector, businesspeople."

Rashed, like much of the staff, is a real liberal. His columns have been translated into English to demonstrate that liberal opinion does have a strong place in Arab media, if not all of Arab society. Indeed the network adopted this perspective not because the business model assumes a larger market share—Al Arabiya, like Al Jazeera, has never run anything but deficits—but because it suits Saudi financial and political interests ill served by the jihad that Saudi princes back elsewhere. With so much at stake, the Saudi royals have virtually total control over the content of the media they own, and London-based Saudi journalists winding down in a Soho pub on Friday nights are accustomed to fielding phone calls from members of the royal family with last-minute edits.

In the end, satellite news networks have little to do with opening up public space for the Arab masses; Arab media is a conversation between Arab elites, used to influence opinion, promote interests, and tinker with the internal design of rival regimes. As Al Jazeera is an instrument of Qatari foreign policy that allows its owner, the emir of Qatar, to project more power than the size and resources of the tiny emirate would naturally dictate by targeting conservative Arab regimes, the Saudi-owned liberal media advances the pro-business, pro-U.S. aspect of Saudi policy.

One of the common misconceptions about the U.S.-Saudi relationship is that Riyadh supplies Americans with most of their energy resources. In fact, while Saudi Arabia is the swing producer of oil, only about 20 percent of our oil comes from the Gulf; our presence there is in order to prevent any disruption that would send oil prices everywhere soaring and to secure the free flow of fossil fuels that supply most of western Europe, Japan, China, and India with their energy needs. If it seems strange that the Bahrain-based U.S. Fifth Fleet plays watchdog for the rest of the world's oil, it is worth remembering that American trade and commerce depend on the stability and prosperity of other nations and the global economy as a whole. U.S. hegemony in the Persian Gulf is a vital national interest for every American regardless of the size of his or her automobile and has been so ever since Franklin Delano Roosevelt struck a deal with King Abdul Aziz Al-Saud in a February 1944 meeting on Egypt's Great Bitter Lake.

Oil is not just the lifeblood of the world economy; it also determines Washington's ability to wage war, a pursuit that requires a lot of fuel, and we were particularly keen to protect it from the Soviets during the Cold War. But because the United States advertised itself as anti-imperialist—a prerogative that helped us ruin the British position in the region—we couldn't very well administer an empire ourselves. Instead, Saudi Arabia and the Shah's Iran became the twin pillars of our Gulf security strategy.

Getting local allies to protect U.S. interests and do the dirty work so that Washington doesn't have to dispatch troops is called "off-

shore balancing," a strategy that worked well in the eastern Mediterranean, where Israel's might, and staunch American support, have
prevented the outbreak of a full-scale, or state-versus-state, war for
over thirty-five years. However, the Persian Gulf is a different situation, for no matter how many arms we sold Riyadh and Tehran,
Washington had no Gulf proxy strong enough to patrol the region
on its behalf or even, as the 1979 Islamic revolution in Iran showed,
capable of saving themselves.

In 1980, a year after Khomeini's overthrow of the Shah removed
one pillar of U.S. security in the Persian Gulf, President Jimmy
Carter laid out the Carter Doctrine. It stipulated that "an attempt by
any outside force to gain control of the Persian Gulf region will be
regarded as an assault on the vital interests of the United States of
America, and such an assault will be repelled by any means necessary, including military force."[3] This policy was bolstered in 1981
while the Iran-Iraq war was in full swing and Ronald Reagan pledged
that the United States would use force to protect the Kingdom of
Saudi Arabia.[4]

The fall of the Berlin Wall almost a decade later provided an
opportunity to rethink our Gulf strategy: With the Soviets gone, who
threatens the Gulf oil that the industrialized nations depend on? As
Khomeini had shown in 1979, it was local actors who posed the
biggest threat to Gulf stability. And so it should not have been a very
big surprise when Saddam Hussein invaded Kuwait in 1990 and
threatened to make a run at the grand prize, Saudi oil fields.

After Operation Desert Storm, Washington left a large force in
Saudi Arabia to deter local threats, but as we now know, thanks to
bin Laden's helpful explanation, the presence of infidel troops compromised the Islamic bona fides of the state and destabilized the
royal family. That fact should have alerted Washington to the strategic dangers of Gulf schizophrenia. If the world's largest known
reserves of oil were imperiled by domestic elements in Saudi Arabia,
which can neither protect itself nor be protected without threatening

the legitimacy of the royal family, then the regime that Washington considered the cornerstone of its Gulf security strategy is inherently unstable. The Saudi royal family could very well meet the fate of the Shah.

In time, American policy makers saw the situation was even worse than they had imagined when, after 9/11, the schizophrenic nature of Saudi policy at the same time became plain: while members of the Saudi royal family relied on U.S. military might to protect them from foreign enemies, their domestic security depended on their ability to redirect the political furies of domestic rivals onto those same Americans who protected them. The Bush administration was rightly furious with the Saudis but had little leverage in compelling them to choose a side once and for all. Ideally, the White House would have liked to play balance-of-power politics and use Iran to pressure Riyadh, but given the nature of the regime in Tehran, that was tantamount to playing Russian roulette with a U.S. vital interest, for the Persian Gulf, one of the world's most important waterways, is essentially an American lake.[5] Even the overthrow of Saddam Hussein, paradoxically, did not strengthen Washington's hand, since Saddam, who in 1990 had seemed poised to overrun Riyadh, had in the years since become a linchpin of Saudi regional security. He not only contained Iran but also, as his fall from power in 2003 demonstrated, papered over Sunni weakness.

It is generally believed that the United States' greatest concern over the Iranian nuclear program is for Israel, a conviction that Washington has done little to correct. By limiting their public concerns to what WMD in the hands of the clerical regime meant for Israel, the Americans refrained from putting the Gulf Arabs in an awkward position. The truth, after all, is that Israel has a nuclear deterrent and can defend itself, and the GCC states can't. They depend entirely on the United States for protection from their Shiite rival. If the nightmare scenario of an Iranian nuclear program is that it poses an existential threat to the Jewish state, in its more practical day-to-day application, a doomsday device in the hands of Tehran's revolutionary regime would allow it to set the Middle East's political, cultural, and financial agenda, tipping the scales in favor of the Shia Persians and against the Sunni Arabs, who have been the regional power for almost a millennium and a half.

Iran's nuclear program is not in itself the main issue; it is merely one of Tehran's assets—along with Hezbollah, Hamas, and such—but it is the most prominent, and the fear and noise surrounding the program have distracted Washington and the international community from recognizing that it is merely one instrument with which Iran can accomplish its strategic aims: to overturn the U.S.-backed regional order, send the Americans packing, and become the strong horse in the Persian Gulf.

And so with no other choice, Washington found itself stuck with the Sunnis, and forced to leave its dispute with Riyadh till later. For the Saudis the situation was more desperate: with their American protector tied down in Iraq, where U.S. forces had taken down their man Saddam and crippled their expeditionary force in Al Qaeda, the only instrument of power the Sunnis had left at their disposal was an oil weapon they were loath to use, and their media.

As a result, beginning in late 2005, the Sunnis turned up the heat on the resistance bloc, with Al Arabiya playing a leading role. In a winter 2005 interview, the former vice president of Syria accused Syrian president Bashar al-Assad of killing the former Lebanese prime minister Rafiq al-Hariri. In spring 2006, in another interview, Hosni Mubarak addressed the Iran question in baldly sectarian terms. "Most of the Shias [in Arab countries] are loyal to Iran," said the Egyptian president. "And not to the countries they are living in." Egypt's Shia population is virtually nonexistent, but Mubarak articulated the fears of GCC rulers, who typically regard their large number of Shia subjects as a potential fifth column. In May 2008, during Hezbollah's takeover of Beirut, Al Arabiya assiduously presented the Sunni version of events on the ground. It documented some of Hezbollah's less successful operations and prominently featured footage of a terrified couple and their infant son, images intended to put Hezbollah's actions in West Beirut on par with the Israeli occupation of the West Bank. The Dubai-based network helped create the regional Sunni consensus, which was that Hezbollah and its Iranian patron needed to be flogged.

The Saudi-owned media made much of the fact that Al Jazeera, house organ of the resistance bloc, was owned by an Arab ruler hosting the U.S. military. The emir of Qatar was among those chiding the Americans for refusing to recognize and assist Hamas as the legal representatives of the Palestinian people. Interestingly, the harangues of a tribal chieftain/hereditary monarch who had deposed his father, which accused the United States of hypocrisy for not living up to its own standards, were not entirely without merit.

Of course the fact that American pressure won the Palestinians their ability to choose their own leaders does not therefore require Washington to fund and befriend whomever the Palestinians chose to elect. Citizenries that elect their governments are accountable for the policies they choose at the ballot box, Palestinian voters no less than American ones. The Arabs did not understand the principles of representative government, but the White House's freedom package included no instructions on how democracy actually works. Instead, it was handed off like a toy on Christmas morning, like an iPhone left out for the Arabs to figure out on their own.

When the Americans showed a lack of faith in their own ideas, Arab pathologies filled the vacuum, and Washington came to accept the schizophrenia of the Arabic-speaking Middle East as a suitable condition for democracy. U.S. policy makers, from the president on down, justified their laissez-faire attitude with the argument that Arab democracy would not look like ours anyway but would embody the traditions and morals of Arab society. It was inevitable after all that the Arabs would take a pass on some of the social values that Americans tend to associate with a democratic way of life, like gender equality and other issues like "anti-religious speech and behavior."[6]

But you can't have it both ways. You can't host a book fair and ban books, or an international sports tournament and block participants from countries you don't like. And you can't call a form of political organization that draws red lines on freedom of expression and persecutes Middle Eastern minorities like atheists and women Arab democracy. If democracy is not universal, if all men are not created equal with certain inalienable rights, then it is not democracy in any meaningful sense of the word. The special pleading on behalf of "Arab democracy" should have made it clear that Arab societies were simply not equipped, not at this time anyway, for the transformation that the White House had envisioned. Likewise, it was obvious that the Americans didn't know where they were going either or, even worse, where they'd come from.

The White House's freedom agenda was at cross-purposes: while it demanded from Middle Easterners what was effectively a political and cultural revolution from the bottom up, the American strategy was to install democracy from the top down. Democracy would democratize the Arabs, just as technology would release their rich creativity, and the new Arab media would lead to freedom of expression. But these are by-products, not starting blocks, and the notion that they are capable of activating a society's progressive impulses without the efforts of real human beings to transform those societies is absurd. Democracy does not liberate a captive people; it is the system of governance with which a society of free men and women that agrees on the equality of all chooses to express its political energies. Without those underlying ideas, democracy, like media and technology, is just a neutral value that can be used to good or bad ends.

The virtues of any technology depend on the condition of the culture using it, a fact that Washington, as well as others, sometimes does recognize—or else the international community, including the Arabs, would not be so intent on keeping the Islamic Republic of Iran from acquiring a nuclear program. Democracy is not, as President Bush liked to say, transformative. Elections did not make the Arabs free; they just made the Palestinians free to vote for Hamas.

The new Arab media will not liberate the masses; it is merely another instrument that Arab leaders use to fight each other. And as for technology, on 9/11 Arab fighters used airplanes, a Western technology designed to bridge distances and nations, to kill almost three thousand people.

"There are a hundred years' worth of bills that the Arabs haven't paid," said Hazem Saghieh, the Lebanese-born columnist for *Al-Hayat*, the London-based pan-Arab daily, and one of the leading voices of contemporary Arab liberalism. We were having breakfast in downtown Beirut, an area rebuilt after Lebanon's fifteen-year civil wars, an eruption of forces still resonating throughout the region. Despite his warm, quick laugh, he describes himself as a pessimist by nature. "In Iraq," he says, "the Americans thought the problem was Saddam's regime. Once you get the regime out of the way, then things would be okay. But they're not. The Arabs on the other hand have always thought the problem in the region was colonialism, Europe, the United States, but it's not. The problem is the society.

"The main issue facing the Arabs," Saghieh continued, "is not about democracy, but much more basic and primitive. The idea was that the only problem is at the political level, and the solution is to reward Arab society by giving it democracy, and that democracy can let it reveal its energies. The problem with democracy is not that there's not enough supply, but not enough demand for it. The problem is at a cultural level."

Democracy is not an application, but the manifestation of a worldview that holds certain values dear, values that, since they were fought and sacrificed for, cannot be easily transferred from one culture to another.

"Globalization put the Arabs face-to-face with their contribution to modernity," says Saghieh. "The Arabs did not contribute to its production, but only consumed it. So we got the technical side of it, meaning we only got it in negative ways. We have the Internet and globalization without a cultural revolution, or what has to happen prior to globalization and the Internet."

The energies that might have led to such a revolution were dammed up long ago. The nineteenth-century Muslim reformers inoculated their audiences against the set of ideas that gave birth to the technological innovations of Western modernity, as well as its forms of political organization, like liberal democracy. Muhammad Ali Pasha sent the Arabs westward to learn what the Europeans were making, and the Salafis, led by Afghani and 'Abduh, encouraged Muslims to accept those scientific advances to improve their lives and strengthen the *umma*. Throughout the course of the twentieth century, the Arabs availed themselves of goods, from consumer electronics to military hardware, while disdaining, as the Salafis had also counseled, the values that accompanied these products, values they associated with the West.

The battle lines in the Middle East's war of ideas are drawn over this simple question: Should the Arabs reject or accept the values that are the building blocks of political and technological modernity? In effect, the Americans had taken the wrong side in the debate in failing to see that the manifestations of a free society, including democracy, are its flower and not its roots. Liberalism and liberal reform are the work not of technology but of real human beings, men and women with a stake in their own societies, like the Arab liberals, inheritors of a tradition that had begun more than a century ago, back in Cairo.

CHAPTER 8

The Battle of Ideas: The Conqueror of Darkness and the Arab Voltaires

I f the Americans were looking to transform the region, it would come not through technology or elections but by aligning themselves with the men and women who had identified the problems of the Arabic-speaking Middle East long before Washington even understood there was a battle of ideas. I'm not talking about so-called Arab moderates, or the men like Fatah's Mahmoud Abbas whose temperament and personal culture differ from, say, the leaders of Hamas in degree rather than kind. I mean Arab liberals, whose intellectual tradition, like Salafism, had its origins in the first modern meeting between the lands of Islam and the West. But unlike Salafism, Arab liberals saw no fundamental conflict between themselves and Europe, and indeed welcomed the encounter.

T he Shepheard Hotel was burned down in the anti-British riots in the winter of 1952, half a year before Nasser's coup, and the reconstruction, far from the original site, seemed to concentrate most of that once-famous spot's Anglo-imperial charm into a dark, wood-paneled tavern now filled mostly with paunchy Egyptian businessmen seated at the bar rail. In the orange glow of the dark room in back, Naguib Mahfouz, the only Arab ever awarded the Nobel Prize in Literature, pressed his eyelids together like a cat dozing in the sun.

It was one of the regular meetings of the Mahfouz circle, a weekly gathering of his friends and hangers-on—all of them from the secular intelligentsia's younger set, or at least younger than Mahfouz, since the writer had survived his peers by decades. Yet this younger generation—journalists, professors, novelists, and professionals—was old enough to have taken sides in the Cold War, and these men, and one woman, of the left were not exactly the liberal, free-market thinkers that the White House's freedom agenda for the Middle East had hoped to galvanize. The Mahfouz circle laid into the Americans, questioning the sincerity of their intentions, until the old man told them to wise up. "It's not a problem if the Americans want us to have democracy," Mahfouz said. "Sometimes our interests and theirs coincide."

The circle's one American regular was Raymond Stock, the novelist's biographer and translator. Stock had lived in Egypt for a dozen years and was as close to Mahfouz as anyone else in the country. It was he who had invited me, and I asked along Raouf, for whom Mahfouz was as much a part of his inheritance as the Pyramids, and this living monument was showing wear. The novelist had fallen earlier in the day, a Band-Aid was hanging from his large, bony eyebrow, and he looked fragile, like a stack of china tottering in the middle of Cairo traffic.

Still, Mahfouz enjoyed these nights out, to smoke, talk, and mostly, at his age, listen, though he was so hard of hearing that his interlocutors took turns sitting next to him to shout directly in his ear in order to be heard. "*Naguib Bey,*" they hollered. "*Naguib Bey.*"

That night, the Mahfouz circle was discussing *Children of the Alley*. An Egyptian weekly newspaper had just excerpted sections of the novel without the consent of Mahfouz or his publisher, and the writer was angry. The last thing Mahfouz needed was trouble from the Islamists again, and he had promised the sheikhs at Al-Azhar that the book would not be published in Egypt without their permission.

"It is obvious why the men of religion don't like the book," Raouf leaned over to tell me. "The characters' names refer to specific prophets, and the last prophet is named after science. This is very controversial since Muhammad is supposed to be the last prophet." When one of Mahfouz's friends put a cigarette in the old man's mouth and lit it for him, Raouf reached for his pack. He pulled a cigarette out for himself and then handed another to me and lit them hurriedly. Now we were smoking with Naguib Bey.

Raouf thought that *Children of the Alley* was Mahfouz's best book. "Better than the Bible and the Quran," he whispered. I told him he should let Naguib Bey know that. "I'll have to shout it out loud," he said. "And everyone will look at me."

Raouf was an extremist of self-effacement. He burned everything he wrote, all his stories and articles, and later relished telling me about the Western and Arab sources he had drawn on, the historical analogies and careful arguments he used to make his case— before he set a match to it. When I asked him why he kept destroying his work, he shrugged his shoulders and laughed. "Who am I writing for except myself anyway?" he said morbidly. "What's worse, if no one understands what I'm saying or if they do understand it?"

The history of Arab liberalism gave Raouf plenty of reason to regard his hero Mahfouz with mixed emotions, like awe, admiration, pity, and a horror of someday winding up in the same place. Alienation and dangerous notoriety have been the fate of all independent Arab voices, dating back to Abu al-'Ala al-Ma'arri, an eleventh-century poet-philosopher regarded as Islam's first Voltaire. "He was not optimistic about human nature," Raouf says. "I have a lot of sympathy for that position." Abu al-'Ala was also a "freethinker," a coded word for atheist or heretic, whose dislike of Islam, and all religion, has made him a touchstone of Arab dissent for close to a millennium:

> *The earth has people of two kinds:*
> *The ones who think have no religion;*
> *the others do and have no minds.*

Like Abu al-'Ala and all the freethinkers, skeptics, infidels, and liberals, Mahfouz had paid for his outspokenness of many years. "He looks sad," Raouf said. "He's had a hard life." He's also a man in his nineties, I said. He's just old. "That, too," Raouf conceded halfheartedly. Why pursue that sort of life if in spite of the popular acclaim the result is distance from those closest to you? In the end it was safer to destroy your work lest it be the cause of your destruction.

Mahfouz was born in 1911 and raised in a working-class Cairo district among the monuments of the ancient city's Fatimid period, where he first learned to listen to the generations of Egypt, and heard their warnings, dreams, and petitions of the past and their echoes in the present. He graduated from Cairo University in 1934, a time of social ferment and hope steered by the country's liberal intellectuals, writers whose work he had immersed himself in since adolescence. They derived their ideas from classical liberal principles, the work of French and English political philosophers, and thus could hardly see themselves as anti-Western. Rather, they struggled with the challenge of the West, a generation that, among its many other cultural achievements, made the novel into an Arab art form. Mahfouz and the Arab novel are almost exact contemporaries; the first modern Egyptian novel, *Zeinab,* was published three years after Mahfouz was born. His first novel was published in 1939, and he went on to write forty novels and short-story collections, dozens of screenplays, and literary criticism. And Mahfouz was not merely the scribe of modern Egyptian history, for he also participated in it, albeit unwillingly, when the Islamists came for him.

Children of the Alley first appeared in serial form in 1959. Its depiction of God and the prophets so outraged the religious authorities that Mahfouz agreed not to have the book published in Egypt, though it has been in circulation elsewhere in the Arab world and in dozens of other languages ever since. A year after Mahfouz's 1988 Nobel Prize, Omar Abdel Rahman, onetime spiritual adviser to al-Gama'a al-Islamiyya, noted that had someone punished Mahfouz for his famous novel, Salman Rushdie would not have dared to publish *The Satanic Verses*. In 1994, one of Sheikh Omar's acolytes acted on the hint and stabbed Mahfouz in the neck, nearly killing him. And thus caught between the state authorities on one side and the men of religion closing in on the other flank, Mahfouz joined a long line of Arab writers and intellectuals who had been persecuted for their work and their ideas. This line included the greatest figure in modern Arab literature, greater even than Naguib Bey.

Taha Hussein, born in 1889, the seventh child of a modest family in a village in Upper Egypt, was early recognized as a man of promise. When he was still in his teens, he began contributing to a leading Egyptian newspaper whose editor prophesied that the young polemicist would be "our Voltaire." Over his long career, Hussein published novels, short stories, essays, translations, and a three-volume autobiography regarded as his masterpiece, *Al-Ayyam* (*The Days*), one of the cornerstones of modern Arabic prose. As a public figure, he was frequently embroiled in controversy thanks to his passionate advocacy of what were often considered Western ideas of freedom. Critics like the Arab nationalist ideologue Sati' al-Husri saw Hussein as a dangerous turncoat who wanted the Arabs to forgo their Arabism in order to walk, as Hussein himself put it, "in the path of the Europeans so as to be their equals and partners."

In Hussein's view, contact with the West was altering Egypt's moral and physical landscape for the better. As he records in his autobiography, ignorance and faith in folk remedies had cost the lives of his youngest sister and an older brother, so what was the value of tradition if it forced Egypt to sacrifice its children on the altars of their fathers? "God has bestowed on us a boon to compensate for our misfortune and calamities," he wrote. "The world has struggled for hundreds of years to attain the present stage of progress. It is within our power to reach it in a short time. Woe to us if we do not seize the opportunity!"[1]

Hussein's career was a culmination of the brief liberal era's reformist impulses, exemplary in its successes and even more so in its failures. He died in 1973 with his wife, Suzanne, a French Catholic, at his side—the "sweet voice," he called her in his autobiography. They'd met some fifty years before when he was writing his dissertation on Ibn Khaldun at the Sorbonne (Émile Durkheim was his supervisor) and needed someone to read to him aloud. Hussein, often referred to as the dean of Arabic letters, had been blind since early childhood, and hence the other epithet accorded him, the Conqueror of Darkness.

Like many able blind boys in Egypt, Hussein was encouraged to pursue Quranic recitation as a career. Reciters didn't have to read the book, just learn it by heart and then deliver passages at feasts and funerals. Hussein, who'd lost his sight at the age of three, learned the Quran in its entirety, forgot it, and memorized it again, thus earning the nine-year-old the title of "Sheikh." In *The Days,* Hussein relates how his father sent him with an older brother to study at Al-Azhar. There the great Muhammad 'Abduh, "the Imam," as Hussein calls him, was revitalizing the curriculum with electives in "modern sciences," like literature. "I know of nothing in the world," Hussein writes, "which can exert so strong an influence for freedom, especially on the young, as literature."[2]

'Abduh, as we've already seen, was a central figure in the Salafist movement, but his influence as a reformer was so wide that he also inspired a circle of liberal and mostly secular intellectuals, journalists, and activists, whom Hussein joined after cutting his ties at Al-Azhar. The liberal intellectuals' main concerns were the treatment of women and minorities, the separation of religion and the state, and the right to freedom of expression, inquiry, and religion. They also proposed a theory of liberal nationalism that, in contrast to Arab nationalism, was based on an Egyptian identity derived from the country's long and ancient history and territorial integrity dating back to the pharaohs. Hence the liberal nationalists—Muslims as well as Christians and Jews and other ethnic groups that had been a part of the Egyptian mosaic for thousands of years—were also sometimes referred to as the Pharaonists.

Whereas Arab nationalism had taken its cue from nineteenth-century German nationalism, liberal nationalism followed the school of thought that originated with French and English political philosophy, from Locke to Rousseau and Mill. Where the Germans believed that the nation existed independently of the state and of the choices people made, the French and the English tradition held that nationalism was chosen and consensual. In the liberal tradition, nationalism begins with the state, or those legal and political institutions that a given people chooses to form; and nationhood, the people's sense of belonging to a nation, is a consequence of the responsibility they take upon themselves to uphold the commonweal.

The problem was that even though the liberal nationalists had a theory, the British occupation meant that they had few of the independent political institutions that could embody it. They justified, or endured, the British presence by reasoning that under the guidance of London's enlightened despotism those independent political institutions would eventually be created and by assuming that it was only a matter of time before the crown granted Egypt full independence and sovereignty. The liberal nationalists may have deluded themselves about the intentions of their imperial overlords, but given the choice between being ruled by London and being ruled by the Ottomans, they opted for Europe as their model future. Many of them had lived in Europe, like Hussein, who studied in Montpellier and Paris as Europe was in the throes of World War I.

Once Hussein returned to Egypt, his first job at what is now called Cairo University was to teach a course in Greek history, of which geography was a central fact, but how could a blind man describe how Greece looked? His wife showed it to him, in one of the most beautiful love scenes in all of modern literature, East or West:

> She had taken a piece of paper and shaped it to conform to the natural contours of Greece. Her aim was to illustrate the mountains and the plains, where narrow and where extensive, and the surrounding coasts. She did this in relief on the same paper. Then she took my hand and guided it over the paper, after making clear to me that she was beginning with the south and moving northwards. She turned east and west too, to indicate to me where the sea was and the dimensions of the plains, narrow defiles and the broad spaces and the sites of ancient cities.[3]

This is a perfect cameo of the Platonic ideal, and it's no accident that Greece is its topos, a site where the East and the West, a man and a woman, eros and intellect, all meet and are bound as one in love. "The dominant and undeniable fact of our times," Hussein would later write, "is that day by day we are drawing closer to Europe and becoming an integral part of her, literally and figuratively."

In Hussein's view, Egypt was an essential part of the classical legacy. The land of the Nile had been subject to both the Greek and the Roman empires, and hence much of its history was written in Greek and Latin. Moreover, Egypt was the mother of civilization, *umm al-dunya,* one of the foundations of Greek art, architecture, and philosophy. Hussein's Egypt was therefore already of the West as well as the East, part of a larger Mediterranean culture, and it was only a matter of time before it was wholly reintegrated into the Europe that it had been a part of for thousands of years.

Hussein the autobiographer saw unities everywhere, but the novelist chronicling the progress of an ancient civilization becoming a new nation also captured the rifts in the social fabric, and much of his work dealt with one of the most difficult issues in Arab Muslim society, namely, the role of women. In one story a daughter turned modern woman in the capital comes home to the countryside to bury her mother, whose heart was broken when her husband brought a second, younger wife into the family home. And in Hussein's most famous novella, *The Nightingale's Prayer,* the central event is an honor killing.

The Nightingale's Prayer opens with three women, a mother and two daughters—the youngest, Amna, is the narrator—who must leave the village because their father has been killed after he was caught with another woman. As the three move from town to town trying to scrape together a living, the elder daughter finds work at the house of an engineer. He seduces her, another in a series of his conquests, and soon dismisses her. The women again pick up and leave, pursued ominously by an uncle from their old village. He surmises that the girl has dishonored the family and slaughters her in front of her mother and sister. Amna vows revenge, not against the uncle, but against the engineer, who had effectively sent her sister to her death. Concealing her identity, she secures her sister's old job in the engineer's house, where she plans to kill him. When Amna realizes she is incapable of taking the man's life, she plots what she believes is an even worse fate for him—to make him fall in love with her until he is so miserable in his unrequited ardor that he is compelled to kill himself. Naturally, it is as she is withholding her affection from the man that she begins to fall in love with him in earnest. As soon as she reveals her identity to the engineer, the uncle reappears to finish off yet another female child destined to shame the family's honor.

It was no coincidence that Hussein made one of his protagonists an engineer, for engineering had become one of the signature professions of modern Egypt's rising middle class, showing that the country was no longer entirely dependent on the West for technical skill and the ability to design its own future. (An entire Cairo neighborhood, Al-Mohandiseen, was named for the engineers who realized Nasser's visionary project, the Aswan High Dam.) In the movie version of *The Nightingale's Prayer*, released in 1959, a year before construction on the dam began, the engineer hurls himself against the symbolic maelstrom of ignorance and violence of the traditional countryside to take the bullet meant for the beautiful young girl.

The book, however, ends a little differently. An Egyptian woman read it to me in its entirety one afternoon. When she was done reading, I looked up to see tears streaming down her broad cheekbones. She rose from the couch and started gathering up my things, handed me the book, and told me to leave.

Lana and I had met for the first time during Ramadan when we sat on a hotel roof overlooking the city at night as cars sped from one *iftar* meal to the next, and feluccas and large riverboats lit the dark Nile below. The waiter demanded her passport, and I vouched for her that she was a foreigner, since state law prohibits Egyptians from drinking alcohol in bars and restaurants during the month of fasting. We sat and talked through the night as tobacco smoke and a second, sweeter smoke, like burning garbage or rotted crops or 9/11, filled the evening air along with the music of Umm Kulthum. "I wish you could understand every word she's singing and what it means to me," Lana said. She translated a line: "Bring your eyes close so my eyes can get lost in the life of your eyes." As I walked her back to her apartment in the early morning hours, I leaned in to kiss her good night. "No, don't," she said, pulling away. "I want you to, but I don't want the policemen to see."

There were policemen everywhere in Cairo, many of them merely self-appointed guardians of Muslim morality. "Eighty million people in this country, and every single one thinks they are the Prophet of Islam," Lana said. It was customary for men to walk down the street holding each other's hands, but if a man and a woman did so, male passersby walked in between to break them up or called out bravely from afar, "*Whore*."

Lana took pity on the real policemen, most of them country kids in shabby white uniforms that hung on them like *galabeyas,* and so overwhelmed by the customs of the big city they could not help but look down at the feet of pedestrians. They had never seen so many shoes. Lana was a doctor and these were her favorite patients, the fellaheen, poor, hardworking peasants. "Their eyes," she said, "are wrinkled in the corners from so much time in the sun. It's like their eyes have a permanent smile."

A childhood illness had permanently damaged her spine. "I spent most of a year unable to move, and my parents would come into my room and tell me what a lucky little girl I was," she said. "God must love me since he blessed me with such good parents who have money to make me better. 'Look at all the other sick children who weren't as lucky,' they'd say. I didn't feel lucky lying on my stomach for a year. And if God thought I should be grateful, then I didn't want anything to do with him. But I couldn't tell my parents I didn't believe in God anymore. It would've hurt them, so I kept it to myself."

I wondered if the handicap that had thrown her back so far inside herself and alienated her from those closest to her had also played a part in making her moral intellect whole and clear, as the solitude of blindness had with Taha Hussein. Unlike those of most Egyptians, Lana's affections were neither restricted to her family nor so abstractly expansive as to encompass all the *umma.* She loved Egypt and she loved Egyptians, and criticized and cursed her country and its people—and then despised me for giving her so much room to say whatever she wanted about Egypt. She knew the rules dictated that she wasn't supposed to say such things in front of a foreigner. She wanted to know why I liked her. Was it vanity, because of how she openly criticized the Arabs and praised the West? Did I just want an Arab to mirror my thoughts back to me? Sadness covered her face like a gloved hand and forced her eyes shut.

"Of course I want what the West has to offer," she said. "Freedom and all the things that come with it, but why can't I have that in my culture, my language, my city? Sometimes I just wish Arabs could stop thinking about the West," she said. "I wish we could be alone to figure out what we're doing. But the Westerners I've known have been like a lifeline to me. I can't imagine what it would be like to be cut off."

Lana attended a private German-language secondary school in Cairo (German was her second language, English her third) and then medical school. She took a job in a large hospital where a colleague courted her by announcing his interest in German philosophy, Nietzsche in particular. "Then one day," she said, "he started talking about Islam, and he sounded like a fundamentalist. So I asked him how he could reconcile Nietzsche with Islam. He said he wasn't about to, and that he didn't care for Nietzsche at all. He used Nietzsche to get my attention and to lead me back to Islam—where all the answers are. He wanted to save me from myself."

More often, it is women who must save men from themselves. Women do not veil to protect their own virtue, but to take responsibility for male desire. The veil's purpose is not to render women modest before God but rather—as the one instance of veiling in the Quran shows—to manage male sexuality and keep men from succumbing to their animal instincts. As such, men are accountable not for their own actions, say, for rape, but for safeguarding honor, the family's, the tribe's, the nation's, and their own. Honor killing and Arab nationalism have the same taxonomy: as the honor of a clan takes priority over the life of an individual woman, the rights of the individual human being are nothing next to the honor of the Arab nation.

Women without close male kin to ensure that the family name remains honorable are both vulnerable and dangerous, like Amna and her sister in *The Nightingale's Prayer*, and like Lana. Lana's father had died several years before, leaving her, her mother, and two brothers, who were powerless to ward off undesirable suitors, like an American. The elder brother suffered from a drug addiction, and the younger was a high-school student only old enough to want answers to questions he had not yet learned to ask. Lana overheard cassette tapes of fundamentalist preachers coming from her younger brother's room and wanted to talk to him, to guide him, but her mother, fearing the deracination of another of her children, warned her off. She was protecting her son to doom him.

Masculine energy is a powerful force. It creates civilizations and destroys them. In every society there are only two internal checks to the inchoate charisma of its young men lest they lose themselves in free-floating violence that takes everyone down with them: there are the male elders, and, even more important, there are the women, mothers and wives. Every society must decide how to best use its manhood to create, govern, and defend itself; none can afford it when either the elders or the women urge their young men to take them to the brink of extinction. Unfortunately, it isn't just the male elders who have been pushing young men to violence. Perhaps the unhappiest fact of the Arabic-speaking Middle East is that Arab women have been as well.

A 9/11 joke: A woman sees a man coming out of a men's room in Cairo (or Riyadh, or Damascus, or Beirut, or Baghdad) and asks him, "Are you Osama bin Laden?" "Why, no," says the man. "Why would you think such a thing?" "Because," she says, "he's the only man left in the Arab world."

It's just a joke, but it gets at something important about the Middle East, which is that often Arab women hold men in contempt if they are not willing to kill and die for Arab honor. Arab women are complicit in the violence of Arab societies, and so it should come as no surprise that of late Arab women have picked up the mantle of martyrdom and chosen to suicide themselves while killing innocents. After all, many have been sending their men to their deaths for years. "The womb of the Arab woman is my strongest weapon," Yasser Arafat is supposed to have said.[4] Arab women are victims of outrages like honor killings and female genital mutilation, and also victims of the law, but they are not innocent, or no more innocent than the infant boys that they raise to adolescence and manhood. This is why the education of Arab women is so controversial, because the guardians of tradition want them to become stronger, healthier, and smarter reproductive factories of Arab resistance. Arab liberals have had a very different project in mind.

"The evidence of history confirms and demonstrates that the status of women is inseparably tied to the status of a nation," wrote Qasim Amin, a late-nineteenth- and early-twentieth-century Egyptian liberal.[5] Amin's first, tentative feminist arguments were set down in his 1899 book, *The Liberation of Women*. He argued that women's emancipation was a patriotic duty that would serve all Egypt, men and women alike. Amin was reluctant to offend his audience, so he appealed to traditional Muslim sources and focused on the veil. He acknowledged that the veil was "one of the permanent cornerstones of morality." But, he argued, in its modern context the way the veil was now used was not true to the original message of Islam. Despite his caution, Amin still came under attack. So two years later, he made his criticisms even sharper.

In 1901, Amin published *The New Woman*, a pamphlet that makes few concessions to Islam and draws instead on Western political philosophy and social theory. Man, Amin wrote, treated woman like a slave and thought she "was not capable of moral or intellectual development," a prejudice that he tied directly to the veil. "This is the secret behind the imposition of the veil upon women and for its continued existence. The first step for women's liberation is to tear off the veil and totally wipe out its influence."[6] It was a bold argument. Unfortunately, it's also one that a century later Arab liberals are still having to make.

It's worth noting that within two years Amin took the two different positions available to Muslim reformers, even down to the present day. In his first effort, Amin showed himself aware of the problems of the Muslim societies, even as he was loath to criticize the customs of the *umma* lest he alienate his local audience and provide ammunition to the foreigners watching and judging. In his next time out, he seemed eager to dismantle Muslim tradition entirely.

We have seen these same two sides represented most recently by two European Muslim activists: Tariq Ramadan, the European Salafist and grandson of Hassan al-Banna; and Ayaan Hirsi Ali, the former Dutch parliamentarian and outspoken critic of many Islamic practices, from the treatment of women to *takfir*. Western commentators have tended to portray their clashing viewpoints as a debate between an authentic spokesman of the Muslim Arab masses and an elitist intellectual who has no street credentials because she sounds too much like a Westerner.[7] However, Banna's grandson is no more genuinely Muslim than the intellectual progeny of Qasim Amin. And it is not a lack of legitimacy that makes liberalism a minority position in Muslim and Arab societies today. It is Arab violence.

It is a piece of received wisdom that the Arab world is still awaiting its Voltaire, but the search for the Arab Voltaire overstates the role European polemicists played in creating a modern, secular culture in the West. The real pioneers of secularism were not the polemicists. They were the scientists like Galileo, who had no real ax to grind with Christianity or even the Church, but whose observations led to data that finally didn't square with religious dogma. And they were rationalists like Descartes, who looked to defeat obscurantism not with satire or polemic but with reason and enlightenment. This was the kind of figure Taha Hussein sought to be, and since literature was Hussein's field of research, he tried to bring an empirical approach to texts of all kinds—including the Quran.

In 1926, Hussein published a short book, *Fi ash-sh'ir al-jahily* (On Pre-Islamic Poetry), about the poetry that predates the advent of Islam. This body of work represents the pagan Arabian ethos that Muhammad's revelation was supposed to have transformed into a devout monotheism. Nonetheless, these poems are vital documents that establish the basis for certain traditions, stories, and even words that are central to orthodox interpretations of the Quran. But in his book, Hussein made a startling argument: the poems were actually written after the Quran and had been invented by religious scholars. He also cast doubt on parts of the Quran itself and made fun of the idea of jinn. Perhaps most damningly, he discussed the passage in the Quran that takes up the biblical narrative of Abraham, ordered by God to sacrifice his son. In the Quran the son is not Isaac but Ishmael, a variation that Hussein called a "fabrication."

Perhaps it seems improbable that a book discussing poems that were fourteen hundred years old could make much of an impact. But in his preface to the book, Hussein made his ambitions clear:

> I wish to introduce into literature the same philosophical method created by Descartes at the beginning of the modern age for inquiry into truth. Everybody knows that the fundamental basis of this method is that the inquirer should give up all previous knowledge and approach his subject with a completely neutral mind . . . We should not allow ourselves to be tied by anything, nor should we submit to anything save authentic scientific method. For if we do not forget our nationality, our religion and everything related to them, we are apt to be tendentious and prone to emotional judgment. Our minds will then be fettered to conform to our nationality and our religion.[8]

In other words, Hussein's investigation was designed to touch off an earthquake by confronting revelation with reason. It did, and Hussein barely survived it. He was called an apostate, death threats were published, and he was tried for attacking the religion of the state. Though the charge was eventually dismissed, Hussein revoked the book and reissued it the next year without the passage about Abraham and Ishmael. The damage, though, had already been done, and the intellectual who poked at the foundations of Islam had been successfully terrorized.

Hussein retired to France for a year with his family, where he wrote *The Days* in a little more than a week. All of the liberal intellectuals, meanwhile, most of whom had defended Hussein during his ordeal, found themselves under attack not just by the official religious authorities like Al-Azhar but also by the Salafis. The backlash put Arab liberals on the defensive. And in all the years that followed, they were never really able to get off it. Instead, it was men like Hassan al-Banna, Sayyid Qutb, and Omar Abdel Rahman who would set the Arabs' intellectual, cultural, and political agenda. And they would do so not through force of argument but through force of arms.

S o why didn't liberalism carry the day in the Arabic-speaking Middle East? When the old man stood, the meeting of the Mahfouz circle was done; Raouf put out his cigarette, then pulled an idea out of his ashtray. "Maybe the question is not what went wrong with Islam and the Arabs," he said, "but what went right with the West."

Raouf was right. To ask what's wrong with the Arabs is to take the West as the historical norm and imagine that its progress is a trajectory that all societies must inevitably follow, leading toward freedom, democracy, and respect for the inherent dignity of the individual human being. But since we have been handed all of these things for free, it is easy to overlook the sacrifices many generations made in blood along the way. Likewise, to forget how we got here is to trivialize the efforts of others elsewhere who strived for the same ideals but met with little or no success, like the Arab liberals. As with all stories of heroes, the life and career of Taha Hussein, a blind boy from a poor Egyptian village who became the leading Arab intellectual of the twentieth century, both highlight and obscure the practical difficulties that waylay more ordinary men.

According to many scholars of the period, liberalism failed because it was not a traditional source of political legitimacy and, as the Muslim Brotherhood's popularity proved, Islam was. To be sure, Islam is a cogent ideological force that binds Arab *assabiya,* but ideas like legitimacy and authenticity taken from the sourcebooks of Western political science and journalism miss the point.

Arab liberals, the intellectual heirs of Taha Hussein, are not less authentically Arab than the Salafists. Liberals and Salafists can both date their origins back to the same historical moment. They have a common ancestor in Muhammad 'Abduh, and both movements arose in response to the challenge of the West. What makes Salafism more potent, and liberalism a minority position in Muslim and Arab societies today, is not an absence of authenticity among liberals. If liberals cannot win, it's at least in part because Arab politics is an affair between armed elites, the regimes and their insurgent rivals, who will kill and die for their causes.

Liberals in the Middle East have been loath to use violence to make their ideas reality. This was intellectually consistent, and, in its way, admirable. But the consequence has been that Arab liberals have been condemned to a fragile existence, dependent on the whim of whatever strong horse was in power. After 9/11, the question that many started asking was whether American intervention in the region might change this dynamic. In other words, was it possible to revive Arab liberalism—which had been crushed in Egypt in the 1920s—as a real cultural and political force in the region, if the Americans were willing to play the strong horse on behalf of those who shared their values? The battleground where this question was asked most seriously was Lebanon.

PART III

"Your Children or Your Guns": The Cedar Revolution and the Fight for the Future of Lebanon

I f Lebanon was a country where genuine democracy seemed to have a chance of flourishing, it was perhaps because it was a country that had already been at war with itself for fifteen years, from 1975 to 1990, and had come out of the fire with the knowledge (or hope) that there were other ways to settle your problems than with violence. Lebanon not only contained the kernel of a democratic polity, but its history presaged much of what occurred in the region after 9/11. But the fact that the United States had been burned there before, taken together with the war in Iraq, was enough to keep Washington from getting close enough to Lebanon again that force would be required.

In 1958, Eisenhower sent the Marines to protect the government of the Christian president, Camille Chamoun, from domestic and foreign rivals. At the time, the U.S. ambassador to Lebanon, Robert McClintock, boasted that the Marines stayed three months without "a single shot having been fired in anger."[1] Twenty-five years later, American soldiers would not be so lucky. They had been dispatched as peacekeepers to keep the warring parties apart, an impossible role that made them vulnerable to every side in the Lebanon wars. In October 1983, this neutrality cost 241 Marines their lives.

It was in the wake of that Hezbollah attack and the subsequent withdrawal of troops from Beirut that Defense Secretary Caspar Weinberger laid out the precepts that should define the use of American force, guidelines later abridged as the Powell Doctrine. It is understandable that a Washington still reeling from Vietnam was chastened by its experience in Lebanon, but to articulate principles that policy makers should observe while deciding whether to use force, and to proclaim that troops should only be committed as a last resort, were to advertise a weak hand.

More important for Lebanon, by declining to engage the Party of God in earnest and choosing instead to withdraw after the Marine barracks bombing, the Americans had given the strong horse a free rein. Consequently, during the 1990s, under the patronage of Syria and Iran, Hezbollah grew in stature and power. While most of the Lebanese had had enough of violence, Hezbollah and its allies became more willing to use it, for they were at war not only with the West (most obviously Israel) but also with all those in Lebanon who subscribed to the values that the West prized and embodied.

Perhaps it seems strange to think of this tiny country on the Mediterranean of fewer than four million as a bellwether for the rest of the region, but more than Iraq or any other Arab society, Lebanon exemplifies most clearly, and starkly, the disparity between two different Middle Eastern worldviews: one is a culture of tolerance, freedom, and coexistence that has hopes of opening onto democratic horizons; and the other is a culture of those who, in the words of Hezbollah's secretary-general, Hassan Nasrallah, love death more than life.

Fawaz's father had been abducted by Hezbollah during the wars and ransomed for half of the family's savings. The rest of it was stripped, after his father's death, by his father's side of the family, leaving Fawaz with no choice but to find his way alone and without a name. In Lebanon you are first of all a name. Your father's name, your family's, the name of your community, town, region, and sect, but Fawaz made his own name. During the 1990s, as a six-foot-six power forward, he was the mainstay of the Christian-dominated Sagesse basketball team at a time when the Christians were paying a high price for their role in the wars. Fawaz and Sagesse were among the few bright spots for the community when the Syrian occupation went after Christian opposition figures and tried to smother under the blanket of Arab nationalism the identity of a sect that predates the Islamic conquests. (Christ, after all, preached the gospel in Lebanon.) During Sagesse games against the top Sunni team, the Muslims waved the green Saudi banner emblazoned with the *shahadah*—"There is no God but God and Muhammad is the Messenger of God"—while the Christians showed the white and gold flag of the Vatican. Fawaz wore a beard signaling that he was rebellious, an intellectual, and celebrated victories strutting around with a cigar. "When we won the Arab championships," he says, "I danced in front of the Algerians' bench and Lebanon went crazy. Grandmothers thanked me for restoring our hope, for reminding them what Lebanon stands for."

Fawaz's vision of what Lebanon stands for—as a model of Middle Eastern coexistence and openness to Western as well as Arab influences—was shaped by Lebanese history. There were the Maronites, an Eastern Catholic rite, whose ancient ties to the Vatican had kept channels open between Lebanon and the rest of the Mediterranean basin for hundreds of years.[2] There were also the Druze, a minority Muslim sect whose early-seventeenth-century leader, Fakhr ad-Din (1572–1635), found refuge from the Ottomans in Florence with the Medicis—the influence of whom can be seen in the architecture of Beiteddine, a Tuscan-inspired Ottoman palace in the Shouf Mountains, the Druze heartland. Typically credited as the father of modern Lebanon, Fakhr ad-Din, as some historians have argued, opened up his country to Europe.

Even the Sunnis along the Lebanese seacoast were different from their co-religionists across the region. They were merchants and traders whose commerce was not with the great ocean of the Arab sands, its desert ports stretching from Jerusalem to Damascus to Baghdad and the Arabian Peninsula, but facing outward, to the Mediterranean Sea. In the twentieth century the Sunnis would try to join Lebanon to the larger Arab nation, which is why the Christians resisted them and fought their Palestinian proxies, but unlike many of the other Arab states Lebanon was never ruled by an Arab nationalist regime. Instead, after the country's 1943 independence, Lebanon had a constitution, a national pact laying out a power-sharing scheme between the country's eighteen sects that allotted the largest shares to the largest communities (the Sunnis, Maronites, and Shia), and the makings of democratic governance. Fifteen years of war and another decade and a half of Syrian occupation had tested the theory of Lebanon as a model of coexistence, but by the time I got to Beirut a few months before the Cedar Revolution in the winter of 2004, the White House's talk of democratic reform in the region had found an eager audience here. The Lebanese believed that Washington had learned from 9/11 what it should have learned in Lebanon in the 1980s—that you can't blink in the eye of terror. Now the Americans were back and were serious about protecting their own citizens, interests, and regional allies, and Beirut was flush with possibility.

Of course, the buoyancy of that moment wasn't always easy to distinguish from the normal course of Lebanese joie de vivre, in the spirit of which at least a few women are sure to jump up on the bar to dance during any evening out. This was part of the Lebanese difference, what distinguished the Land of the Cedars from the rest of the Arab world: a tradition of intellectual curiosity and ambition reflected in the country's highly competitive, if not altogether free, press that represents all of the many political parties and even features the region's first gay lifestyle magazine; a thriving book-publishing industry; a large, well-trained middle class educated in either the Arabic, the French, or the American system; an internationally renowned cultural milieu distinguished by architects like Bernard Khoury and fashion designers like Elie Saab; a French- and Ottoman-inspired cuisine; a local wine industry that dated back several thousand years; and the most famously beautiful women in the region, maybe all the world.

"Maybe it is the wars that make them so beautiful," Fawaz conjectured. "The hardness of it leaves only the strong. But there is no doubt that Lebanese women know how to present themselves." Even in the small mountain towns—all contending that their daughters, wives, and sisters were the most beautiful—the women dressed in the latest fashions, long fur-lined leather coats and high heels, and in the cities, well, women danced on bar tops. Ground zero of the Lebanese avant-garde was Torino, a small, loud, and smoky club in Gemmayze, a nightlife area in East Beirut only a fraction the size of the East Village but many times more alluring simply because it was in an Arab city pulsing with eros. Musicians, filmmakers, actresses, writers, and students became more scandalous by the drink, a posture that in reality revealed their sweetness and naïveté as they walked the tightrope between traditional Arab mores and Western trends.

The Saudis loved Lebanon as much as anyone. They relaxed and enjoyed themselves openly here as they could not even in Cairo or the other Arab cities they visited for recreation. The men in their long white robes hunted in packs for Lebanese women, or they dined with their families, or both. The Saudi women also loved the country. Some were cloaked entirely in black, others simply covered their hair, their dark eyes dilated with smoke from the water pipes they sucked on publicly. Almost everything was allowed in Lebanon, even for Saudi women, some of whom wore their hair teased like Jersey girls out for a Saturday night in the West Village and dressed themselves in tight jeans and gaudy black stiletto-heeled boots that clacked on the cobblestoned streets by the clock at Nejmeh Square.

The Saudis were protective of Lebanon, a refuge that they'd

helped rebuild after the war through the offices of Rafiq al-Hariri. Born in the southern Lebanese port city of Sidon, Hariri went to Saudi Arabia and got involved in construction work, so impressing the royal family with his energy and ability to finish on time and under cost that they made him their man in Lebanon. In 1994, he founded Solidere, a company for the reconstruction and development of the Beirut Central District, where boutiques and luxury chain outlets lined the crowded sidewalks along with dozens of restaurants, Lebanese, Moroccan, Italian, French, and American chains like T.G.I. Friday's, where the waitstaff sang "Happy Birthday" to patrons in Arabic, French, and English.

Fawaz and I spent nights downtown in the wet Mediterranean air, watching women and tourists, and eating and smoking cigars among rows of colorful Ottoman-era limestone villas, bullet pockmarked from the wars. This part of downtown had been controlled by the Palestinians, Fawaz explained, and then fell into the hands of Christian fighters, led by one of his neighbors, an old family friend in his late fifties now with powerful hands and gray thinning hair bearing no traces of the furious Afro he wore in a photograph of him and his cadre, among them a beautiful, lethal young woman brandishing a Kalashnikov.

During the first years of the war, the Christians and Palestinians came down here at night with their guns and drugs and fought, and then by day went about their ordinary business, until the conflict erupted into a full-scale war. A rumor grew up among Fawaz's fans and rivals that during the wars he was a captain in the Lebanese Forces, the main Christian militia. This seemed to explain why after Sagesse victories, large, piston-fingered men with shaved skulls and leather coats walked onto the court to embrace him. In reality, he'd spent part of the conflict sharpening his basketball skills at a junior college in Kansas. His father was ecstatic that his boy was going to learn firsthand how the Americans valued work and rewarded merit. "Even in the Lebanese league," says Fawaz, "I always played against the Americans. I always got the toughest matchup on defense, and that meant some guy from an American college." In Kansas, the Greek Orthodox Fawaz attended his first Baptist service, and he was the first Arab his classmates had ever met. "I had Palestinian posters all over my room, and the school administration brought me in for a talk."

It wasn't until after his return to Lebanon that his political transformation began as he started to reconsider the Arab nationalist commonplaces he had been reared on in what was then a mixed West Beirut neighborhood. The problems of the Middle East, he realized, weren't the result of colonialism, imperialism, Zionism, or the United States. They were the product of the inability of Arab societies to respect the individual and the difference of every individual. Still, the Americans could help, he figured. And they had to since it was in their own interest to do so. "I have to admit it, but when the planes hit the towers September 11, I was happy," he says. "I knew that the Americans could no longer afford to ignore the problems of the Middle East. The bargains you'd made with dictators, and the political culture it had given rise to, was untenable. Finally, you had to deal with the real problems."

Fawaz cheered on the invasion of Iraq, which he saw as a war to bring down a pillar of Arab nationalism, a totalitarianism as destructive of the individual human being as communism. The onetime leftist who used to sport Che T-shirts now took as his role model a former Soviet dissident, Natan Sharansky, whose book *The Case for Democracy* became President Bush's manual for Middle East reform. A state that does not respect the human rights of its own citizens, Sharansky argued, will not behave better toward its neighbors or peers in the world community. Freedom for the Arabs would mean security for the rest of the international community—including Israel, where Sharansky had moved after the Soviets released him from prison.

If Sharansky's nationality made some of Fawaz's Lebanese

friends uneasy when he pushed the book on them, Fawaz himself saw the Jews of Israel as just another Middle Eastern minority, like the Christians, Shia, Druze, and Kurds. Fawaz had met a reporter from one of the major U.S. papers when he came through Beirut and seemed surprised at the journalist's patent dislike of Israel. I noted that the journalist was uncomfortable, if not hostile, like many American Jews about the idea of a Jewish state. "Then that is a problem with his personal identity," said Fawaz. "But it has nothing to do with the region. If he's hostile toward the idea of a Jewish state in the Middle East, it means he can't understand us either. The Jews were here before the Christians, who were here before the Muslims, so if the Jews don't belong in the Middle East, then neither do Oriental Christians, and that is not possible, because we definitely belong. My father is buried here, as was his father, and his father before him. And I will be, too."

Fawaz related the history of his ancestors, their fights against the Ottomans and storied figures like Ahmad al-Jazzar, "the Butcher," an Ottoman official with a reputation for violence that struck fear into the hearts of the Christians. "But it wasn't just the Christians who were terrorized by the Ottomans and the Sunnis," Fawaz said. "It's all the minorities, all of us here. It's our story—fear of each other. If you were walking on the same side of the street as a Sunni," Fawaz explained, "they'd tell you to move over and get to the left, *ishmal.*

"But if they killed a Christian," he continued, "the Christians would take their revenge, and the Ottomans would chase them as far as the mountains. If they followed them up the steep passes, they'd be cut to ribbons. My grandfather used to be involved in that game, but my grandmother gave him a choice: it's either your children or your guns."

All of Lebanon is armed, every family in every sect in every quarter of every town, but only Hezbollah was allowed to hold on to its heavy weapons after the conclusion of the civil war. There had been a national agreement and several UN Security Council resolutions calling for all Lebanese parties to disarm, but the international community was not going to disarm the Party of God, and neither was the government of Lebanon, since it had become a Syrian puppet regime ever since the war's end, and Damascus had no interest in weakening Hezbollah, even if foreign officials were eager to be deceived otherwise.

When Israeli prime minister Ehud Barak, for instance, decided in 2000 to end his country's eighteen-year-long occupation of Lebanon, he thought it was both possible and necessary to get Syria to stop supporting Hezbollah. If not, he thought, "there was the unmistakable risk that attacks from Lebanon would continue even after withdrawal, especially because Syria always used Lebanon as a pressure point against Israel."[3] It apparently never occurred to the Israelis, the Americans, or any of the other pillars of the international community that this was precisely why the Syrians would never willingly divest themselves of a valuable strategic asset. Their sponsorship of Hezbollah meant that all parties had to go through Damascus even to discuss concessions, and disarming Hezbollah would force Syria to forfeit that leverage.

Hezbollah, meanwhile, had its own reasons for keeping its guns. The Islamic Resistance's self-described raison d'être is to defend Lebanon against Israel, and as Hassan Nasrallah's gloating over Israeli corpses proves, Hezbollah takes real joy in killing Jews. However, its deepest fear is not of the Zionist state founded in 1948 but of the Sunni sea that has engulfed the Shia for more than thirteen hundred years. The Christians may be terrified of the Sunni majority, but in Sunni orthodoxy Christians and even Jews enjoy a protected status as "people of the Book." The Shia, on the other hand, are considered merely heretics, or worse, a point that the Al Qaeda in Iraq leader Abu Musab al-Zarqawi made in his last published statement before his death in the spring of 2006. He said he saw through Hezbollah's charade. It was just a cover for Israel and protected the Jews from the wrath of the genuine, Sunni resistance. The Shia were not real Arabs, only the Sunnis were; he called the Party of God Zionists.[4]

Hezbollah's warring against Israel shows that, despite Zarqawi's invective, the Shia are Arabs in good standing and warrant a place in a Sunni-majority Middle East that has been at war with the Zionists since 1948. Indeed, after Israel's withdrawal from Lebanon in 2000, and later after the July 2006 war, Hezbollah was able to claim with some justice that only it had ever made Israel taste defeat, a triumph denied the various Sunni defenders of Arabism over the last half century of their loss and humiliation.

Most historical accounts of Hezbollah, authored by the group itself or by fellow travelers among the Western left, claim that the resistance was indigenous, rising out of the Shia community's natural right to fight the Israeli occupation of southern Lebanon. In fact, from the very beginning Hezbollah was a collaborative venture between Iran and Syria. The Party of God binds their four-decade alliance and made these two non-Sunni regimes—Syria is ruled by Alawis (a non-Sunni Muslim minority sect) and Iran is Persian Shia— relevant in a Sunni-dominated region. Backing Hezbollah also permitted them to make war against the Jewish state and burnish their resistance bona fides without risking war on their own borders. Fighting through Lebanon was natural for them: Iran's ties to the Lebanese Shia community dated back to the fourteenth century, while Damascus had never considered Lebanon anything but a Syrian province.[5] Moreover, Beirut's weak central government made Lebanon a clearinghouse of resistance.

Lebanon's status as a forward base for non-state actors was formalized in 1969, when, under the auspices of Egyptian president Gamal Abdel Nasser, the Lebanese, some reluctantly, granted the Palestinians the right to attack Israel from Lebanese territory. The Palestine Liberation Organization used that prerogative after it was thrown out of Jordan in 1971—the Palestinians set up shop in

Lebanon and quickly renewed their campaign against Israel. Eventually, this provoked Israel's 1982 invasion of Lebanon to drive the PLO out of southern Lebanon. The inhabitants of the region were happy to be rid of the Palestinians, whose resistance had goaded Israeli retaliation against Lebanon in the first place. Shia laborers found employment in northern Israel, and they also fought for Israel's proxy force, the South Lebanon Army.

Other Lebanese Shia, though, were not so enamored of Israel. And so in June 1982, with Syrian permission, Iran sent a large group of Iranian Revolutionary Guards to the Bekaa Valley, where they trained Lebanese Shia to field the militia that would become Hezbollah. The Party of God's motto at the time was "The Islamic Revolution in Lebanon," and Hezbollah was one of the few early successes Iran's clerical regime had in exporting its revolution. (Tehran's ambitions were stalled in the 1980s when Saddam Hussein waged his decadelong war against Iran in the name of Sunni Arab honor.) In seeding Hezbollah, and preparing the ground to become regional hegemon, Iran demonstrated that it could bridge the Persian-Arab divide. Hezbollah's fight against Israel won the hearts of the Sunni Arab masses and provided Arab cover for Iran's grander project to overthrow the Sunni order. Hezbollah was equally valuable to Syria, since with the PLO and the stubborn Arafat gone, Syrian president Hafez al-Assad was now co-holder of the exclusive franchise for resistance in Lebanon.

Assad's task was made easier by the fact that once the Reagan administration withdrew the remainder of U.S. troops from Lebanon in 1984, Washington effectively contracted Lebanon policy out to the Syrians. Despite (or perhaps because of) Hezbollah's bombing of the Marine barracks, the United States had no appetite for confronting the group. American policy makers rationalized this decision by citing experts who told them Hezbollah was nothing to worry about.[6] It was not an Iranian-backed militia, academics explained, or Damascus's Praetorian Guard, but a "national resistance" movement steadily integrating into Lebanon's national fabric and in the process of becoming a regular political party. Sympathetic, or gullible, journalists highlighted the "social services" that Hezbollah provided for the Shia, and ignored the fact that Hezbollah forced the government out of Shia areas in order to build its own state within a state.

There was little that Rafiq al-Hariri could do about Hezbollah's growing power during his three terms as prime minister, for like the rest of Lebanon's political class, outside of a small group of Christian leaders, he was under Syria's thumb. And so, while Hezbollah fed the resistance against Israel with Shia martyrs, Hariri rebuilt Beirut with Sunni money from the Gulf states and weaned the Sunni community off of perpetual war with the Zionist state by refocusing its energies elsewhere. (Incidentally, Hariri's experience as an Arab expat in Riyadh and his return to Lebanon as a moderate influence are enough to disprove the notion that it is Saudi Arabia alone that is responsible for radicalizing Arab societies.) And Hariri tried to foster better relations between Arabs and the West, especially after 9/11. His private foundation sent tens of thousands of students off for college and advanced studies in Europe and the United States.

Lebanon's two different Muslim communities took two radically different paths. In reshaping the Sunni community, Hariri left resistance to Hezbollah and the Shia, and paved the way for a rapprochement with the Christians and the Druze. Implicitly, at least, he was pushing the idea that Lebanon was a nation with a distinct character and destiny, and not merely a cog in the wheel of the Arab nation.

Damascus, however, was ill disposed to see the rules change in Lebanon, and as Hariri began to challenge Syrian president Bashar al-Assad and move ever closer to the opposition, he was in increasingly greater danger.

It's a curious fact that many of those who had typically blamed the West for all the problems of the Middle East also argued, after 9/11, that it was laughable for the Bush administration to try to impose democracy on the region from without. In their view, apparently, foreign powers are all-powerful in the Middle East when they're pursuing evil ends. But when they're trying to bring about positive change—like creating democracy—they're impotent. This makes little sense, as Lebanese history makes clear. In fact, in Lebanon's history, outside forces have had both positive and negative legacies. There were the Ottomans, whose five centuries in the region had a deep impact on every aspect of the Levant, including relations between the sects. France had been a political and cultural force in the Christian community dating back to the sixteenth century, when the Catholic kings anointed themselves protectors of the Maronites in a region often hostile to Christians. France's decision to send forces in 1982 was a reprise of 1860, when it dispatched a contingent to defend its wards against the Druze. This earlier civil war led to the creation of Mount Lebanon, a semiautonomous Ottoman region, leaving France the dominant Western nation in Lebanon for another century. The French built schools and universities, and under the yoke of France's post–World War I mandate for Lebanon, French administrators influenced some of the country's democratic political institutions, most importantly Lebanon's constitution, modeled after that of the French Third Republic. The Francophone era effectively ended in 1983 with an attack by Hezbollah on a squad of French paratroopers (a bombing simultaneous with that on the Marine barracks), an attack that ushered in the Iranian moment, pushing Lebanese Shia toward radicalization. Within the space of a few decades the Iranians turned Shia precincts in the south, the Bekaa Valley, and the southern suburbs of Beirut into outposts of the Khomeinist revolution, where portraits of the late ayatollah hung alongside posters of Lebanon's Shia martyrs.

Granted, what the Americans offered was different from what other foreign powers had brought to Lebanon—not guns, or money, or political institutions, but something less concrete, a political order. Moreover, imposing democracy from the outside seemed to contradict the essence of consensual politics. However, the Lebanese already had a tradition of democracy. There was also a long-standing relationship between Lebanon and the United States. In 1866, the American missionary Daniel Bliss founded the Syrian Protestant College, on a cliff overlooking the Mediterranean, "the finest site in all Beirut."[7] That school later became the American University of Beirut, the second-oldest U.S. institution of higher education in the Middle East, and, oddly, a famous petri dish for Arab nationalism.

Relations with the United States had helped foster other intellectual trends as well, including a liberal nationalist current, named after the ancient seafaring people of the Mediterranean from whom the Lebanese claimed descent, Phoenicianism (much like the Egyptians' Pharaonism). That notion of a continuous, distinct, and historical Lebanese identity was possible largely thanks to Lebanon's early relations with America. Or consider the example of Kahlil Gibran (1883–1931): the author of *The Prophet* is Lebanon's most famous writer, a distinction that only makes sense because he and others helped define the idea of a Lebanese national identity, constructed not only in the hills of Gibran's native Lebanon but also in the immigrant enclaves of New York and Boston, where he spent a large part of his life with other Lebanese exiles.

At the turn of the twentieth century, refugees from the Ottoman Empire—mostly Christians and other minorities—started pouring into America, seeking shelter from persecution and famine as the empire was veering toward its violent demise. This created a peculiar problem: since there were no nation-states under the Ottomans, no national identities as such, most of these Middle Easterners had little sense of identity outside of their religious or sectarian affiliations, and therefore did not know how to describe themselves in American terms. When they were asked upon their arrival at Ellis Island what they were, there was no ready definition at hand. Until 1899, the U.S. Bureau of Immigration usually labeled them "Turks from Asia."[8] But they were not Turks, for, among other reasons, they did not speak Turkish. They spoke Arabic, but at the time few Arabic-speaking Middle Easterners thought of themselves as Arabs. So, what were they?

In the anti-immigration mood of the early twentieth century, some American politicians wanted to limit immigration of "undesirable races." The Ottoman immigrants wanted to show that they were useful and Western oriented, meriting a place in America, and so they claimed kinship with one of the founding nations of Western civilization, the Phoenicians, ancient forefathers of the Lebanese.[9] In fighting for space and privilege among other newly hyphenated Americans—the Germans, Italians, Irish, and Jews—they came to ask, if the family next door is Italian-American, then what kind of American am I? They deliberated about their identity long before their compatriots at home were doing the same, and forged an identity separate from the Ottomans and more expansive than the one they'd known from town, sect, and tribe. In a sense, Lebanese-American identity preceded a purely Lebanese one. This American/Lebanese interdependence cuts to the heart of both peoples' self-image—one as a land of immigrant opportunity, the other as a separate and distinct nation in a region where it is often fatal to be different.

The Americans had a reason to fight for Lebanon, but ironically it took the French—and in particular Jacques Chirac—to show them why. The French president's opposition to the Americans' plans to invade Iraq seemed so extraordinary in its pitch and intensity that U.S. opinion makers were forced to conclude that our good ally's histrionics was nothing less than a keening index of the Bush administration's recklessness; in reality, Chirac's position was characteristic of French Middle East policy. For almost fifty years, ever since the loss of its Algerian colony and throughout the Cold War, France's regional policy was to offer a "third way"—neither

American nor Soviet—a strategy that, since Paris lacked the military and economic weight of a superpower, required a soft touch. Chirac, a major figure in French politics for many decades, mastered the personalized style of Arab diplomacy, where length of tenure is at least as important as competence, and befriended regional leaders, like Arafat, Saddam, and Hafez al-Assad. The late Syrian president's son Bashar made Paris the first Western capital he visited when he came to power, but he crossed the French president several times on financial matters and bullied the Arab leader Chirac liked most, Rafiq al-Hariri.

Chirac knew that Washington was furious with Damascus for interfering in Iraq and saw ganging up on Syria as an opportunity to mend fences with the Americans. After all, with Saddam out, and Arafat and Hafez dead, the United States had virtually run the board in the Middle East, and the only way for France to project power in the region was to stay close to the Americans. And so when Bush visited Normandy for the sixtieth-anniversary commemoration of D-day in June 2004, Chirac proposed Lebanon as a focal point of joint action against Syria.

The White House was hounded for its unilateralism in Iraq, and going against the will of traditional friends, like Paris, but Bush's Lebanon/Syria policy was a model of multilateral consensus, built in partnership with France, regional players like Saudi Arabia, and the United Nations. UN Security Council Resolution 1559, demanding the withdrawal of Syrian forces from Lebanon and the disarmament of Hezbollah, was co-sponsored by Paris and Washington.

"The U.S. and France seized on Lebanon," said Elliott Abrams, the Bush administration's deputy national security adviser for global democracy strategy. We spoke in his office a few weeks before the end of the Bush administration's term. "The overall relationship between the two countries was bad," Abrams said. "And this was something to do together to crawl out of the hole of Iraq. We recognized Lebanon as a building block for Franco-American relations, and finally the two presidents could speak about something. Chirac was personally sad and infuriated about Syrian interference in Lebanon. For us, there was Lebanon as a long-term interest and also in the short term—the war on terror, Iran, and Hezbollah. And obviously there was the freedom agenda, too."

Abrams is a controversial figure in American politics owing to his role in the Reagan administration's Iran-contra affair. But many Lebanese saw him as their champion in Washington. In Lebanon, ordinary media consumers know the name of the Lebanon desk officers at the State Department, the Pentagon, and the National Security Council staff; and U.S. embassy officials out for a coffee or glass of wine in downtown Beirut are treated like celebrities. That's partly due to the esteem so many Lebanese have for the United States, as well as their residual fear that Washington is going to sell out Lebanon as it did in the 1990s when the George H. W. Bush White House green-lighted Syrian hegemony in Lebanon in exchange for Hafez al-Assad's agreeing to send troops for Operation Desert Storm. Accordingly, the Lebanese read every small sign out of Washington as if it meant the United States was preparing to let the Land of the Cedars once again become a Syrian satrapy.

Abrams thought that these fears were overblown. He argued that the United States has always had a pro-Lebanon policy. "It goes back to 1958," he said. "It's based on idealism, and geopolitics. It didn't change with the Bush administration; it deepened and intensified with the setting. The conditions were ideal. The brave and courageous Lebanese were trying to take their country back and they went to the street. How could that not elicit support from the U.S.? And then the other context was the war on terror. The murder of Rafiq al-Hariri looms very large in the annals of terror."

The impact of Hariri's murder can't be overstated. On February 14, 2005, the former prime minister and twenty-two others were killed in a massive car-bomb explosion. The immediate verdict in Lebanon was that the Syrians were responsible, and that judgment was seconded by the international community. A preliminary UN investigative team charged the Assad regime with creating the backdrop for the assassination. "The Government of the Syrian Arab Republic bears primary responsibility for the political tension that preceded the assassination of the former Prime Minister."[10]

Before his death, Hariri was criticized for his business dealings, some questionable even by Lebanese standards. And until the very day of his murder the Christians, in characteristic intra-sectarian Lebanese fashion, cursed him for the enormous mosque he was building downtown, a blue-domed neo-Ottoman structure whose minarets were higher than the spires of the Maronite church next door. But after his death, the Christians bestowed on Hariri the honorific "martyr," and took to the streets on his behalf as they had—even at the risk of imprisonment, torture, and murder—for other victims of the Damascus regime over the last fifteen years. The Druze community marched alongside the Christians as they had ever since their leader Walid Jumblatt broke with Damascus after more than two decades of Syrian tutelage. Strangely, Hariri's own sect, the Sunnis, took no part in the huge, almost daily, demonstrations in Martyrs' Square, where their leader's corpse was laid to rest. That changed after Hezbollah, on March 8, held a massive rally at which its secretary-general, Hassan Nasrallah, expressed gratitude to Syria and defiance to the rest of the world, including most of Lebanon. "The resistance will not give up its arms," said Nasrallah, "because Lebanon needs the resistance to defend it."

The Sunnis were finally motivated. Incensed to see the Shia gather to thank the regime that had killed their leader, the Sunnis were ready to go to the streets. The next week, March 14, a month after the assassination, the Sunnis joined the Christians and Druze for the largest protest ever in Lebanon, and perhaps the largest noncompulsory political demonstration ever in the Middle East, with estimates running from 1.2 million to 1.5 million people, or one-third of the entire country, and the independence intifada took root.

Fawaz wrapped the red and white scarf of the Cedar Revolution around his neck and went downtown to march and chant for freedom, sovereignty, and independence, but remained suspicious about what many Lebanese meant by national unity. "Lebanon's a democracy; we're not supposed to all agree." National unity sounded a little too much like Arab nationalism. "Anyway, all this stuff about Lebanese unity is folklore," Fawaz said. "The Christian cross, the Muslim crescent, and the white skullcap symbolizing the Druze all in one tableau—what does it mean? Where is our unity? What do the Lebanese agree on? We agree on one thing; after fifteen years of civil war we agree to no longer settle our problems with violence."

That was more than enough for the Americans. Against bin Ladenism, Lebanon offered a multi-sectarian coalition with more than a million Arabs who'd gone to the street to protest peacefully against an act of terrorism. Instead of justifying violence as a means to redress their grievances, and instead of murdering their opponents, Lebanon's pro-democracy advocates were abiding by the rule of law, and investing their hopes for justice in international law, embodied by a series of UN Security Council resolutions demanding a Syrian withdrawal, disarmament of Hezbollah, and an investigation into Hariri's murder that would "identify its perpetrators, sponsors, organizers and accomplices."

All of this, not surprisingly, made Syria worried. Damascus feared that if indictments in the Hariri murder led up the chain of command as many suspected, the young Syrian president's future was at best going to resemble Slobodan Milosevic's last years as an international pariah. At worst, he, his brother Maher al-Assad, head of the Syrian Presidential Guard, and his brother-in-law Asef Shawkat, chief of military intelligence, would be toppled in an internal coup. And so, on April 26, twenty-nine years and two weeks after the Syrian army first entered Lebanon, it left. At the time it seemed like an extraordinary victory for democracy, and the Lebanese youth who'd carried the weight of the Cedar Revolution exulted in the Syrian withdrawal.

Even as the youth celebrated, though, the elder generation remained circumspect. Walid Jumblatt, for one, wanted to know when the Americans were leaving Iraq.

Jumblatt is head of Lebanon's Druze community, which—thanks in part to the legacy of Fakhr ad-Din, the Druze emir who is thought of as the founder of modern Lebanon—wields more power in the country's sectarian system than would seem to be warranted by its numbers (approximately 300,000). Scattered elsewhere throughout the Levant—Syria, Jordan, and Israel—the Druze, a Muslim minority sect dating back to eleventh-century Egypt, have around a million adherents. A community with such small numbers, and that does not accept converts, owes its long existence to two factors: the martial skills of its people, and their unerring ability to discern a real strong horse from an impostor. For instance, in Israel, many Druze aligned themselves with the Zionists before the 1948 war of independence against the Arabs, and since then have continued to produce some of the Jewish state's most valued warriors. And so Jumblatt, despite his well-documented history of anti-Americanism, didn't want the Americans to leave Iraq. His question was designed to gauge the level of Washington's commitment to the region so that he could figure out how far he could afford to stick his neck out without having the Syrians cut it off.

Fawaz and I visited Jumblatt at Mukhtara, his family's Ottoman-era stone palace in the Shouf Mountains. He was sitting in his living room beside a large golden Buddha, a souvenir of his father, Kemal, a Buddhist as well as a warlord. Like his father, whom he replaced as Druze leader after Kemal was assassinated by the Syrians in 1977, Jumblatt embodied contradictions—an aristocratic leftist and a tribal chieftain, the owner of a vineyard and a battle-hardened military tactician, whose study and library were decorated with trinkets from the former Soviet Union, like a Soviet naval officer's uniform, mementos from when Moscow trained his militia and was his main weapons supplier during the civil wars. Jumblatt's chief rival then had been the Maronites, against whom he waged a brutal campaign in the Shouf during the 1980s, but now he was allied with them, as well as with the Sunnis. And after the murder of Hariri, he had become the public face of the pro-democracy movement that took the name of March 14, and was clearly galvanized by the democratic currents sweeping through the region.

"It's a good thing Saddam was brought down," Jumblatt said, smoothing his mustache and the famous shock of wiry gray hair sticking out from his balding head. "It should've happened thirty years ago. And the Americans shouldn't have stopped with Saddam, but should've brought down the dictator in Damascus, too."

Jumblatt hadn't always been opposed to the Syrians. After the assassination of Kemal, Jumblatt kept the peace with his father's killers, while profiting from their occupation. That changed in 2000, when the Israelis withdrew from the south and Jumblatt decided it was time for the Syrians to depart as well. "I defended Syrian interests," Jumblatt said. "Now I'm fed up. I am following my father, and I feel free for the first time in my life. I have a free conscience now, and I can sleep at night. We want our system, freedom of speech, freedom of the press. Let the Syrians have the system they want, but let them leave us free. We're the only country in the Arab world that has freedom of press and speech. If we succeed in preventing Lebanon from becoming a police state, and set up a democracy like it used to be, we'll be an example in the region. The liberals in the region are waiting for us. If we fail, it will return to the status quo. But in the long term, these regimes cannot stay."

It was inspiring to hear a man who knew so much about the violence and authoritarianism of the region express hope that democracy might actually triumph. But for Jumblatt's vision of the future to have been realized, the United States would have had to support it with strong horse tactics. Instead, it flinched. A little more than a month after the withdrawal of Syrian troops, Damascus and its local allies renewed their campaign of terror against Lebanese democracy. Bombs were set off in commercial and residential areas, and a series of assassinations targeted civil society activists, government ministers, parliamentarians, and journalists, with writers like Samir Kassir and Gebran Tueni killed in car-bomb explosions, and May Chidiac maimed in another. Washington castigated the Syrians for their actions, but did nothing to correct them, and the combination of words without actions only pointed to Washington's lack of resolve.

"The Americans," Jumblatt later told an American audience, "should send car bombs to Damascus." Jumblatt said he had only been joking, but the point was a crucial one: without deadly American reprisals for the Syrian regime's violence, Lebanese democracy was vulnerable. A hundred and thirty thousand American troops stationed close to Syria's border had helped embolden the Cedar Revolution. But without their help, the Lebanese were without a strong horse of their own, and left alone to face one of the most ruthless regimes in the region.

CHAPTER 10

The Capital of Arab Resistance: Damascus's Regime of Terror

Syria's war against Lebanese democracy left the Bush White House torn. Even though the Americans had come to recognize that Lebanon was a strategic interest in its own right, because it was a way to push back against Iran and push the freedom agenda forward, the administration's overriding interest was Iraq. While some in the White House argued for punishing Damascus, the military saw a strike against the Syrians as opening another front in the war on terror, and it already had its hands full in Iraq. The civilians responded that deterring Damascus would also make the military's job easier in Iraq, where the Syrians were helping insurgent groups kill U.S. soldiers. And while Washington had leverage on the Syrians with the international tribunal for the Hariri assassination, international law meant nothing unless someone was willing to enforce it through force of arms. If the Americans wanted to empower democratic energies in the region, they would have to show they were willing to protect the few genuine and useful allies they had, and continue to go after the groups and regimes that were doing all they could to crush any genuine liberal upsurge in the region, regimes like the one in Damascus. If Washington was unwilling to do that work, it should have refrained from supporting a popular uprising and then turning and effectively handing the palace hangman the noose.

In the end, of course, the White House refused to go after Syria and thus declined to shield Lebanon. In doing so, the United States guaranteed that Lebanon's experiment in popular liberalism would become a short-lived one. While American diplomats worked with the Lebanese government to extend the power of the state over all its territory and disarm Hezbollah, Syria and its Lebanese allies were using violence to bring the government down. And as the American military was struggling to put down an insurgency in Iraq and help build a state, its efforts were subverted by a state sponsor of terror. In short, what Syria proved was that in the Middle East today, there is no substitute for the strong horse. Or, rather, it proved that the only way a democratic alternative can survive is through strong horse means.

Damascus is the beating heart of Arabism, which in the Syrian version is a revivalist movement meant to reprise the first Arab empire, the Umayyads, memorialized in the city's most famous landmark, the Great Umayyad Mosque. The dynasty began in 661, when Mu'awiya, the governor of Syria, overthrew Ali, the last of the *rashidun,* and moved the caliphate here to Damascus. Nearly a century later, the political malcontents whom the Syrian rulers had exiled to Iraq eventually brought down the Umayyads in 750, ushering in the rise of the Baghdad-based Abbasids. This relationship was reversed after the 2003 U.S. invasion of Iraq, when Damascus became the headquarters of exiled Iraqi Baathists, who fomented turmoil and violence in their old country in an attempt to kick out the Americans. The Syrians were more than happy to help the insurgency—both the Baathist and the Al Qaeda branches—since doing so solidified Damascus's role as the self-described capital of Arab resistance, where resistance is terrorism that serves Syrian interests.

For thirty years, Damascus has been a warehouse of resistance, hosting the leaders of the Palestinian rejectionist front, Hezbollah, the Iraqi insurgency, and the global jihad, some of them openly, like Hamas chief Khaled Meshaal, others clandestinely, like the late Hezbollah legend Imad Mughniyeh, and others more secretly yet, behind bars. It is an apt metaphor for the Syrian terror state that prison is its workshop and iron forge, where the mukhabarat tortures Syrian oppositionists and cultivates the agents of worldwide resistance.

Ghassan al-Mufleh spent twelve years in Syrian jails. The forty-eight-year-old writer and opposition activist was imprisoned for communist activities but styles himself after the iconography of American rebellion—long black hair, an upturned collar of his black leather jacket, and a squint like James Dean even when he isn't chain-smoking. We met in the European city that he's made his home in exile, and he explained how the Syrian mukhabarat recruits its terrorist assets in prisons, a process he saw firsthand.

"Remember that Syria is a proudly Arab nationalist state, and it requires no visas from Arab visitors," says Mufleh. "So almost every Arab fighter heading off to do jihad comes through Syria. If they return from jihad alive and want to head home—Egypt, Saudi Arabia, Morocco—they just say that they were in Syria, working, vacationing, and their record is clean. But when they are heading through the Damascus airport, Syrian security detains some of the ringleaders in prison to see if they can use them. They give them a choice—either they can agree to work for the Syrian services, or they will be turned in to their own home intelligence agency. It is an easy choice."

After Mufleh explains that the regime has been manipulating jihadi fighters dating back to the 1970s, I note the possibility that Hafez al-Assad had inadvertently assisted in bringing down his Soviet patron by facilitating the flow of Arab fighters in and out of Afghanistan. Mufleh notes the deeper irony that he was jailed for taking Marxism seriously. "We Marxists couldn't get money to publish our pamphlets," he said. "So how do terrorist groups get money for weapons? You can't keep these organizations afloat without money from states. The Europeans know this," says Mufleh, citing the intelligence service of his new home country. It brought him in for questioning when he first moved there. "Terrorism is not spontaneous. It is not stateless. I am sure that the Americans know this, too, that the Syrians sponsor terror."

Perhaps it seems strange, then, that during the Bush administration's second term many of the harshest critics of Bush's Syria policy were former CIA hands, or journalists with extensive CIA sources, who complained that the White House was making a mistake by isolating Damascus. Since members of the intelligence community have done so much liaison work with Damascus, they argued that the Syrians could help us with Al Qaeda since they shared a common interest with the United States in putting down jihadis. They contended, with many in Washington, that Damascus couldn't possibly be working with Sunni Islamists: first of all, Syria's was an Arab nationalist regime that had no love for Islamists; second, Damascus had as much to fear from Sunni fanatics as anyone else since Syria's ruling clique was drawn from the minority Alawi community.

Since 1966, Sunni-Arab-majority Syria (some 70 percent of the country's seventeen million inhabitants) has been governed by the Alawis, a small syncretic sect that is ostensibly an offshoot of Twelver Shia Islam.[1] The name of the community is derived from that of the last of the *rashidun,* Ali, in whose person the Alawi faithful believe God manifested himself. This heresy, together with the Alawi observance of Christian holidays, lends credence to the idea that the Alawi faith owes perhaps as much to Christianity as it does to Islam.[2] In any case, few Alawis are initiated into the deeper workings of the faith. Anti-Alawi polemicists describe it as a fertility cult based on worship of the vagina, and claim that once a year the Alawis observe debauched pagan rituals where they engage in sex with anyone they want, including relatives and members of the same sex, all to satisfy the voracious sexual appetites of their women. Bin Laden's mother is

apparently an Alawi, even as one of Sheikh Osama's intellectual god-
fathers believed that the members of this sect were "more infidel
than Jews or Christians, even more infidel than many pagans." Ibn
Taymiyya, whom we have met before, believed that "war and punishment in accordance with Islamic law against [the Alawis] are among
the greatest of pious deeds and the most important obligation."[3] To
this day the Sunnis consider the Alawis heretics.

During the post–World War I French mandate of Syria, Paris
played on Alawi anxiety and resentment to carve a military, security,
and intelligence apparatus out of the minority sect to serve French
interests. As plans were being drawn for post-mandate Syria, the
Alawis called in their claims to French favor and petitioned to have
their own state, or to be attached to Lebanon, the refuge of minorities, or for the French to stay in Syria—anything but to be cast off as
part of an independent Syria that would leave them at the mercy of
the Sunnis. A group of Alawi leaders, apparently including the great-
grandfather of Syria's current president, wrote to the then prime
minister of France to explain that the Alawis were afraid "to be joined
to Syria for it is a Sunni state and Sunnis consider them unbelievers;
ending the mandate would expose the Alawis to mortal dangers."[4]

The French remained impervious to Alawi appeals. And so, as the
mandate came to an end, the Alawis had little choice but to find a
way of living with the Sunnis. Their solution was to forge a common
national identity with their potential persecutors, an identity forged
almost entirely around opposition to Israel. By unifying to make war
with the outsider, Syrians would forgo campaigning against each
other. The Alawis therefore draped themselves in the mantle of
Arabism, and by making war on another regional minority, the Jews,
they almost managed to disguise their own anxious status as Muslims. Following the turnover of yet another Sunni government—
post-mandate Syria had endured a chain of coups and countercoups
from the very beginning—an Alawi military regime brought stability
with Hafez al-Assad's ascent to the presidency in 1971. Assad's regime

clinched the Alawis' place in Syria, but it also augmented Sunni ire. Throughout the mid-1970s and early 1980s, Syria's branch of the Muslim Brotherhood waged a war against the Alawi regime, culminating in an attempt on Assad's life. The regime retaliated by leveling Hama, a Muslim Brotherhood stronghold, where security forces killed anywhere from ten thousand to forty thousand Syrians.

Given this history, it wasn't entirely shocking that after 9/11, the White House and the Alawis essentially agreed that the central problem with the Arabic-speaking Middle East was Sunni violence. (This changed, of course, once the Bush administration came to see that bin Laden was less of a threat than Iran.) After all, this was a point of view that the Alawis had held for hundreds of years, even if Washington had just recently stumbled upon it. For most of the twentieth century, Americans had been accustomed to thinking of the Sunnis as allies and friends in whom they had vested their interests in the region. But 9/11 left the White House feeling betrayed by the Sunnis, and made many in Washington believe that Assad could become an important asset in the war on terror—even though Syria had been on the State Department's list of "state sponsors of terrorism" since it was first compiled in 1979. While it was true Damascus supported Hezbollah and Hamas, people argued, it would never back Al Qaeda and other networks of "stateless" terrorists, because they targeted not only the United States but Arab regimes as well.

The problem was that even though the Syrian regime believed that Sunni violence was a threat to its interests, that did not mean it would be willing to work seriously with the United States in quelling it. Indeed, the notion that Syria was a potential ally against Al Qaeda rested on a pair of mistaken assumptions: first, that Arab nationalists and Islamists are always at war and would not dare to work together; and second, that the Alawis' fear of the Sunnis compels them to make perpetual war against them, when in fact it is often easier and quite productive, if still dangerous, to manipulate Sunni Islamists instead of fighting them. This kind of manipulation, after all, is a central part of power politics in the region, with the various Arab rulers using terrorist organizations as cat's-paws in their struggles with each other. For instance, the coups that overturned Syrian governments throughout the 1940s, 1950s, and 1960s were typically backed or instigated by outside actors, among them Iraq, Egypt, and Jordan. So, when Hafez al-Assad came to power, he decided to act preemptively by interfering with other regimes before they could interfere with him. He backed the rivals and enemies of, among others, the Jordanians, Egyptians, Arafat, Saddam, and the Saudis, working with both Arab nationalist and Islamist terrorist organizations. In short, Arab terrorist outfits do indeed target Arab regimes, which is precisely why they are often funded by those regimes' intra-Arab rivals. Arab rulers either set up their own cutouts or bought off existing organizations, just as Saudi princes paid off hostile Arab journalists, and redirected their energies onto other regimes. Syria's history made it clear that, far from being unwilling to partner with Sunnis or Islamists (or both), the Alawis were happy to do so when it served their interests. And that meant any alliance with the United States against Al Qaeda was unlikely to amount to much.

Why did so many policy makers, officials, and analysts continue to insist that Syria was not the problem but part of the solution? Here again we can see how policy often dictates analysis. In the 1990s, both the Bush and the Clinton White Houses hoped to capitalize on the end of the Cold War, and Operation Desert Storm, by pushing for Arab-Israeli peace. In order to keep the Syrians at the table, Washington pursued a policy known as "constructive engagement," which meant that so long as Damascus made gestures toward peace, or just kept talking, the United States would overlook its occupation of Lebanon and its support for terrorist organizations. During this era, which you might call the golden age of peace processing, U.S. secretaries of state were frequent guests of Hafez al-Assad in the Syrian capital—James Baker made twelve trips to Damascus; Warren

Christopher, thirty-four; and Madeleine Albright, seven.[5] It would, of course, have been unseemly for America's chief diplomats to be seen so assiduously wooing a state sponsor of terror, and so the Americans simply buried the fact that Syria was supporting a wide array of terrorist organizations, from Kurdish nationalists in Turkey to Palestinian Sunni jihadis in Lebanon. Who was responsible for arming and funding these groups and giving them logistical support? Not Syria, the United States insisted—it was a peace partner. As a result, the myth took hold that no state was responsible for arming and funding terrorist groups: these groups were not shaped and supported by Middle Eastern states pursuing their strategic interests; rather, they were all just rogue networks of stateless operators motivated by a wide array of grievances.

The reluctance of many U.S. policy makers to acknowledge Syria's complicity in terrorism was nicely illustrated in the winter of 2007, when former U.S. national security adviser Zbigniew Brzezinski was in Damascus meeting with Bashar al-Assad, even as on the other side of town Imad Mughniyeh, a Hezbollah commander, was killed in a car-bomb attack. Mughniyeh was thought to be responsible for many acts of international terror, including the 1983 Marine barracks bombing in Beirut, and the fact that he traveled freely to Damascus made it obvious that Syria was providing shelter to terrorists, even to those with American blood on their hands, and under the nose of a visiting American dignitary no less.

Brzezinski, along with Democratic lawmakers like Speaker of the House Nancy Pelosi, who also visited Bashar in Damascus, was one of those pundits and policy makers who chastised the Bush administration for isolating Syria, an opinion institutionalized in the bipartisan gravitas of the Iraq Study Group, co-chaired by James Baker. These attacks made it sound as if the Bush administration had willfully ignored Damascus's overtures toward an alliance. The truth was more nearly the opposite: the Bush White House had tried to improve its relationship with Damascus after 9/11. It had dispatched several high-level envoys, like Secretary of State Powell, whose April 2003 visit was intended to secure Assad's cooperation in Iraq and a promise to shut down the Damascus offices of Hamas and Islamic Jihad. But that visit ended in disarray—when Powell convened a press conference to boast of his success, reporters quickly discovered that the bureaus of the Palestinian groups were still open for business. And needless to say, Assad never cooperated over Iraq. Even so, the administration kept the doors open: in January 2005, Deputy Secretary of State Richard Armitage made a last visit to Damascus. But a few weeks later, Hariri was assassinated in Beirut, making it all too clear that Assad had no interest in altering his behavior. A day later, Washington withdrew its ambassador.

The fact that the United States spent more than a decade trying to cajole Damascus would have been bad enough had it only been a waste of American money, time, and prestige. What made the U.S. efforts even more problematic was that by trying so hard to work with the Syrians, American policy makers had effectively encouraged terrorism. The reason they were so intent on working with Syria, after all, was that they believed the Syrians had the ability to spoil peace efforts in the region. That sent a clear message: the easiest way to get the attention of world leaders and prove that you are indispensable to peacemaking is by killing people. To be sure, American policy makers sought to frame it differently, and tried to come up with explanations for why Syria, given the right carrot, would stop sponsoring violence throughout the region. But in doing so, the United States ended up, as it so often has in recent decades, excusing those who make violence their initial response to anything that offends them, and legitimizing terrorism.

"If the Americans try to do to Syria what they did to Iraq," says Ibrahim, "we will fight them. Syrians are tough."

And the Iraqis are not? I ask him.

"Not like Syrians are tough," he says. "And we will all fight as one."

Ibrahim usually laughed when he was caught blustering through a lie. The first time I walked into his store in the Old City of Damascus he flattered the American's sense of business propriety by telling me he set a fair price for rugs and furniture, and never bargained. I told him I wanted to be there when he told the next Arab customer who came through that he refused to bargain. Then there was the afternoon I brought a friend around from New York who asked about the Jewish quarter close by, and Ibrahim confided that his name was in fact Abraham. He was a Jew, he said in hushed tones, one of a mere hundred or so remaining in the city after centuries of a major Jewish presence here in the heart of the Holy Land now scattered to the Syrian Jewish diaspora in New York and New Jersey—maybe my friend knew some of his relatives. Ibrahim kept a straight face throughout, but my friend still didn't buy anything from Abraham the landsman.

Ibrahim's criticism of the Iraqi resistance didn't sound all that convincing, either. At the very least, it was not something you heard from many Syrian Sunnis, since between their fight against the Americans and the slaughter of Iraqi Shia, the Iraqi Sunnis had come to be regarded as rock stars by many Syrians, as they were in the Damascus cabaret that Ibrahim and I visited one night. The top-notch cabarets are staffed mostly by Russian girls, with the blondes fetching the most attention from the Gulf tourists, but where Ibrahim goes, the girls are Arab, Egyptian, Syrian, and Iraqi, and so self-conscious that I began to wonder how many of them were veiled before they started to earn a living in their ill-fitting prom-dress knockoffs and chunky high heels. The MC swapped dirty jokes with a small group of Iraqis. One of them, a compact man sitting in front of a bottle of Absolut, wore a turtleneck, brown leather coat, and a mustache characteristic of the Arab officer class. He was pouring himself shots of vodka and loudly toasting the MC, who took a small bow and returned the compliment. "To Iraq," said the MC, "and the proud sons of the resistance of Fallujah." When the blood drained from Ibrahim's face and he suddenly asked for the check from a middle-aged Egyptian woman in a bathing suit, I began to wonder if maybe he really was Jewish after all.

"Fighting the Americans in Iraq is very dangerous," Abd al-Halim Khaddam told me. "But it also makes Bashar popular. Anything under the banner of resistance is popular."

Khaddam knows all about Syrian resistance policy—the terror that advances Syrian interests abroad while it consolidates domestic support in the capital of Arab resistance. Khaddam served as Hafez al-Assad's foreign minister and vice president, a post he held under Bashar for five years before he split with the regime and left Syria. Shortly after he moved to Paris, he told an Al Arabiya interviewer that Bashar was directly responsible for the Hariri assassination. Damascus responded by claiming that Khaddam's charges were compromised by the millions he'd stolen while in power. Obviously Khaddam had helped himself to the kitty, but only a regime as vainglorious as the Syrian Arab Republic's could suppose that calling a high official with a quarter century of service dirty would not make the entire government look rotten from the head, Hafez and Bashar al-Assad, on down.

Still, it was curious to see Khaddam refashioning himself as a champion of democracy. The short, aging, white-haired man in a turtlenecked sweater with the kind eyes and the gracious manner sitting before me in a Brussels hotel room had been responsible for a lot of human pain. He managed Syrian interests in Lebanon before Bashar took over the Lebanese file himself.

"Bashar got his influence back in Lebanon through Hezbollah," said Khaddam. "But the Americans say they want him to cut his ties to them and Hamas, which is also an important card and they expect him to throw it away. The Americans see appearances without seeing the fundamental issues. They want an agreement between Syria and Israel, but the Americans are naive. They want to change the regime's behavior, but behavior is an index of human nature. A dictator has the soul of a dictator. It is in the nature of a dictator. How can you ask him to change his behavior? Is it objective to separate the dictator's behavior from the nature of the regime?"

Khaddam had worked for the dictator's father, who was also a dictator and equally vicious, if smarter. I asked him how he rationalized it, now that he was a democrat, after all. Khaddam avoided the question of morality and instead contrasted the strategies of the father and the son.

"In the '70s, Syria had a very balanced policy," he said. "We stood with the U.S.S.R., but we always kept channels open with the West. We were opposed to the U.S. but not in conflict, we knew what our limits were. We saw that in 1974 we could not fight Israel once Egypt was out of the picture. We compensated by supporting resistance."

Much of that resistance was waged against the other Arab states as well as Israel. The Syrians made it especially hard for Egypt after Sadat signed the peace treaty with Israel.

"But we never went against the region," said Khaddam. "With Bashar and his alliance with Iran, that changed."

It was Hafez who had initiated the relationship with the Iranian Islamists even before Khomeini came to power, but Khaddam said that Hafez always knew he couldn't afford to antagonize the Arabs. "Whenever the situation deteriorated between Iran and Saudi Arabia, we told Saudi that if anyone is against Saudi, we will stand with Saudi. And we went to talk to the Iranian leadership and calm things down, to say how dangerous the potential for conflict is."

Khaddam explained that it was the Hariri assassination that pushed Syria irretrievably into the Iranian camp. The Saudis blamed the murder on Bashar, and his response was a steady stream of insults directed at the Sunnis until the only friends he had left in the region were the Iranians. "He can't get out of the Iranian basket even if he wanted to," said Khaddam.

For the past thirty years, since the Islamists took over Iran and allied with Syria, Western policy makers have sought to "split" Damascus from Iran, wasting countless hours, money, and lives (Arab, Israeli, and American) in the effort. Describing the ties between the two states as "unnatural" or a "marriage of convenience," Western officials choose to ignore what the Syrians and Iranians say themselves—that it is a strategic alliance with deep roots and a shared ideology. It is true that one state is a Shia theocracy and the other an Arab nationalist regime, but the ideology they share is resistance. Both support armed resistance; both are expansionist powers—Iran desirous of exporting the revolution, and Syria with designs on Lebanon; and both are opposed to the Sunni Arab order and determined to drive its American underwriter from the region once and for all. It is on behalf of Iran that Syria has confronted, enraged, and alienated the Sunni states in the region, doing so because it has calculated that Tehran is winning. Yet the Europeans, many Americans, and even a few Israelis believe that Damascus may yet move away from Iran, abandon Hezbollah and Hamas, and thereby forsake its ideology, its self-image as the capital of Arab resistance and steadfastness, and everything else that allows it to project power in the region—all in exchange for a peace with Israel that it can't make, a regional profile as meager as Yemen's, and a U.S. bribe.

"The alliance with Iran puts Syria in the middle of the very dangerous conflict," said Khaddam. "Iran has ambitions to control the region, from the Mediterranean to Afghanistan, which is against the interest of the Arabs and the West. And Bashar fought in Iraq on behalf of the Iranians."

This was, to be sure, a gamble on Assad's part, since he could not be sure how the White House intended to respond, and with troops on the Syrian border the United States had the ability to do something drastic. But he had an advantage, namely, that as bad as he was (and is), Washington feared that if he fell, what came after him would be worse: either a Sunni Islamist regime or a semi-failed state. In either case, the White House believed, Syria would actually become more likely to export terrorism. This was almost certainly wrong, resting as it did on the assumption that terror is the work of rogue networks of stateless actors who flourish in failed states, rather than relying heavily on the sponsorship of regimes and their mukhabarat. But effectively, the United States, chastened by its experience in Iraq, chose the devil it knew over the devil it didn't, and Assad's gamble paid off.

This wasn't entirely shocking. The Arab regime, after all, is a resilient beast. And in the past five years, Syria has sustained several significant blows to its prestige—its presumed responsibility for the murder of Hariri, its withdrawal from Lebanon, the Mughniyeh assassination conducted on its front doorstep, and Israel's raid that destroyed the Al-Kibar nuclear facility in northwestern Syria. Through it all, the Alawis have stayed in firm control, suffering no real damage to their power and, to date, minimal international repercussions.

And so, even after the surge, the Syrians continued to push their luck by sending foreign fighters across the border, as though to signal to the incoming Obama administration that Damascus had to be dealt with—after all, the Syrians were capable of putting out fires they'd started. And so in the spring of 2009, the U.S. military discovered a network of Tunisian fighters thought to have been warehoused in Syrian prisons before they were dispatched to Iraq; and a Syrian national detained, according to the Iraqi police, in a Syrian jail was apprehended in Kirkuk before he could detonate his explosive vest in a Shia mosque.[6] During one period, U.S. military sources found that more than 90 percent of the foreign fighters in Iraq came through Syria, as Damascus International Airport became the transit spot of choice for jihadis, who flew straight into the beating heart of Arabism and were processed through to the Iraq frontier.[7]

For all of the assistance Assad gave the insurgents, this doesn't mean that he was the *cause* of the violence in Iraq. Syria merely helped describe the phylogeny of the region. For Assad and the Alawis, the Iraqi insurgency amounted to a debate over the nature of the Middle East. The Bush administration thought that the region was ripe for democracy and pluralism, and that its furies could be tamed by giving Middle Easterners a voice in their own government. Syria countered that the Middle East could only be governed through violence. Its support for the insurgency was, at least in part, intended to give Washington no choice but to put away dangerous ideas like Arab democracy.

It is of course true that the Bush administration did not fully comprehend the dangers of sectarianism around the Middle East, but the fact is that even the Al Qaeda home office did not understand what was happening out in the field.

In a letter captured by the Americans in 2005, Ayman al-Zawahiri sent his greetings and congratulations to Abu Musab al-Zarqawi, but also queried him on certain matters raised by his jihad in the land of the two rivers.[8] Zawahiri conceded that the Shia, adherents of "a religious school based on excess and falsehood," were indeed calumnious and destined in the fullness of time to reap the rewards of their heresy. But he was nonetheless compelled to note, "Many of your Muslim admirers amongst the common folk are wondering about your attacks on the Shia." He admonished Zarqawi to focus on the Americans and leave the Shia for later because Al Qaeda fans did not understand his obsession with killing those who were presumably co-religionists.

There was something to this: I remembered Raouf's mother in Cairo, who sat at home all day watching the new Iraqi cable stations that revealed a different world to her that she knew nothing of previously—it was a Shia world. She was moved to tears when she heard for the first time the tragic story of Hussein's martyrdom. "Why are you crying, Mother?" Raouf's Islamist sister asked her. "Okay, it's a sad story, but it's not our story. We're Sunnis."

Perhaps Zawahiri, like Raouf's mother, could not fathom the depths of sectarian loathing, for it was he, hiding in a cave somewhere mulling over grand strategy, who misread public opinion, and Zarqawi had tapped into something essential. He was playing to his Sunni Arab base throughout the sectarian states, and they loved it. His audience wasn't just *takfiris* and fellow travelers but also mainstream Sunnis around the region who might not have entirely approved of all his tactics, but agreed that someone had to put the Shia back in their place lest they misunderstand what was in store for them once the Americans left. Bin Laden killed Americans, and the Palestinians and Hezbollah killed Jews, but Zarqawi was the man in the trenches who slaughtered the heretics that Sunni Arabs have successfully kept in their place for a millennium now and have to live with every day.

Compared with Zarqawi, Zawahiri and bin Laden were just mainstream Arab demagogues. Washington, they say, is the only thing standing between them and the fall of the infidel regimes in Cairo, Riyadh, and elsewhere. But only a *takfiri* Boy Scout could really believe that a few stalwart souls camping out in caves could topple authoritarian states like Egypt and Saudi Arabia, states managed by massive security services devoted exclusively to preserving their own power. Zarqawi, by contrast, showed that to bring down the established order, you don't fight the regimes; you set the region in flames by tapping into sectarianism and force the people to fight each other.

This is what the Syrians, and the Iranians, did in Iraq—but the Americans were also at fault, and not just because we failed to provide enough security early on. We should have given more consideration, and even respect, to the theory the Arabs had about us. While Washington may have thought it was laboring to bring democracy to the region, the Arabs believed we were on a deliberate course to set them at each other's throats, with the goal of dividing and conquering. The sectarian warfare in Iraq that Zarqawi was waging was therefore seen as just the first of many more conflagrations to come, con-flagrations that the Arabs thought would be to our benefit, and of course to that of the Israelis.

Sometimes shows of power and diplomacy are, in fact, connected aspects of one player's coherent and comprehensive Middle East pol-icy. But often what appears to be a grand strategy is just a fantasy that Arab analysts, journalists, and café society have projected onto the map of the region in order to pass time and keep the mind nim-ble, like a narrative version of backgammon. That was the case with the Arab interpretation of U.S. policy in Iraq. We didn't want to set the Sunnis and Shia against each other—we just wanted to take a few pieces off the table. But the Arabs find it impossible to believe that we do not understand the nature of the Middle East, and they there-fore assume that our guile matches our power.

The assumption that democracy was all a plan to set the Arabs at each other's throats also made sense to many Arabs because it fit with the way they see their own societies. For the Americans, democ-racy meant investing the Arab man, woman, and child with the rights due every human being. From the Arab nationalist perspec-tive, empowering the Arab individual would necessarily come at the expense of the Arab nation. And weakening the unity of the nation would animate the sectarian monster that has stalked the region for a millennium.

Nowhere were these fears stronger than in Damascus. For the Syrian regime, democracy would mean an end to the domestic peace cultivated through coercion and repression since the founding of the modern Syrian state, and the unleashing of violence at unprecedent-edly lethal levels. Majority rule, meanwhile, would obviously not only spell the demise of the Alawi regime but also threaten the very exis-tence of the Alawi community. As they watched what was happening in Lebanon and Iraq, it was easy for the Arabs to conclude that if rep-resentative government meant brother slaughtering brother, then the Americans could keep their precious democracy to themselves.

Hatred of America's freedoms, the Bush White House liked to say, is why jihadis commit acts of terror against the United States. The Syrian regime reminded the Arab mainstream that it wasn't American freedoms that they hated, but their own. The Arabs feared each other.

CHAPTER 11

Middle East Cold War and the Israeli Strong Horse

All throughout June 2006, in the streets of Beirut you could find the flag of any of the thirty-two nations playing in that summer's World Cup. Shop owners, of course, tailored their stock to their clientele—there were no Iranian flags to be found in the Christian areas, no star-spangled banners in the Shia regions. And yet partisan sympathies did not always follow sectarian lines. One of Hezbollah's MPs declared that he was for the Brazilians, even if they wound up facing the Party of God's Iranian patron, which was fielding a side in the tournament for the first time in years. Fawaz had an Italian passport and his sister lived in Paris, but he supported the Germans, as did most of the Sunnis, turning their noses up at the weak Saudi team. My Saudi neighbor affixed a Brazilian flag to his car antenna.

I saw the championship final at a country club high in the mountains, where the crowd was split evenly between France and Italy, the two European powers playing for the cup. France is the historic protector of the Christian community, but Lebanese regard themselves as temperamentally more similar to their stylish northern Mediterranean cousins, the Italians. There were several big screens in the banquet hall, where long rows of cafeteria tables were loaded with hamburgers, fries, hummus, and other Lebanese dishes. It was cool in the mountains that night, so whenever a group of teenagers opened the doors to the balcony looking out on the stars and the capital below sparkling in the bay, a strong gust whipped through the room, and the elders clutched their French and Italian flags to themselves like blankets. With France's chances for victory all but lost in the closing minutes after the star midfielder Zinedine Zidane was sent off for head butting a trash-talking opponent, a middle-aged woman with dyed blond hair and the French tricolor draped over her shoulders puffed on her cigarette and sighed. "What do you expect?" she seemed to ask no one in particular. "He's an Arab."

Thanks to Italy's victory, the next morning Lebanon woke up Italian. The following morning, Hezbollah fired rockets on Israeli villages and kidnapped two Israeli soldiers while killing another eight, and Lebanon was again divided.

In the year and a half after the Hariri assassination and the withdrawal of Syrian troops, the Lebanese political class and ordinary citizens alike pointedly ignored their country's own problems. For instance, very few Lebanese thought to look to Hezbollah as a possible culprit in the Hariri assassination, even though the group had pioneered the use of the car bomb. It was impossible to the majority of Lebanese that the Party of God had had anything to do with the murder of the former prime minister—the resistance that had liberated Lebanese lands from Israel wouldn't dare turn their weapons on fellow Lebanese, they thought. When they were not laying blame for everything at the feet of Syria or Israel, they were worrying local details as though the world outside merely reflected what was happening in their particular corner of Lebanon—in a country the size of Lebanon, too small to field a superior national football team, politics is the national obsession.

Saturday mornings I sat in the ABC mall in Ashrafiyeh, the heart of Christian East Beirut, with a group of Lebanese who debated

Maronite politics and the Maronite presidency, as if Washington and Riyadh, Tehran and Paris, Jerusalem and Damascus were beholden to the machinations of this ancient yet tiny community. Fawaz drew on his long cigar and shook his head in disagreement. "Our problem," he said, "is with the Islamist organization in the south that is courting war with a powerful enemy."

It was difficult not to recognize what Hezbollah was up to. In the months leading up to the eruption of open hostilities, Hezbollah had made several unsuccessful attempts to kidnap Israeli soldiers on the border. That winter, one of the party's Palestinian affiliates operating out of southern Lebanon had fired at Israel, which had countered by attacking Hezbollah positions. The Israelis had warned that the next flare-up on their northern border would bring much more severe retaliation. But Syria needed its allies in Lebanon to keep fostering conflict in order to distract the international community's attention from the Hariri investigation, and by the summer it had become clear that a major confrontation was coming. In June, Hamas kidnapped an Israel Defense Forces (IDF) soldier on Israel's southern border, a provocation that tested the resolve of Ehud Olmert's politically insecure Israeli government, and one, most importantly to the Israeli public, that had no military credentials. When, a month later, Hezbollah decided to join the fray, only the Lebanese were surprised by Israel's response, including Hassan Nasrallah, as he later disclosed.[1]

When I first felt the reverberations of the Israeli bombs falling on the Beirut airport ten minutes away from my apartment, I thought of Kristina, a DJ at a club in my neighborhood. One night after her set had ended, we sat quietly and chatted at the bar while the crowd was emptying into the night.

"Do you think it's strange," she asked, "that the Lebanese party so much when we have all these problems in the country?"

No, I told her. I said it was one of the things I loved most about the Lebanese, that despite all their hardships they pushed on and enjoyed their lives to the fullest as though nothing else mattered. It was only now, thinking back, that I understood the look in her eyes: she thought I was as delusional as her countrymen.

Israel's July war of 2006 with Hezbollah was by some accounts the ninth Arab-Israeli war, including the two wars of 1948 (one against the Palestinians and another against the combined Arab armies), Suez in 1956, the Six Day War of June 1967, the October 1973 war, the First Lebanon War from 1982 to 2000, the first intifada from 1987 to 1990, and the second intifada, 2000–2003. But it was more than this. What the Israelis call the Second Lebanon War should also be seen as the first salvo in a much larger, region-wide cold war that would eventually encompass the entire Middle East, bringing in marginal players like Sudan and non-Arab actors like Turkey, and of course Iran, whose push for hegemony in the Middle East was driving the conflict.

On one side of this conflict was the Iranian-led resistance bloc, which also included Syria, Hezbollah, and Hamas; on the other was the U.S.-backed regional order, comprising the Sunni powers Egypt, Jordan, Saudi Arabia and the other Gulf Arab states, and Israel. When Israel's 2007 attack on the Syrian nuclear facility and subsequent assassination of the Hezbollah legend Imad Mughniyeh were received by these Arab states with silence, that further clarified the battle lines. And by December 2008, when Israel laid siege to Gaza and the Egyptians insisted that Hamas could not come out of the conflict victorious, it was obvious that this war was different from any other in the modern Middle East—for Israel was not just reestablishing its deterrence against its Arab enemies but also playing strong horse on behalf of Washington's Arab allies, even if the Arabs were loath to admit it.

Critics of U.S. Israel policy—at least those who are not constitutionally anti-Zionist—tend to fault Israel as a strategic liability. Their argument is that because the Arabs and the Muslim world generally dislike the policies or even the fact of a Jewish state in the Middle East, U.S. support for Israel means that we are unnecessarily antagonizing hundreds of millions of people, many of whom live on the world's largest known reserves of oil. Leaving aside the dubious wisdom, never mind the moral clarity, of choosing allies and making policy based on the emotions of other countries' citizens, for whom by definition U.S. interests are not paramount, the reality is that Israel is the United States' greatest strategic asset in the region.

Consider the history: in 1970 the Israelis stopped the Syrians from making a move on the Hashemite Kingdom of Jordan at a time when the United States was too busy in Vietnam to commit troops to protect an Arab ally. In 1981, the Israelis attacked Iraq's nuclear reactor at Osirak, an operation that at the time met with opprobrium from the entire world, including the Reagan administration, but made it possible a decade later for U.S. troops to take action against Saddam and liberate Kuwait and protect Saudi Arabia without fear of an Iraqi nuclear response. In June 1982, Israel destroyed Syria's Soviet-made surface-to-air missile battery in Lebanon's Bekaa Valley—an event that reverberated throughout Moscow defense circles when they realized that Israel's U.S.-made technology was far superior to their systems. And hence some analysts believe that this battle, effectively a proxy war, was part of the "cascade of events" that led to the fall of the Soviet Union.[2] To be sure, there are other features that bind the U.S.-Israeli relationship—intelligence sharing, joint projects between the two countries' defense industries, and of course the overwhelming support of American voters, Jewish and non-Jewish alike, for Israel—but for more than thirty-five years, the core of the alliance has been cold strategic calculation.

During the 1973 Arab-Israeli war, for instance, the United States airlifted tens of thousands of tons of munitions to Israel to ensure its victory, and awe the Soviets, but those arms shipments were delayed by Secretary of State Henry Kissinger in order to show the Israelis who pulled the strings. And the shipments served U.S. interests in other ways, too—by arming Israel to the teeth, the Americans were signaling to the Arabs that there was no way for them to defeat the Jewish state, and that if they ever wanted concessions from the Israelis, they would have to come through Washington to get them. The strategy worked: Anwar al-Sadat got the picture and jumped sides, from Moscow to Washington, and with Egypt now in its portfolio the United States' regional position was further augmented, allowing it to go from Great Power to power broker. This also set in motion the Arab-Israeli peace process, which earned Israel treaties with Egypt and Jordan and negotiations with the Palestinians, and neutered Syria, leaving it with no option, as the former Syrian vice president Khaddam had explained, but resistance. There has been no full-scale Arab-Israeli war since 1973, which is the direct result of Israeli strength and American support. And yet for all the complaints that the United States is too pro-Israel, Washington does not embrace Israel at the *expense of* the Arabs; rather, it is allied with them both, funding and/or protecting every Arab state, except for Syria.

When the government of Ehud Olmert decided to make war against Hezbollah in the summer of 2006, all of Washington's Arab allies, as one former senior administration official explained to me, were overjoyed. With the Americans having taken down a Sunni security pillar—Saddam—and then getting tied down in Iraq, Riyadh, Cairo, and the rest sensed the Iranians were gaining ground and that they were vulnerable. Even though they were incapable of doing anything about it themselves, the Sunni powers as much as anyone wanted to see the resistance bloc rolled back.

The Arab masses felt differently. A week into the war, I crossed over the mountains and found Damascus in full party mode, engaged in an orgiastic carnival celebrating the blood sacrifice of the Lebanese and the bloodletting of the Israelis. Young Syrians packed together in their cars, flying yellow Hezbollah flags and shouting martial slogans to other passersby. This was one Arab state where the regime and the people were in sync, at least when it came to resistance.

Dalia's blood ran thick with resistance against the Zionists. She was a reporter with Syrian TV whose father had been the Syrian ambassador to London during the Hindawi affair, which occurred in 1982, when a pregnant Irish woman boarding a London flight to Tel Aviv was found by El Al security to be carrying a bomb in her carry-on bag, packed by her boyfriend, Nezar Hindawi.[3] After the plot was discovered, Hindawi hid at the Syrian embassy, which, he later testified, had directed the operation. The British briefly broke off diplomatic relations with Syria, and Dalia's father was sent home. "All Syrians support the resistance," said Dalia.

We were sitting in a café in the Christian quarter of Damascus's Old City set up as a kind of shrine to the great Lebanese singer Fairuz. Posters of her were everywhere, and all her CDs and DVDs were on sale. Dalia said she loved Fairuz but was more ambivalent about Lebanon. "It feels cheap to me," she says. "It doesn't have any authentic Arab culture, like we have in Syria. They've gone too far; it's too Western. I don't think they care about their ties anymore to Arab culture, to the Arabs."

I pointed out that her neighbors across the mountains were dying on behalf of Arab causes, whether they supported those causes or not. She seemed surprised or perhaps embarrassed when I said that at least half of Lebanon did not support the resistance and was furious with Nasrallah for dragging them to war. "If you think that the U.S. or anyone can offer the Syrian government a deal to abandon its support for Nasrallah, you are crazy," she said. "They are fighting Israel."

Resistance is the political discourse of insatiable grievance, and it seemed that those grievances blinded Syrians like Dalia to the possible consequences of the pact that their regime had signed them up for. If Iran was glad to spill Lebanese blood in its pursuit of regional hegemony, why wouldn't it use Syrian blood as well?

After Israel's 2009 siege of Gaza, the Sunni powers made precisely this point, that Iran was shedding Arab blood to advance Persian causes. But something more than this was happening: the

Iranians had tapped into deeper, and darker, Arab emotions. The Bush administration thought that what the Arab masses really wanted was democracy and representative government. Iran, though, gambled that what the Arabs really wanted was not reform but resistance. And Tehran's hunch was right. In its proxy war against the U.S. regional order, Iran was succeeding where the Americans had failed: it was driving a wedge between the Arabs and their rulers.

The Iranians found sympathy for their project in the unlikeliest quarters. There was Saad Eddin Ibrahim, the Egyptian democratic rights activist, who came out in support of Hezbollah's war. I had met Ibrahim a few years before while he was awaiting trial for trumped-up charges brought against him by the Mubarak government, a government he had once served as an adviser and speechwriter for Mubarak and Egypt's First Lady. The enmity he felt toward his former jailer was undoubtedly part of the reason he now cheered on Hezbollah—the enemy of his enemy Mubarak was his friend. But Ibrahim always had a soft spot for the Islamists, and his work on Egyptian militants in the 1980s had established his academic reputation. "When I was in school in the U.S.," he told me at a dinner in Cairo, "there was the civil rights movement and the women's movement. When I came back to Egypt, there was the Islamist movement."

Weeks after the July 2006 war's end, Ibrahim would interview Nasrallah and praise him, chastising the Bush administration for isolating Hezbollah's secretary-general. After all, according to Ibrahim, Nasrallah wasn't an extremist like bin Laden; he was a moderate. Ibrahim's assessment was based on polling showing that Nasrallah had won a large cross section of popular support; ergo, he could not possibly be on the extremist fringe. In a survey of seventeen hundred Egyptians, Nasrallah was first on a list of thirty regional figures ranked by perceived importance.[4] What did it mean that bin Laden appeared on only 52 percent of those lists? According to Ibrahim, it meant Nasrallah's 82 percent made Hezbollah "mainstream." The democratic rights activist argued that an armed group that had effectively staged a coup d'état on behalf of an adventurist foreign policy that had put all of Lebanon at risk was of a "civic disposition" and "not inimical to democracy."

It was an odd conclusion. There was no arguing that Nasrallah was popular with the Arab masses. But the broad support for him would be evidence of his moderation only if moderation were a political value universally cherished in the Arabic-speaking Middle East. It is not. What Nasrallah's approval ratings really showed was that a majority of Arabs gravitate toward the strong horse, no matter how violent or risky its tactics. It was shocking that a famous Arab liberal like Ibrahim refused to see this, and ended up carrying water for Hezbollah, an organization determined to destroy any vestiges of a liberal, democratic order in Lebanon. The White House's project for regional transformation was going backward.

More urgently still, Israel did not perform as well as everyone, including the Sunni powers, had expected. The Olmert government had promised to change the regional equation and disarm Hezbollah, but its management of the war was uncertain, if not incompetent. After two weeks of an aerial onslaught, Hezbollah was holding on against the Israelis, and at the same time damaging the prestige of Arab regimes fretting on the sidelines. Arab rulers like Saudi king Abdullah and Mubarak were half men, said Bashar al-Assad, while Hezbollah had shown the Arab masses who was willing to take it to the Zionists, and capable of doing so. Sunni resolve was ebbing. So when the Israelis struck civilian housing near the town of Qana, site of another Israeli raid that killed civilians in a UN compound in 1996, the Sunni regimes could abide no longer and demanded the United States move to a cease-fire immediately.

In strict military terms, the war didn't look like much of a victory for Hezbollah, which had lost at least five hundred fighters, or five dead Hezbollahis for every IDF soldier killed. But Nasrallah's stated aims in the conflict were modest—*if I survive, we win*—so Israel was widely perceived to have lost the war, even if long afterward Nasrallah would seldom come out of hiding for fear of an Israeli assassination attempt. Had the war continued, it's possible Hezbollah would have been severely weakened, but the irony was that Washington had effectively helped rescue Hezbollah, fearing that a continuation of the war would have led to the toppling of the Lebanese government.

The Israelis did not want to distress their U.S. ally further than their poor management of the war already had, and so there is reason to believe the Olmert government sought the cease-fire at least as ardently as the Americans. But the Israelis were still frustrated with the way Washington saw Lebanon. The Israelis thought Bush had created an imaginary Arab country in his own mind. The administration, the Israelis contended, thought they were dealing with Jeffersonian liberals when the Lebanese were just a bunch of clansmen at each other's throats. And the Israelis believed that their reading of Lebanon was later vindicated when leaders of the March 14 movement, including Walid Jumblatt and Prime Minister Fouad Siniora, feted Samir Kuntar after the Lebanese national was released from an Israeli prison where he'd served three decades for murdering a four-year-old girl while fighting with the Palestinian resistance. It was a repugnant moment, and to watch pro-democracy figures celebrating Kuntar's return was nauseating. But the Israelis had it wrong about Lebanon. There was only one tribe doing the killing in that country, and most of the Lebanese—the ones the United States was backing—were willing to abide by the rule of law and put their trust in the international community. The Americans were undoubtedly naive and overly optimistic about Lebanon's prospects. But it was the Israelis who didn't understand what was happening in Lebanon.

That misunderstanding had its roots in Israel's past experience.

The Israelis had always imagined that Lebanon would be the second country to make peace with the Jewish state, after Egypt. Among other things, they saw in Lebanon's large Christian population a community that shared many of the same values and was also at odds with the region's Sunni majority. But Israel's perception of

Lebanon changed when it invaded in 1982 in order to drive out the PLO. Israeli prime minister Menachem Begin met with the country's newly elected Christian president, Bashir Gemayel, to move toward diplomatic relations, but two weeks later Gemayel was assassinated by a Syrian agent. Remarkably, this left the Israelis without a backup plan, showing that they had an incomplete understanding of Lebanon, and of the region as a whole: even if they wanted peace with Lebanon and saw the Christians as their partners, that choice was not for minorities like Christians and Jews to make. Decisions of that magnitude can only be made by the Sunnis.

In fact, the Israelis knew this—their two peace treaties were with Sunni powers—and generally refrained from basing their regional strategy on what they had in common with Arab minorities: that they were all despised by the Sunni Arabs. Their past Lebanon policy of reaching out to the Christians was an aberration, and a miscalculation they were determined not to make again. Hence they considered the Americans sentimental for being taken in by the prospect of Lebanese democracy.

The Lebanese understood the region perfectly in all its complexity. They knew what effect pulling one lever here would have over there, and how the regional powers interacted. But for all that, they could not see the forest for the trees. They were too subtle, too convinced there was a backdoor way to solve their problems. Because they, understandably, did not want another civil war, they would not take on Hezbollah. Instead, they told themselves that eventually Hezbollah would simply give up its arms—if only they could find the right incentive, the correct political recipe to make it do so. The truth should have been clear after Israel's 2000 withdrawal, when the resistance declared its arms were still needed to fight for a thin piece of land in an obscure corner of Lebanon near the Israeli border, the She-baa Farms.[5] Hezbollah was never going to give up its weapons. Who has ever willingly given up their arms, except after having been defeated?

The result of all this was that Hezbollah marched on, effectively setting its own foreign policy, regardless of what the rest of the country or its government desired. The only consolation left to the Lebanese was the belief that Hezbollah would never turn its weapons on other Lebanese. That delusion was shattered in May 2008, when Hezbollah mounted a coup targeting Sunnis in Beirut and Jumblatt's Druze in the Shouf Mountains. Even before this, it should have been obvious that Hezbollah was more than willing to sacrifice fellow Lebanese to its own interests—after all, how much of a difference is there between shooting your neighbors yourself and starting a war and then hiding behind your neighbors when the enemy returns fire?

Of course, it wasn't clear to the Western media and policy circles until after the Gaza conflict in 2009 that the resistance bloc used human shields as a matter of course. During the summer of 2006, the question was still open to debate, even though it should have been obvious that the reason Hezbollah had built a state within a state was to avoid responsibility for its actions and prevent enemies from engaging it as they would the military of a sovereign nation. All of Lebanon was a human shield.

It was easy to feel like a human shield that summer. The Israeli Air Force dropped circulars across the country warning civilians to vacate potential areas of interest. The papers were pressed together into large balls that would break apart in midair and scatter the flyers over a wide area. One such mass failed to open and fell hard to the earth in the middle of a soccer field near my apartment. Kids stripped the warning ball down sheet by sheet.

I went up to Fawaz's house in the mountains. His balcony overlooked the valley down below by the water, where Hezbollah was entrenched in the southern suburbs of Beirut. The Israelis, it seemed, had found the building where Nasrallah was holed up, hidden somewhere in its recesses, and they were pounding away at the nine-story structure to get at him. During the civil wars, the men now under siege below in the southern suburbs had kidnapped Fawaz's father.

"We owned a tile store in West Beirut," Fawaz told me. "My family lived there for a long time, through most of the war even—I still vote in that district—it was a mixed neighborhood, and my father was used to working with anyone. He had hired this young Shia kid who told Hezbollah about the money my father had in his safe, and they took him hostage." They released him a day later, but not before cleaning out half of the family's money. "Right after that," said Fawaz, "we moved up here to the mountains."

The year before we had been sitting out on the same deck from where we now watched buildings being turned to dust. Last year the noise came from a bunch of teenage girls hosting a pool party for some neighborhood boys. Fawaz had said he was envious of them. "I wish that we had that experience, too," he said. "But we grew up different. We didn't know what it was like to throw parties, to meet girls in a regular way. And so my generation is kind of stunted emotionally; we grew up in a non-normal environment. Everyone is always so close together you have no room for yourself, your thoughts. You don't have the time or room to figure out who you are and how to grow up."

Fawaz's three young nephews were visiting from Paris, and they made the best of a strange summer vacation, taking turns petting Fawaz's big golden retriever, the children and the animal soothing each other after each explosion. We went back and forth between the TV set in the living room and the balcony; there was nothing else to do. "During the war," Fawaz remembered, "there were entire days you couldn't leave the house, and all we could do was sit around and play cards. I can't even stand to look at a deck of cards now. Any card game reminds me of the war."

An entire generation of Israeli men fought in Lebanon. They frequently refer to the First Lebanon War as their Vietnam— except it was more traumatic. Continents separate America from

Southeast Asia, but Lebanon is on Israel's northern border. And when I came to Israel in the middle of the July 2006 war, almost every man I met asked about Lebanon, because they, too, had lived there. Some had gotten as far north as Beirut, though most were confined to the southern part of the country, where they occupied the security zone and fought Hezbollah. Many liked the country. Some Israeli men wanted to talk about the women, others about the beach, and others yet the mountains. In Jerusalem, I met Asher Kaufman, who had served in Mount Lebanon with the Maronites, and went on to become an important scholar of Lebanese intellectual history and culture. Another Israeli told me how his time served in Lebanon had made him rich. After his tour in the army he traveled, like many Israeli kids just out of the service, and wound up in Tokyo. To support himself, he sold posters on a street corner until a local street tough told him he was poaching on his territory. When the Japanese man turned to answer a call on his cell phone, the Israeli stripped the primitively large device from his hands and beat him with it. The street tough's boss admired his nerve and hired him. "I didn't even think about the consequences when I hit the guy," he said. "I had just left the army, and when you are a teenager, crazy things go through your mind—anything could happen to you in Lebanon."

Levanon is the most mournful word in the mouth of a Hebrew-speaking mother, and I confess that when I first heard the word uttered, it terrified me, too, the biblical name of a country I had come to love.

I met Fawaz's hero in a café in West Jerusalem. Natan Sharansky was surprised to hear of the reception his book *The Case for Democracy* had with Lebanese readers. He didn't know there were neoconservatives like Fawaz in Lebanon. In fact, Sharansky admitted, there weren't that many neoconservatives in Israel either. If Israeli intellectuals and policy makers agreed with Sharansky that democracy would make the Arabs better neighbors, few thought the Arabs were even capable of it. Now, after the war against Hezbollah, an Islamist group that was elected to take part in the government, I asked him if he still believed in Arab democracy. "The White House was unwise to rush to elections rather than build democratic institutions first," he answered. I said I was not sure that was the only issue.

Societies that have democratic institutions are built by men and women who seek such an order and are willing to sacrifice for it. Societies that do not have them have instead the regimes that they themselves have designed, through either active participation or acquiescence. In book 8 of *The Republic,* Plato writes, "The States are as the men are. They grow out of human characters." The failure to wrestle with this fundamental observation was the greatest error of U.S. post-9/11 Middle East policy, which in its push for Western-style democracy overlooked the fact that while all men may be entitled to life, liberty, and the pursuit of justice, they do not all seek it, for some, as the resistance proudly proclaims, love death more than life. Ultimately, the problem with the region was not the regimes, nor was it Islam, nor even the Islamists, but the Arab societies of which they were a part.

There were exceptions. I thought of Fawaz up in the mountains watching his birthplace on fire. He said that if he didn't live to see democracy, then his children would, or their children would. I thought of Raouf, the German Idealist, and Ahmed the Sufi, Abdul Rahman the weeping giant of Homs, and all the other Arabs who believed the same, and wanted what Lana the Cairo doctor said she wanted—all the things the Americans have to offer, but in her city, her culture, and her language. But it wasn't going to happen now, and perhaps not ever.

It was not that the Arabs were incapable of democracy but that most of them did not want it, and those who did want it had not the means to win it. To be sure, the Arabs wanted to choose their leaders—who does not?—but as for the accommodations and compromises between contending points of views, which is the signature of a democratic and secular society, these tenets had no foundations in a region where history had convinced people that there was always good reason to fear your neighbor. The politics and culture of a society that cannot share power and cannot transmit it from one body to another without violence and repression are what led to 9/11, and so the Americans, who have trouble believing that anyone given the choice would not prefer to settle differences through peaceful means, through talk, were finally incapable of doing much for the Arabs. Nor in the end did we owe them anything in exchange for 9/11.

"In the long run," said Sharansky, "democracy is the only option."

I told Sharansky how much my friend Fawaz would've liked meeting him. I told him that Fawaz was a careful student of the Soviets and communism and all the last century's totalitarian movements, including Arab nationalism, a corporatist ideology built on more than just a twentieth-century idea to eradicate the individual self. Fawaz would've enjoyed talking with Sharansky and learning firsthand what the Soviet Union was like, and, most important, how Sharansky and the rest of the dissidents had triumphed in the end. That would have been inspiring. But the impossibility of such a meeting, Fawaz crossing the border for a cup of coffee, is precisely what is wrong with the Arabic-speaking Middle East. A man who says he wants peace with his neighbor, not a peace that comes through destruction and elimination, but a real peace, is a traitor.

Conclusion

I t was more than a year after the July 2006 war that I returned to Beirut. For the destruction and death Hezbollah had brought them, the Lebanese seemed angrier at the Party of God than ever; and they couldn't, or wouldn't, do a thing about it. Hezbollah and its allies had occupied the downtown area, turning it into a squatters' village and further burdening an already fragile economy by closing down dozens of businesses, shops, and restaurants. But life goes on in Lebanon. Cash continued to pour in from the Gulf states, much of it earmarked for real estate; most of it went for luxury high-rises by the water, while some more was detailed for rebuilding the Shia areas turned to rubble in the war (the Arabs, as well as the Americans, vainly imagined these goodwill gestures might separate the Hezbollah-dependent Shia from their Iranian sponsors). Gemmayze was packed with more bars and restaurants than before—some of the establishments that had closed downtown simply moved over to the relatively secure East Beirut neighborhood—for the Lebanese, in spite of their trials, or because of them, would not forgo their nightlife. And Fawaz was engaged to be married. Maybe his son, named after Fawaz's father, or his son's son, who would invariably be named after Fawaz himself, would get to see a peaceful, flourishing Lebanon. Or maybe Lebanon would just keep going through these seemingly endless seasons of violence one year and peace and prosperity the next. For the Arabic-speaking Middle East, that was a kind of stability after all.

The Arabs are a feuding people, as the historian Kamal Salibi remarked to me in Beirut, but they are not a warlike people. Of course, even in this century alone the Arabs have gone to war among themselves repeatedly—as the previous chapters show—but they have no taste for all-out conflagration, or the kind of total war that Arab nationalism, as a tribal pact, tends to preclude. Perhaps the more serious concern is that the Arabs will *not* fight each other, and choose instead to bind together, such as it were, or be bound by others, in a regional pact in order to focus their energies elsewhere, like against the United States, again. That is one feud they cannot afford to continue. Another 9/11, or even a series of attacks, would not represent an existential threat to the United States, even if weapons of mass destruction were employed. But American retaliation against such attacks could very well constitute an existential danger to the Arabs.

The British historian Arnold Toynbee noted that most civilizations die by their own hand, a lesson that originates with Ibn Khaldun, whose cyclical theory of history explains that civilizations in their final stages are incapable of defending themselves—in other words, they lose their will to live. The issue with the Arabs is not that they will not fight, but their appetite for warfare disguises the fact that the Arabs are losing their will to live. Never before in the annals of history has suicide played such a large role as it has in the last quarter century of Arab warfare.

Hezbollah laid the groundwork for 9/11, which was simply a suicide car bombing raised to the next level. In November 1982, the first car-bomb "martyrdom operation" killed seventy-four Israeli soldiers and fourteen others, the first in a series of spectacular Hezbollah attacks, culminating in the 1983 Marine barracks bombing. Amal,

another Shia organization, saw that Hezbollah's martyrdom operations were winning it prestige and power, and so it had no choice but
to match its rival. Amal's first suicide car bombing came in June
1984.[1]

With Lebanon's Shia community in competition for young men
willing to sacrifice themselves to defeat the foreign (Israeli or American or French) occupiers, clerical authorities delivered rulings mud-
dying the distinction between dying at the hands of others and dying
by one's own hands. From the very beginning the Shia clerics understood they were walking a fine line between martyrdom and suicide.

It is in the nature of religion to forbid suicide. The world, religion tells us, is not meaningless but the divine order of an almighty
creator who gives life and takes it away—and only he gives it and takes
it away. Therefore, specific religious prohibitions against suicide are
superfluous, except as reminders that despair and existential bore-
dom have been significant concerns for every society from the beginning of time, or else there would be no need for measures to keep
those inclined to take their own lives from doing so.

With the increasing secularization of the postindustrial Christian West, the prospect of eternal damnation has become less of a
deterrent to suicide at the same time that the temporal realm has
become more appealing, with the result that man may be less
desirous of leaving it. Our lives are filled with pleasant, beautiful dis-
tractions, including consumer goods and entertainments, and, for
parts of the professional class anyway, there is spirituality in work, a
self-creation begetting meaning. The Arabic-speaking Middle East
has not become more secular, and in contrast to the West it perceives
the temporal realm as having gotten not better but worse, always
worse, at least according to the region's own account of itself. Worse
since the founding of Israel, worse since the period of European colonialism, worse since the Ottomans, worse since the Mongols overran
Baghdad, worse since the Abbasids replaced the Umayyads, worse
since the death of Hussein, worse since Ali's defeat at the hands of

Mu'awiya, and much worse since the death of the Prophet of Islam. If the Arabs are humiliated and desperate, it is not because of the West but because of their own historical narrative of decline and decadence, a story about a God who has turned his back on the Arabs and allowed them to be humiliated. To explain the self-inflicted deaths of Arab youths in terms of their despair and humiliation is not a rationale for martyrdom, but a suicide note scribbled across the pages of a fourteen-hundred-year-old history.

As Hezbollah and Amal fed the resistance with the bodies of their young men, their struggle was now waged on two fronts, against the foreign enemy and against each other. With their competition for martyrs escalating, more and more were being sent out on ill-conceived operations that failed to kill any of the enemy's numbers and only accomplished the deaths of the martyrs, whose suicides were tactically futile, but useful in demonstrating the commitment of their fighters. The clerics tried to reimpose limits.

"We believe that self-martyring operations should only be carried out if they can bring about a political or military change in proportion to the passions that incite a person to make of his body an explosive bomb," wrote Hussein Fadlallah in 1985. Fadlallah had at one time been Hezbollah's spiritual adviser, until his unrivaled religious authority among Lebanon's Shia community antagonized the Party of God's Iranian sponsor. "The self-martyring operation is not permitted unless it can convulse the enemy. The believer cannot blow himself up unless the results will equal or exceed the [loss of the] soul of the believer. Self-martyring operations are not fatal accidents but legal obligations governed by rules, and the believers cannot transgress the rules of God."

It was the elders themselves who had overridden the defense mechanisms against self-annihilation, and when they realized the mistake they'd made, it was already too late. When the martyrdom operations stopped, Hezbollah and Amal turned on each other, and then fratricidal war tore apart families and villages. Where once suicide had destroyed only the individual body, now it ravaged the corporate one.

The Lebanese wars reprised the history of the Arabic-speaking Middle East: terror as a political instrument; terror in the name of Islam; sectarian violence; wars within wars; Arab rulers interfering in another domain to advance their strategic interests abroad and secure the realm at home; the murder of innocents. And the wars were also a preview of what was to come in the region, like suicide, for that was new.

Hezbollah's war in the summer of 2006, and Hamas's war in the winter of 2008–2009, marked the birth of the suicide nation. Where once the martyrdom operation was a matter of one man, or a cadre, going after the enemy and dying, now an entire society would stand and absorb the blows as a whole, sacrificing itself in large numbers—from suicide bomber to a society of suicide. The paradox is that for the culture of suicide to win, someone had to be left standing. "We are going to win because they love life," said Hassan Nasrallah, "and we love death."

"He mocks those who love life," said Fawaz, as we were walking through the cool night in the mountains overlooking Beirut. It was New Year's Eve, and the city below was sparkling in the bay. "But the party of life will fight to keep it."

And a culture that loves death will also ultimately win what it prizes most, death.

In short, Arab violence should not be confused with Arab strength. Indeed, the war in Iraq and its aftermath have exposed all the fault lines in the region—sectarian, political, cultural, and so on—and have left the Arabs more fragile than at any time since the Western powers liberated them from the Ottomans. So what role, if any, should the United States play in the Arabic-speaking Middle East? Or, where do Arab interests and those of America converge?

First of all, let's do away with the notion of a return to the pre-9/11 status quo. For all the mistakes of the Bush administration, one of the things we have learned the last several years is that it is dangerous to entrust American interests to our Sunni allies. For Arab regimes, regional stability means exclusively their own stability, which almost always comes at the expense of someone else's security, which is how we got 9/11. The Sunni regimes cannot protect our interests, and, as we saw when the United States had to protect the Gulf states from Saddam, and when Israel campaigned against Hezbollah and Hamas, they are not even capable of fighting for themselves.

We share with our Arab allies two interests alone—energy and nonproliferation. As such, our greatest concern in the region is that of our allies—the Iranian nuclear program. Getting the bomb would turn Tehran into a regional hegemon capable of setting the political, cultural, and economic tempo of the Middle East, and touch off a proliferation nightmare in a region as volatile as this one. Moreover, it would push Iran's regional assets into even deadlier conflicts with Israel and other regional powers, like Egypt, which considers Hamas an enemy, and the Arab states where Hezbollah has established a beachhead outside of Lebanon, including Iraq and the Arab Gulf states. If Washington is not prepared to do everything to bring a halt to Iran's nuclear program, including military action, then our regional partners will seek other solutions. The Israelis are very likely to take matters into their own hands, which may let the Arabs breathe easily for a while, but in time they, too, will go their own way separate from Washington.

Whether or not the United States is sufficiently determined to stop the Iranians raises the issue of American resolve, or the lack of it—that is to say, American weakness. After all, a broad consensus of American opinion makers, including the policy establishment, academics, and journalists, maintain that the United States' position throughout the Middle East has been weakened, diplomatically, politically, morally, and militarily, largely because of the war in Iraq. Let me offer a different perspective.

Between October 2001 and April 2003, American armed forces invaded and occupied two Muslim states and sent their leaders scurrying for cover. Unlike Middle Eastern rulers who would have scorched the land of their vanquished foes as an enduring lesson to anyone else thinking of trying to attack their citizens, interests, and allies, the United States decided to democratize them instead. It did this for the sake of those two countries' men and women, in the hope that Iraq and Afghanistan might be beacons of democracy for their neighbors, and because good governance in lands many thousands of miles away was a vital interest of the United States as well as that of the entire international community.

These were the actions not of a weakling but of a country so confident, or haughty, that even as it was recovering from a spectacular national tragedy, it thought it could turn an untested political theory—the democratization of the Middle East, a region with no history of democracy—into a national security strategy. And despite the setbacks in Iraq, the reality is that American power is as great as it ever was. The question is whether we will recognize this, for if instead we perceive ourselves to be uncertain or weak, the region will act as if we were. Perception will become reality. The only power capable of dislodging us from our position in the region is our own.

It is still far too early to know how Iraq will turn out, and while it touched off a number of political, social, and cultural upheavals perhaps comparable, as some commentators noted, to Napoleon's 1798 invasion of Egypt, the uncertainty in Iraq and Lebanon makes it clear that democracy is not going to catch on anytime soon in the Arabic-speaking Middle East. Nonetheless, just as the Reagan administration pushed the Carter White House's human rights agenda, albeit to a different degree and with its own emphases, it is unlikely future administrations will be willing to wholly cashier the Bush team's freedom agenda, or capable of doing so.

It is in the nature of U.S. foreign policy to promote democracy because it is in the character of our people to believe, incorrectly I would argue, that what we have accomplished is not extraordinary and others, too, are capable of it. Perhaps it is partly the minority-rich composition of the Middle East that has led American observers to believe that by bearing a passing resemblance to our multiethnic, multiracial immigrant nation, the region may not be more ready for democracy than others but certainly has more need of it. In any case, our actions among the Arabs have long had a missionary quality, and our enthusiasm for spreading the gospel of the American civic religion is unlikely to subside too much now. The temperament of our society is no more susceptible to immediate about-faces than that of the Arabs.

Nonetheless, the reality is that foreign powers cannot impose political solutions in the Middle East, not for long anyway. This runs counter to the received wisdom of the Western policy-making establishment, which holds that there are no military solutions but only political solutions. For foreign powers, the reverse may be true. The Ottomans, for instance, pursued their interests through their deputies, collected their taxes and tribute, and interfered with internal Arab dynamics rarely, and when they did, it was with a swift and heavy hand. Politics is the public reckoning of how men conduct their lives with their neighbors. Only the Arabs can make the decisions that will lead to political solutions, as in Iraq with the Sunni tribes; as with the two Arab states, Egypt and Jordan, that have made peace with Israel; and as with Arab nationalism, an Arab political solution that keeps the feuding tribes from destroying each other.

The Americans tried a political solution, democracy, and that, along with 9/11, revealed the region's politics for what they truly are. At least the problems of the Middle East are now being fought out where they belong, not in lower Manhattan, but in the region itself, where the Americans, as long as they have the will to stay, should understand that he who punishes enemies and rewards friends, forbids evil and enjoins good, is entitled to rule, and no other. There is no alternative, not yet anyway, to the strong horse.

Notes

Introduction: The Clash of Arab Civilizations

1. G. R. Hawting, *The First Dynasty of Islam: The Umayyad Caliphate* A.D. *661–750* (Carbondale, Ill., 1987), p. 4.
2. Leo Strauss, *What Is Political Philosophy? and Other Studies* (Chicago, 1988), p. 48.

Chapter 1: The Strong Horse

1. A. J. Arberry, *The Seven Odes: The First Chapter in Arabic Literature* (London, 1957), p. 35.
2. Alan Jones, *Early Arabic Poetry, Volume II: Select Odes* (Oxford, 1996), p. 55.

Chapter 2: "An Arab Regardless of His Own Wishes"

1. Edward Said, *Covering Islam: How the Media and the Experts Determine How We See the Rest of the World* (New York, 1981), p. 204.
2. Robert Irwin, *For Lust of Knowing* (London, 2006), p. 293.
3. Ibid., p. 331.
4. Adeed Dawisha, *Arab Nationalism in the Twentieth Century: From Triumph to Despair* (Princeton, N.J., 2003), p. 72.
5. Elie Kedourie, *Islam in the Modern World* (New York, 1980), p. 56.
6. Joshua M. Landis, faculty-staff.ou.edu/L/Joshua.M.Landis-1/syriablog/2004/07/ is-bathism-secular.htm.
7. Edward Said, "The Phony Islamist Threat," *New York Times Magazine,* Nov. 21, 1993.
8. Dawisha, *Arab Nationalism in the Twentieth Century,* p. 63.

Chapter 3: "No Voice Louder Than the Cry of Battle"

1. Michael S. Doran, *Pan-Arabism Before Nasser* (New York, 1999).
2. Miles Copeland was Nasser's handler during the 1950s, a story he tells in great detail in Miles Copeland, *The Game of Nations: The Amorality of Power Politics* (New York, 1970).

3. www.guardian.co.uk/comment/story/0,3604,788470,00.html.
4. Thomas L. McPhail, *Global Communication: Theories, Stakeholders, and Trends*, 2nd ed. (New York, 2005), p. 204.

Chapter 4: The Muslim Reformation

1. www.scholarofthehouse.org/dinistrandna.html.
2. Reynold Nicholson, *A Literary History of the Arabs* (Cambridge, U.K., 1953), pp. 145–46.
3. Bernard Lewis, *The Arabs in History*, 6th ed. (New York, 2002), p. 32.
4. For instance, the *sira*, Muhammad's biography, is drawn from an account composed more than a hundred years after the Prophet's death, a text that is only available in another author's edition published some fifty years later.
5. Kristina Nelson, *The Art of Reciting the Qur'an* (Austin, Tex., 1985), is a lively sociology of Egyptian reciters and their audiences.
6. Ernest Gellner, *Postmodernism, Reason, and Religion* (New York, 1992), pp. 11–13.
7. Elie Kedourie, *Afghani and 'Abduh: An Essay on Religious Unbelief and Political Activism in Modern Islam* (1966; London, 1997), p. 44.

Chapter 5: "The Regime Made Us Violent"

1. Lawrence Wright, "The Man Behind bin Laden: How an Egyptian Doctor Became a Master of Terror," *The New Yorker,* Sept. 16, 2002.
2. Nadav Safran, *Egypt in Search of Political Community* (Cambridge, Mass., 1961), p. 79.
3. Albert Hourani, *Arabic Thought in the Liberal Age, 1798–1939* (New York, 1962), p. 240.
4. Hamid Enayat, *Modern Islamic Political Thought* (London, 1982), pp. 69–83.
5. Johannes J. G. Jansen, *The Dual Nature of Islamic Fundamentalism* (Ithaca, N.Y., 1997), p. 33.
6. Cf. Paul Berman's excellent discussion of Qutb in *Terror and Liberalism* (New York, 2003), pp. 52–102.

Chapter 6: Bin Laden, the Father of Arab Democracy

1. Elie Kedourie, *Politics in the Middle East* (Oxford, 1992), p. 172.
2. For the illiteracy rate, see www.state.gov/r/pa/ei/bgn/5309.htm.
3. Miles Copeland, *The Game of Nations: The Amorality of Power Politics* (New York, 1970), p. 99.
4. www.brookings.edu/articles/2006/02middleeast_wittes.aspx.
5. www.washingtonpost.com/wp-dyn/content/article/2005/09/08/AR2005090800151.html.
6. Peter W. Rodman, *More Precious Than Peace: The Cold War and the Struggle for the Third World* (New York, 1994), pp. 85–86 and nn. 77, 78. Eisenhower said this in 1967 to Richard Nixon and to Israel's ambassador Avraham Harman, www.meforum.org/article/420.
7. Bob Woodward, *Plan of Attack* (New York, 2004), p. 150.
8. Eli Lake, "How the Outbreak of War on 9/11 Rattled Gadhafi, Other Tyrants," *New York Sun,* April 6, 2006, www.nysun.com/article/30504.
9. *Al Mussawar,* June 2002.
10. Richard Perle, "Ambushed on the Potomac," *National Interest,* Jan.–Feb. 2008, p. 8. For an overview of when, and how, the freedom agenda kicked in, see Douglas Feith, *War and Decision: Inside the Pentagon at the Dawn of the War on Terrorism* (New York, 2008).

11. "President Bush Presses for Peace in the Middle East," www.whitehouse.gov/news/releases/2003/05/20030509-11.html.

12. "President Bush Discusses Freedom in Iraq and Middle East," remarks by the president at the twentieth anniversary of the National Endowment for Democracy, Nov. 6, 2003, www.whitehouse.gov/news/releases/2003/11/20031106-2.html.

13. Steven R. Weisman, "Rice Acknowledges Surprise over Hamas: Many Were Caught Off Guard, She Says," *International Herald Tribune,* Jan. 30, 2006, www.iht.com/articles/2006/01/30/news/rice.php.

14. www.hudsonny.org/2009/01/hamas-and-the-palestinians.php.

15. "Al-Zawahiri: U.S. Talking to Wrong People in Iraq, Urges 'Holy War' Against Israel," Associated Press, Dec. 20, 2006, www.foxnews.com/story/0,2933,237678,00.html.

16. Cf. Milton Viorst, "Fundamentalism in Power: Sudan's Islamic Experiment," *Foreign Affairs,* May/June 1995, www.foreignaffairs.com/articles/50969/milton-viorst/fundamentalism-in-power-sudans-islamic-experiment.

17. Peter W. Rodman, "Policy Brief: Don't Destabilize Algiers," *Middle East Quarterly,* Dec. 1996, www.meforum.org/article/420.

18. The Georgetown professors John Esposito and John O. Voll and the former CIA analyst Graham Fuller were among the most enthusiastic advocates of Islamist democracy.

Chapter 7: The Schizophrenic Gulf

1. For instance, see Hugh Miles, *Al-Jazeera: The Inside Story of the Arab News Channel That Is Challenging the West* (New York, 2005); and Marc Lynch, *Voices of the New Arab Public: Iraq, Al-Jazeera, and Middle East Politics Today* (New York, 2006).

2. Cf. Qaradawi's judicious advice concerning "how to give up masturbation" on his Web site, www.IslamOnline.net: www.islamonline.net/servlet/Satellite?pagename=IslamOnline-English-Ask_Scholar/FatwaE/FatwaE&cid=1119503543914.

3. Jimmy Carter, State of the Union address, Jan. 23, 1980, www.jimmy carterlibrary.org/documents/speeches/su80jec.phtml.

4. Also known as the "Reagan Corollary" to the Carter Doctrine. Cf. Edward J. Marolda and Robert John Schneller, *Shield and Sword: The United States Navy and the Persian Gulf War* (Annapolis, Md., 2001), p. 13.

5. Martin Kramer, "America's Interests: A Bedside Briefing," paper presented at the Harvard University symposium "After Bush: America's Agenda in the Middle East," Sept. 23, 2008.

6. Kenneth Pollack, *A Path Out of the Desert: A Grand Strategy for America in the Middle East* (New York, 2008), p. 235.

Chapter 8: The Battle of Ideas

1. Taha Hussein, *The Future of Culture in Egypt* (Washington, D.C., 1954), p. 14.

2. Taha Hussein, *The Days* (Cairo, 1997), p. 217.

3. Ibid., p. 391.

4. www.fareedzakaria.com/ARTICLES/newsweek/081301.html.

5. Qasim Amin, *The Liberation of Women and the New Woman: Two Documents in the History of Egyptian Feminism,* translated by Samiha Sidhom Peterson (Cairo, 2004), p. 6.

6. Ibid., p. 134.

7. Ian Buruma and Timothy Garton Ash engaged in a lively debate with Paul Berman and Pascal Bruckner about the comparative relevance of the Islamist

thinker Tariq Ramadan versus Ayaan Hirsi Ali, the Somali-born Dutch parliamentarian whose sharp criticism of Islam and Europe's Muslim community brought her under fire from the European left. Cf. Paul Berman's article in the *New Republic:* "Who's Afraid of Tariq Ramadan? The Islamist, the Journalist, and the Defense of Liberalism," June 4, 2007.

8.   Lewis Awad, *The Literature of Ideas in Egypt: Part One* (Atlanta, 1986), p. 143.

Chapter 9: "Your Children or Your Guns"

1.   Miles Copeland, *The Game of Nations: The Amorality of Power Politics* (New York, 1970), pp. 202–4.

2.   Egypt's Copts are believed to number anywhere between four and twelve million out of eighty million Egyptians.

3.   Dennis Ross, *The Missing Peace: The Inside Story of the Fight for Middle East Peace* (New York, 2004), p. 509.

4.   Donna Abi Nasr, "Hezbollah, al-Qaida Mirror Islamic Split," Associated Press, June 24, 2006, www.lebanonwire.com/0606MLN/06062423AP.asp.

5.   Heinz Halm, *Shi'ism,* 2nd ed. (New York, 2004), p. 71.

6.   Consider, for instance, the opinion of the CIA's John Brennan: "It would not be foolhardy, however, for the United States to tolerate, and even to encourage, greater assimilation of Hezbollah into Lebanon's political system, a process that is subject to Iranian influence . . . The best hope for maintaining this trend and for reducing the influence of violent extremists within the organization as well as the influence of extremist Iranian officials who view Hezbollah primarily as a pawn of Tehran is to increase Hezbollah's stake in Lebanon's struggling democratic processes." John Brennan, "The Conundrum of Iran: Strengthening Moderates Without Acquiescing to Belligerence," *Annals of the American Academy of Political and Social Science* 618, no. 1 (2008), pp. 168–79. It is unclear why the author saw Hezbollah worthy of a larger part in Lebanon's democratic processes in an article published two months after the party attempted a coup against the government and overran the western sector of Beirut, leaving a trail of blood in its wake.

7.   Robert Kaplan, *The Arabists: The Romance of an American Elite* (New York, 1993), p. 35.

8.   Asher Kaufman, *Reviving Phoenicia: The Search for Identity in Lebanon* (London, 2004), p. 72.

9.   In correspondence with Asher Kaufman.

10.   United Nations Security Council, "Report of the Fact-Finding Mission to Lebanon Inquiring into the Causes, Circumstances, and Consequences of the Assassination of Former Prime Minister Rafik Hariri," executive summary, Feb. 25–March 24, 2005, domino.un.org/UNISPAL.NSF/3822b5e39951876a85256b6e0058a478/79cd8aaa858fdd2d85256fd500536047!OpenDocument.

Chapter 10: The Capital of Arab Resistance

1.   Since the constitution stipulated that the president of Syria had to be a Muslim, in 1973 Hafez al-Assad aligned himself with one of Lebanon's Shia leaders, Musa al-Sadr, who declared that the Alawis were recognized as "brothers" of the Shia. This cover later facilitated closer relations with the Islamic Republic of Iran's Shia theocracy. Cf. Fouad Ajami, *The Vanished Imam: Musa al-Sadr and the Shia of Lebanon* (Ithaca, N.Y., 1986), p. 174.

2.   Daniel Pipes, *Greater Syria: The History of an Ambition* (New York, 1990), p. 160.

3.   Ibid., p. 163.

4.   Ibid., p. 167.
5.   www.state.gov/secretary/former/index.htm.
6.   www.aawsat.com/details.asp?section=4&issueno=11114&article=517594.
7.   Karen DeYoung, "Papers Paint New Picture of Iraq's Foreign Insurgents," *Washington Post*, Jan. 21, 2008, p. A1.
8.   www.dni.gov/press_releases/20051011_release.htm.

Chapter 11: Middle East Cold War and the Israeli Strong Horse

1.   "Nasrallah Sorry for Scale of War," BBC News, Aug. 27, 2006, news.bbc.co.uk/2/hi/middle_east/5291420.stm.
2.   www.geocities.com/d_elazar/USA/bekaa.pdf.
3.   news.bbc.co.uk/onthisday/hi/dates/stories/october/24/newsid_2478000/2478505.stm.
4.   Saad Eddin Ibrahim, "The 'New Middle East' Bush Is Resisting," *Washington Post*, Aug. 23, 2006.
5.   In fact it is not clear whether the Shebaa Farms are Lebanese or Syrian. For example, Walid Jumblatt said in the winter of 2008, "The Shebaa Farms are not Lebanese. They become Lebanese when the Syrian government agrees to delineate these Farms with the Lebanese government, and we send the joint document to the UN." See www.psp.org.lb/Default.aspx?tabid=107&articleType=ArticleView&articleId=10134.

Conclusion

1.   This account is greatly indebted to Martin Kramer, "Sacrifice and 'Self-Martyrdom' in Shi'ite Lebanon," in *Arab Awakening and Islamic Revival* (New Brunswick, N.J., 1996), pp. 231–43. Also available at www.geocities.com/martinkramerorg/Sacrifice.htm.

Index

ABOUT THE AUTHOR

LEE SMITH is a Middle East correspondent for the *Weekly Standard*.
He has written for *Slate*, the *New York Times*, the *Boston Globe*, and
a variety of Arab media outlets. He is also a visiting fellow of the
Hudson Institute. A native of New York, he lives in Washington, D.C.